A CONCORDANCE OF BIBLE READINGS

A
CONCORDANCE
OF
BIBLE READINGS

Compiled by
Charles R. Joy

THE WORLD PUBLISHING COMPANY
Cleveland and New York

Published by The World Publishing Company
2231 West 110th Street, Cleveland 2, Ohio

Published simultaneously in Canada by
Nelson, Foster & Scott Ltd.

FIRST EDITION

Library of Congress Catalog Card Number: 65-25778

To my children's children
Peggy, Peter, Billy, Stevie, Kenny, Richie, Patti
"They shall dwell in the land."

Preface

This reference book is designed to meet the need for a practical and comprehensive guide to Scripture selections suitable for public reading, group study, or private meditation. More than 5,700 Bible passages are included under 1,560 alphabetically arranged topics. Each reference is followed by a brief quotation or summary phrase, enabling the user to determine quickly whether the content of a given reading fits his individual purpose.

The special purpose of this *Concordance*, in contrast to similar volumes of greater* bulk, lies in its explicit focus on longer passages and on topics of greatest general interest. Thus, all passing references in isolated verses have been deliberately excluded. These carefully selected readings can be read in worship services, in classes of instruction, or on special occasions; they can also be a valuable aid to personal Bible study and devotions.

The topics range from basic themes of faith and life to celebrations of the church year and national holidays. A special effort has been made to eliminate headings of marginal importance and infrequent use. Extensive cross references permit the reader to locate sustained passages on almost any topic of enduring significance and contemporary relevance.

The compilation has been based on the most familiar and widely loved Bible translation, the King James Version, but the reader will find the references equally appropriate for use with modern translations.

The compiler hopes that many ministers, teachers, speakers, and laymen will find as much satisfaction in using this book as he has had in preparing it.

June, 1965   CHARLES R. JOY

---

*For example, the compiler's earlier work, *Harper's Topical Concordance*, New York: Harper & Row, 1940, rev. ed. 1962.

Abbreviations

To achieve economy of space in a work consisting primarily of Bible references, abbreviations have been reduced to the briefest form consistent with clarity and comprehension.

Ac.	Acts	Ja.	James	Ne.	Nehemiah
Am.	Amos	Jb.	Job	Nu.	Numbers
1 Ch.	I Chronicles	Je.	Jeremiah	Ob.	Obadiah
2 Ch.	II Chronicles	Jn.	John	1 Pe.	I Peter
1 Co.	I Corinthians	1 Jn.	I John	2 Pe.	II Peter
2 Co.	II Corinthians	2 Jn.	II John	Ph.	Philippians
Col.	Colossians	3 Jn.	III John	Pr.	Proverbs
Da.	Daniel	Jo.	Joel	Ps.	Psalms
De.	Deuteronomy	Jon.	Jonah	Re.	Revelation
Ec.	Ecclesiastes	Jos.	Joshua	Ro.	Romans
Ep.	Ephesians	Ju.	Judges	Ru.	Ruth
Es.	Esther	Jude	Jude	S. of S.	Song of Solomon
Ex.	Exodus	1 K.	I Kings	1 S.	I Samuel
Eze.	Ezekiel	2 K.	II Kings	2 S.	II Samuel
Ezr.	Ezra	La.	Lamentations	1 Th.	I Thessalonians
Ga.	Galàtians	Le.	Leviticus	2 Th.	II Thessalonians
Ge.	Genesis	Lu.	Luke	1 Ti.	I Timothy
Hab.	Habakkuk	Mal.	Malachi	2 Ti.	II Timothy
Hag.	Haggai	Mat.	Matthew	Tit.	Titus
He.	Hebrews	Mi.	Micah	Zch.	Zechariah
Ho.	Hosea	Mk.	Mark	Zph.	Zephaniah
Is.	Isaiah	Na.	Nahum		

[A]

Abasement, *See* Humility
Abhorrence, *See* Hatred
Ability
Ex. 18:13-24 Thou shalt provide able men
Ju. 7:1-9 Gideon's three hundred men
Da. 3:8-18 Our God is able to deliver us
Mat. 3:1-12 God is able of these stones
Mat. 17:14-20 Nothing shall be impossible unto you
Mat. 20:20-29 Are ye able to drink of the cup?
2 Co. 12:1-12 When I am weak, then am I strong
Ep. 3 The power that worketh in us
Ph. 4:8-13 I can do all things through Christ
1 Pe. 4:1-11 The ability which God giveth
Abnegation, *See* Sacrifice
Abode, *See* House
Abolition
Ex. 6:1-9 I will bring you out from bondage
Is. 2:10-22 The idols he shall utterly abolish
Is. 51:1-6 My righteousness shall not be abolished
Is. 51:11-15 The redeemed of the Lord shall return
1 Co. 15:19-26 The last enemy that shall be destroyed is death.
2 Ti. 1:1-11 Jesus Christ hath abolished death
Re. 21:1-7 There shall be no more death
Abomination, *See* Sin
Absence
Ge. 31:44-49 When we are absent one from another
Ru. 1:1-17 Intreat me not to leave thee
Mat. 25:14-30 Parable of the talents
Lu. 15:11-32 The son took his journey into a far country
Jn. 16:1-16 It is expedient for you that I go away
Ac. 20:28-38 They should see his face no more
2 Co. 5:1-9 Whether present or absent
2 Co. 13 Finally, brethren, farewell
2 Ti. 4:1-8 The time of my departure is at hand
Absolution, *See* Forgiveness

Abstinence, *See* Temperance Sunday
Abundance
De. 30:1-10 The Lord will make thee plenteous
1 K. 17:1-16 Neither shall the cruse of oil fail
Ps. 16 In thy presence is fulness of joy
Is. 11:1-9 Full of the knowledge of the Lord
Is. 28:9-20 For the bed is shorter than that a man can stretch himself on it
Je. 2:1-9 I brought you into a plentiful country
Am. 9:11-15 The mountains shall drop sweet wine
Lu. 6:27-38 Good measure, pressed down
Lu. 9:10-17 There remained twelve baskets
Lu. 12:16-21 Thou hast much goods laid up
Lu. 12:22-32 All these things shall be added unto you
Ep. 1:15-23 The fulness of him that filleth all in all
Abuse, *See* Injury
Acceptance
Ps. 19 Let my meditation be acceptable
Is. 61:1-6 The acceptable year of the Lord
Am. 5:21-24 I will not accept your offerings
Mi. 6:6-8 To do justly, and to love mercy
Mat. 23:13-33 Woe unto you, scribes and Pharisees
Lu. 18:9-14 The Pharisee and the publican
Ro. 12 Acceptable unto God
Access, *See* Door; Hospitality
Accident, *See* Adversity
Acclamation, *See* Praise
Accomplishment, *See* Achievement
Accord, *See* Agreement; Covenant; Unity
Account, *See* Cost
Accuracy
Le. 19:35-37 Just balances, just weights
Ps. 101 He that telleth lies shall not tarry
Mi. 6:10-15 The wicked balances
Ac. 5:1-11 Ananias and Sapphira
Ro. 12:9-21 Provide things honest
Accusation, *See* Condemnation

Achievement
Ge. 1:26-31; 2:1, 2 The heavens and the earth were finished
1 K. 8:12-30 The dedication of Solomon's temple
2 Ch. 8:12-16 So the house of the Lord was perfected
Ezr. 3 The foundation of the house of the Lord was laid
Mat. 25:14-30 Well done, good and faithful servant
Lu. 2:25-35 Mine eyes have seen thy salvation
1 Co. 13:9-13 When that which is perfect is come
2 Ti. 4:1-8 I have kept the faith
Re. 21:1-7 A new heaven and a new earth
Acquaintance, *See* Friendship; Knowledge
Acquiescence, *See* Agreement
Acquisition, *See* Gain; Greed
Action, *See* Deed; Service; Labor Day
Activity, *See* Deed; Labor Day
Addition, *See* Gain
Adequacy, *See* Abundance
Administration
Ge. 41:25-44 Joseph was ruler over all Egypt
1 K. 10:1-13 Thy wisdom and prosperity exceedeth
2 Ch. 14:1-7 Asa did that which was good
Is. 9:2-7 The government shall be upon his shoulder
Mat. 25:14-30 I will make thee ruler over many things
1 Co. 12:1-11 There are differences of administrations
2 Co. 9 Touching the ministering to the saints
Re. 21:1-7 Behold, I make all things new
Admiration
1 K. 10:1-9 The Queen of Sheba admires Solomon
Jb. 9:1-10 Wonders without number
Ps. 19 The heavens declare the glory of God
Ps. 77:11-19 I will remember thy wonders of old
Ps. 107:21-43 These see the works of the Lord
Ps. 136 His mercy endureth for ever
Ps. 139:1-18 Marvellous are thy works
Lu. 4:16-22 All wondered at his gracious words
Ac. 3:1-11 The people wondered

Admission, *See* Door
Admonition, *See* Condemnation
Adoption
Jn. 1:1-14 Power to become the sons of God
Ro. 8:1-17 If children, then heirs
2 Co. 6 I will be a Father unto you
Ga. 4:1-7 The adoption of sons
Ep. 1:1-14 Predestinated unto adoption
1 Jn. 3:1-11 Now are we the sons of God
Adoration, *See* Worship
Adornment, *See* Beauty
Adulation, *See* Praise
Adultery
Ex. 20:1-17 Thou shalt not commit adultery
2 S. 12:1-10 Nathan condemns David for adultery
Mat. 5:27-32 Whosoever looketh on a woman to lust hath committed adultery
1 Co. 6:9-20 Glorify God in your body
Ga. 5:16-26 The works of the flesh are manifest
Advance
Ex. 14 Speak unto them that they go forward
Jos. 1:1-11 Ye shall pass over Jordan
Is. 45:1-8 I will go before thee
Is. 62 Prepare ye the way of the people
Mat. 13:31, 32 The grain of mustard seed
Mat. 13:33 The kingdom of heaven is like leaven
Lu. 2:40-52 Jesus increased in wisdom and stature
Lu. 9:51-62 He steadfastly set his face to go to Jerusalem
Ph. 1:12-27 Unto the furtherance of the gospel
Ph. 3:4-14 I press toward the mark
Advent
Ps. 72:2-19 He shall come down like rain
Is. 9:2-7 The people have seen a great light
Is. 11:1-9 The spirit of the Lord shall rest upon him
Is. 53 Surely he hath borne our griefs
Hag. 2:1-9 The desire of all nations shall come
Mat. 1:18-25 Thou shalt call his name Jesus

Mat. 25:14-30 After a long time the lord of those servants cometh

Lu. 1:26-35 Hail, thou that art highly favoured

Lu. 3:1-18 Prepare ye the way of the Lord

Lu. 8:1, 4-8 The glad tidings of the kingdom

Jn. 1:1-14 The light shineth in darkness

Ro. 8:35-39 The love of God in Christ Jesus

Ro. 13 The night is far spent, the day is at hand

Ph. 1 According to my earnest expectation

Ph. 2:1-11 At the name of Jesus every knee should bow

Ph. 3:7-21 That I may know him

2 Pe. 1 We were eyewitnesses of his majesty

Advent, Second, *See* Christ, Second Coming of

Adventure, *See* Courage; Pilgrim; Pioneer

Adversary, *See* Antichrist; Enemy; Satan

Adversity

Ge. 7:11-24 The flood was forty days upon the earth

De. 28:15-46 The Lord will smite thee

2 Ch. 15:1-7 God did vex them with adversity

Jb. 14:1-14 Man is full of trouble

Jb. 16 He hath broken me asunder

Ps. 34 Many are the afflictions of the righteous

Ps. 90:3-17 We are consumed by thine anger

Ps. 91 Thou shalt not be afraid for the terror

Is. 54:7-17 O thou afflicted, tossed with tempest

La. 1:1-11 How doth the city sit solitary

La. 1:12-22 See if there be any sorrow like mine

Eze. 7:1-15 Sword, famine, pestilence

Eze. 7:23-27 Destruction cometh

Mat. 5:1-12 Blessed are they which are persecuted

Lu. 13:11-17 Thou art loosed from thine infirmity

2 Co. 4:8-18 Troubled, yet not distressed

2 Co. 12:1-10 I take pleasure in infirmities

Advice, *See* Instruction

Advocate

De. 5:1-21 I stood between the Lord and you

Is. 53 He made intercession for the transgressors

Lu. 22:31-38 I have prayed for thee

Lu. 23:27-34 Father, forgive them

Ro. 8:26-39 The Spirit maketh intercession for us

1 Ti. 2:1-6 There is one God, and one mediator

He. 7 A priest after the order of Melchisedec

He. 12:22-29 Jesus the mediator of the new covenant

1 Jn. 2:1-12 He is the propitiation for our sins

Affectation, *See* Hypocrisy

Affection, *See* Love

Affirmation, *See* Agreement; Proclamation

Affliction, *See* Adversity

Affront, *See* Injury; Offense

Aftermath, *See* Result

Age, *See* Generation; Old People's Sunday; Time

Age, Golden, *See* Kingdom, the Coming

Aggressiveness, *See* Ardor; Boldness; Might

Agitation, *See* Confusion

Agnosticism, *See* Christ, Denial of; Christ, Doubt of; Denial; Doubt; God, Denial of; Unbelief

Agony, *See* Pain

Agreement

De. 27:14-26 All the people shall answer and say, Amen

Ps. 133 Dwelling together in unity

Is. 11:1-9 The wolf shall dwell with the lamb

Mat. 5:21-26 Agree with thine adversary quickly

Mat. 18:15-20 If two of you shall agree on earth

Ac. 8:1-4 Saul was consenting

1 Jn. 5:1-8 There are three that bear witness

Aid, *See* Help

Ailment, *See* Sickness

Aim, *See* Aspiration; Purpose

Alarm, *See* Fear

Alertness, *See* Readiness

Alien, *See* Stranger

All, *See* Whole

Allegiance, *See* Loyalty

Allegory, *See* Parable

Alleluia, *See* Praise

Alliance, *See* League; Nations, United

All Saints
Ps. 105 Touch not mine anointed
Mat. 13:24-43 The righteous shall shine as the sun
1 Co. 1:1-9 Called to be saints
He. 11:1-16 These all died in faith
He. 11:17-40 Of whom the world was not worthy
He. 12:1-3 So great a cloud of witnesses
Re. 7:1-10 A great multitude stood before the throne
Re. 7:11-17 They serve him day and night
Re. 19:1-9 The voice of a great multitude

All Souls
Ps. 72 All nations shall call him blessed
Ps. 97 He preserveth the souls of his saints
Eze. 18:1-9 Behold, all souls are mine
Jo. 2:28-32 I will pour out my spirit upon all flesh
Mat. 11:25-30 Come unto me, all ye that labour
Mk. 16:12-20 Preach the gospel to every creature
Jn. 10:1-18 Other sheep I have, not of this fold
Ac. 17:22-31 All men are of one blood
1 Pe. 2:11-25 The Shepherd and Bishop of your souls

Allurement, *See* Temptation

Ally
De. 2:1-7 Forty years the Lord hath been with thee
De. 31:1-8 The Lord will be with thee
1 S. 18:1-4 Jonathan loved him as his own soul
2 K. 6:8-17 They that be with us are more
Ps. 20 Some trust in chariots
Jn. 16:25-33 I am not alone, the Father is with me
Ep. 4:1-25 We are members one of another

Almighty, *See* God, Omnipotence of
Almsgiving, *See* Charity
Alpha, *See* Beginning
Altar, *See* Sanctuary
Alteration, *See* Change; Conversion
Altitude, *See* Height
Altruism, *See* Unselfishness
Amazement, *See* Astonishment

Ambassador
Ps. 119:33-48 I will speak before kings
Pr. 13:1-17 A faithful ambassador is health
Is. 6:1-8 Here am I; send me
Is. 40:1-11 Jerusalem that bringest good tidings
Mal. 3:1-6 I will send my messenger
Lu. 20:9-18 I will send my beloved son
Jn. 1:1-18 John bare witness of him
Jn. 1:19-28 The voice of one crying in the wilderness
Jn. 3:25-36 He must increase, but I must decrease
2 Co. 5:8-20 We are ambassadors for Christ

Ambition
Ge. 11:1-9 Let us make us a name
2 S. 15:1-6 Oh that I were made judge in the land
Mat. 20:20-28 Seats in Christ's kingdom
Mk. 9:33-37 They disputed who should be greatest
Lu. 12:16-21 I will build greater barns
Lu. 14:7-14 They chose out the chief rooms
Ph. 3:13-21 I press toward the mark

Amendment, *See* Conversion
Amends, *See* Restoration
Amnesty, *See* Forgiveness
Ampleness, *See* Abundance
Amusement, *See* Gayety
Anarchy, *See* Confusion
Anathema, *See* Curse

Ancestor
De. 7:7-13 Ye were the fewest of all people
1 K. 8:54-61 God be with us, as with our fathers
Ps. 16 I have a goodly heritage
Ps. 145 One generation shall praise thee to another
Pr. 17:1-6 The glory of children are their fathers
Mat. 3:1-12 We have Abraham to our Father

Anchor, *See* Steadfastness

Angel
Ge. 28:10-22 Behold the angels of God
Ge. 32:24-32 Jacob wrestles with an angel

Ps. 91 He shall give his angels charge over thee

Ps. 103 Bless the Lord, ye his angels

Mat. 4:1-11 Angels came and ministered unto him

Mat. 22:23-32 They are as the angels in heaven

1 Th. 4:13-18 With the voice of the archangel

He. 1 He maketh his angels spirits

Re. 12:7-12 Michael and his angels fought

Anger

Ps. 6 Chasten me not in thy hot displeasure

Ps. 30 His anger endureth but a moment

Pr. 16:21-32 He that is slow to anger

Jon. 4 Jonah was very angry

Mat. 2:1-18 Herod was exceeding wroth

Mat. 3:7-12 The wrath to come

Mat. 5:21-26 First be reconciled to thy brother

Ep. 4:17-32 Let all wrath and anger be put away

Anguish, *See* Adversity

Animal, *See* Beast

Animosity, *See* Hatred

Annals, *See* Past

Annihilation, *See* Destruction

Anniversary, *See* Memorial Day

Announcement, *See* Proclamation

Annoyance, *See* Trouble

Annulment, *See* Abolition

Annunciation

Lu. 1:26-39 Thou shalt bring forth a son

Lu. 1:46-56 My soul doth magnify the Lord

Anointing, *See* Consecration

Answer

Ju. 14:12-18 Samson put forth a riddle

1 K. 10:1-13 Solomon told her all her questions

Jb. 38 Then the Lord answered Job

Ps. 91 He shall call, and I will answer

Pr. 1:20-33 They shall call, but I will not answer

Lu. 2:40-52 They were astonished at his answers

1 Pe. 3:10-22 Always ready to give an answer

Antagonism, *See* Enemy

Anthem, *See* Hymn

Antichrist

1 Jn. 2:15-29 Even now there are many antichrists

1 Jn. 4:1-6 This is that spirit of antichrist

Anticipation, *See* Hope

Antipathy, *See* Hatred

Anxiety, *See* Worry

Apathy, *See* Indifference

Apocalypse, *See* Revelation; Vision

Apocrypha, *See* Secrecy

Apostasy, *See* Christ, Denial of; God, Denial of

Apostle, *See* Disciple

Apparel, *See* Clothes

Appeal, *See* Entreaty

Appearance, *See* Easter; Revelation; Vision

Appetite, *See* Bread

Applause, *See* Praise

Appointment

Ps. 78:58-72 He chose the tribe of Judah

Is. 6:1-9 He said, Go, and tell this people

Is. 42:1-16 Behold mine elect

Je. 1:1-10 I have put my words in thy mouth

Eze. 2 Son of man, I send thee to Israel

Am. 7:7-17 The Lord took me as I followed the flock

Lu. 10:1-17 The Lord appointed other seventy also

Ac. 9:10-22 He is a chosen vessel unto me

Ac. 16:8-15 Come over into Macedonia, and help us

2 Ti. 1:1-11 An apostle by the will of God

He. 1 God hath anointed thee

Appreciation, *See* Praise

Apprehension, *See* Fear

Approach, *See* Door; Hospitality

Approval, *See* Agreement; Praise

Arbitration, *See* Judgment

Archangel, *See* Angel

Architecture, *See* Builder

Ardor

Ps. 119:137-144 My zeal hath consumed me

Jn. 2:13-17 The zeal of thine house hath eaten me up

Ac. 22:1-11 I was zealous toward God

Ro. 12:1-11 Fervent in spirit

2 Co. 5:1-17 The love of Christ constraineth us

Ardor, (cont.)

2 Co. 5:12-21 If we be beside ourselves, it is to God
Ga. 6:6-10 Let us not be weary in well doing
Ph. 3:1-14 I follow after, if that I may apprehend
Col. 3:16-25 Whatsoever ye do, do it heartily

Argument, See Reason

Aristocracy, See Best; Chief

Arm

De. 33:26-29 Underneath are the everlasting arms
Jb. 40:6-14 Hast thou an arm like God?
Ps. 44:1-6 Neither did their own arm save them
Ps. 98 His holy arm hath gotten him the victory
Is. 11:1-9 They shall not hurt nor destroy

Armistice Sunday

Ps. 46 He maketh wars to cease
Ps. 67 Let all the people praise thee
Is. 2:1-5 Let us walk in the light of the Lord
Is. 11:1-9 They shall not hurt nor destroy
Mi. 4:1-7 In the last days it shall come to pass
Mi. 5:1-7 This man shall be the peace
Mat. 5:1-9 Blessed are the peacemakers
Mat. 5:43-48 I say unto you, Love your enemies
Mat. 18:21-35 How oft shall I forgive my brother?
Mat. 26:51-56 They that take the sword shall perish
Lu. 6:27-38 Love ye your enemies
Lu. 10:25-37 Thou shalt love thy neighbour as thyself
Ro. 14:16-19 The kingdom of God is peace
Ph. 4:1-17 The peace of God passeth understanding
Col. 3:1-17 Let the peace of God rule in your hearts
He. 12:12-15 Follow peace with all men
1 Pe. 3:8-16 Seek peace, and ensue it
Re. 21:1-7 A new heaven and a new earth

Armor, See Security

Army

2 K. 6:8-17 The mountain was full of chariots of fire
Ps. 27 Though an host should encamp against me
Ps. 33 No king is saved by the multitude of an host
Is. 2:1-5 They shall beat their swords into plowshares
Is. 31 Woe to them that trust in chariots
Eze. 37:1-10 They stood up, an exceeding great army
Jo. 3:9-17 Beat your plowshares into swords

Arrest, See Captivity

Arrogance, See Pride

Art, See Beauty

Artisan, See Hand; Labor Day

Ascension Sunday, See Christ, Ascension of

Asceticism

Da. 9:1-15 With fasting, and sackcloth, and ashes
Jon. 3 The people of Nineveh put on sackcloth
Mat. 3 His meat was locusts and wild honey
Mat. 6:16-18 Appear not unto men to fast
Mat. 8:18-27 Jesus had not where to lay his head
Mat. 9:10-17 Why do thy disciples fast not?
Lu. 14:25-35 A disciple must forsake all he has
Ro. 8:1-13 Ye must mortify the deeds of the body
Ga. 5:16-26 Crucify the flesh

Ash Wednesday

Ge. 18:23-33 I am but dust and ashes
2 K. 22:16-20 Because thou hast humbled thyself
Jb. 42:1-10 I repent in dust and ashes
Ps. 34 The Lord saveth such as be contrite
Is. 55 He will abundantly pardon
Eze. 18:20-32 Make you a new heart and a new spirit
Mat. 3:1-12 Repent ye
Mk. 2:13-28 I came to call sinners to repentance
Lu. 15:11-32 I have sinned against heaven and before thee
Lu. 18:9-14 God be merciful to me a sinner

Re. 2:1-7 Remember from whence thou art fallen

Aspiration
Ps. 24 Lift up your heads, O ye gates
Ps. 25 Unto thee do I lift up my soul
Ps. 42 My soul panteth after thee, O God
Ps. 121 My help cometh from the hills
Is. 40:1-11 Get thee up into the high mountain
Is. 40:26-31 Lift up your eyes on high
Mat. 5:1-12 Blessed are they which hunger and thirst
Ph. 3:13-17 I press toward the mark
Col. 3:1-15 Set your affection on things above

Assault, *See* Army; Strife

Assembly
Ps. 111 I will praise the Lord in the assembly
Is. 1:10-20 It is iniquity, even the solemn meeting
Mat. 18:15-20 Where two or three are gathered together
He. 10:16-31 Forsake not the assembling of yourselves

Assent, *See* Agreement
Assistance, *See* Help
Association, *See* Ally
Assurance, *See* Trust

Astonishment
Ps. 139:1-18 I am fearfully and wonderfully made
Mat. 7:24-29 The people were astonished at his doctrine
Mat. 15:29-31 The multitude wondered
Mk. 6:45-56 Jesus walks on the sea
Lu. 9:28-36 Jesus is transfigured
Ac. 2:1-13 The day of Pentecost
Ac. 3:1-12 Peter makes the lame man walk

Asylum, *See* Refuge
Atheism, *See* God, Denial of

Atonement
Is. 53 He bare the sin of many
Jn. 1:29-34 Behold the Lamb of God
Ro. 5 While we were sinners, Christ died for us
1 Co. 15:1-22 In Christ shall all be made alive

2 Co. 5 Reconciling the world unto himself
He. 2 Jesus tasted death for every man
1 Jn. 1 The blood of Jesus cleanseth us
1 Jn. 2:1-17 He is the propitiation for our sins
1 Jn 4:1-11 God sent his only begotten Son

Atrophy, *See* Death, Withering
Attachment, *See* Bond; Faithfulness; Love; Loyalty
Attack, *See* Army; Strife
Attainment, *See* Achievement
Attendance, *See* Presence
Attire, *See* Clothes

Attraction
De. 30:11-20 If ye be drawn away and serve other gods
2 S. 22:1-20 He drew me out of many waters
Je. 31:1-9 With lovingkindness have I drawn thee
Ho. 11 I drew them with bands of love
Mat. 4:23-25 There followed him great multitudes
Jn. 6:35-51 Except the Father draw him
Jn. 12:23-36 I will draw all men unto me

Audacity, *See* Boldness
Audience, *See* Assembly; Church
Austerity, *See* Asceticism
Author, *See* Book

Authority
Pr. 29 When the righteous are in authority
Mat. 7 The people were astonished at his doctrine
Mat. 8:5-10 I am a man under authority
Mat. 20:20-28 The sons of Zebedee
Mk. 1:13-34 He taught them as one that had authority
Mk. 10:35-45 Whosoever will be great among you
Lu. 9:1-6 He gave the disciples power and authority
Ro. 13:1-7 Be subject unto the higher powers
1 Th. 5:12-23 Esteem them very highly

Autocrat, *See* Tyranny

Autumn
Ps. 1 He shall be like a tree

Autumn *(cont.)*

Ps. 65 Thou crownest the year with thy goodness
Is. 1:28-31 Like an oak whose leaf fadeth
Is. 40:1-8 The grass withereth, the flower fadeth
Avarice, *See* Greed
Aversion, *See* Hatred
Avowal, *See* Confession
Awakening
Ps. 3 I laid me down and slept; I awaked
Ps. 17 When I awake with thy likeness
Ps. 30 Joy cometh in the morning
Ps. 130 More than they that watch for the morning
Ps. 139 When I awake I am still with thee
Lu. 9:28-36 When they awoke they saw his glory
Ro. 13 The night is far spent
Ep. 5:1-16 Awake thou that sleepest
Award, *See* Reward

Awareness
Jb. 31 Doth he not see my ways?
Is. 11:1-9 Full of the knowledge of the Lord
Mat. 24:42-51 In such an hour as ye think not
Jn. 3:1-13 Except a man be born again, he cannot see
Ac. 9:1-22 Suddenly there shined a light from heaven
Ac. 11:1-10 In a trance I saw a vision
Awe
Jb. 37 My heart trembleth
Ps. 33 Stand in awe of him
Ps. 111 Holy and reverend is his name
Is. 6:1-8 Mine eyes have seen the King
Is. 9:2-7 His name shall be called Wonderful
Ph. 2:1-11 At the name of Jesus every knee should bow
He. 12:18-29 With reverence and godly fear
Re. 4 Holy, holy, holy, Lord God Almighty

[B]

Babel, *See* Confusion
Baby
Ex. 2:1-10 He was a goodly child
1 K. 3:3-14 I am but a little child
Is. 3:1-15 Children will be their princes
Is. 65:17-25 There shall be no more an infant of days
Mat. 11:25-30 Thou hast revealed these things to babes
Lu. 1:26-35 The holy thing that shall be born of thee
Lu. 2:1-19 Ye shall find the babe in a manger
Lu. 18:15-17 They brought unto him infants
1 Co. 3:1-9 I have fed you with milk
1 Pe. 2:1-10 As newborn babes
Babylon, *See* Captivity; Sin
Backbiting, *See* Slander
Backsliding
De. 8 Lest thou forget the Lord thy God
Je. 3:6-19 Turn, O backsliding children
Mat. 26:47-56 Judas' betrayal
Mat. 26:69-75 Peter's denial
Jn. 6:53-69 Will ye also go away?

Ga. 4:1-18 How turn ye again to the weak elements
2 Ti. 4:1-10 Demas hath forsaken me
He. 10:30-39 If any man draw back
2 Pe. 2:9-22 The dog is turned to his vomit again
Re. 2:1-7 Thou hast left thy first love
Badness, *See* Sin
Balance, *See* Measure
Balm, *See* Healing
Banishment, *See* Exile
Banner
Ex. 13:20-22 The pillar of cloud and the pillar of fire
Ps. 20 We will set up our banners
S. of S. 2:1-13 His banner over me was love
S. of S. 6:1-10 Terrible as an army with banners
Is. 13:1-11 Lift up a banner upon the high mountain
Is. 59:9-21 The Lord shall lift up a standard
Is. 62:6-12 Lift up a standard for the people
Banquet, *See* Feast

Baptism
Mat. 3 I have need to be baptized of thee
Mat. 28:11-20 Teach all nations, baptizing them
Mk. 1:1-11 John did baptize in the wilderness
Lu. 12:49-53 I have a baptism to be baptized with
Jn. 3:1-13 Except a man be born of water
Ac. 2:38-41 Repent and be baptized
Ac. 8:26-39 What doth hinder me to be baptized?
Ro. 6:1-11 We were baptized into his death
1 Co. 12:1-13 By one Spirit we are baptized into one body
Ep. 4:1-7 One Lord, one faith, one baptism

Barbarian, *See* Stranger

Barrenness
Ge. 18:1-16 Sarah thy wife shall have a son
Ju. 13 An angel appeareth unto Manoah's wife
Ps. 107:31-43 He maketh a fruitful land barren
Is. 54:1-10 Sing, O barren, thou that didst not bear
Mat. 21:17-22 Christ curseth the fig tree
Lu. 23:27-31 Blessed are the barren
Jn. 15:1-6 The branch that beareth not fruit

Battle, *See* Strife

Beacon, *See* Light

Beast
Ge. 1:20-25 God made the beast of the earth
Jb. 5:19-27 The beasts shall be at peace with thee
Pr. 12:1-10 A righteous man regardeth his beast
Is. 11:1-9 A little child shall lead them
Mat. 12:10-13 A man is better than a sheep
Mk. 1:9-13 He was with the wild beasts
Lu. 12:22-30 Consider the ravens
Re. 14:9-11 They that worship the beast and his image

Beatitude
Ge. 12:1-3 Thou shalt be a blessing
Ge. 17:1-8 I will multiply thee exceedingly
Ge. 32:24-32 I will not let thee go, except thou bless me

De. 28:1-14 All these blessings shall come on thee
Ps. 1 Blessed is the man
Ps. 91 Under the shadow of the Almighty
Ps. 118:22-29 The stone which the builders rejected
Is. 32:9-20 Blessed are ye that sow beside all waters
Mal. 3:8-12 I will open the windows of heaven
Mat. 5:1-12 Blessed are ye

Beauty
Ps. 19 The firmament sheweth his handywork
Ps. 90 Let the beauty of the Lord our God be on us
Ps. 96 Worship the Lord in the beauty of holiness
Ec. 3:1-15 He hath made every thing beautiful
Ec. 10:2-12 Gracious words of wisdom
Is. 33:13-24 Thine eyes shall see the king in his beauty
Is. 61:1-6 Beauty for ashes
Mat. 6:24-34 Consider the lilies of the field
Ph. 4:1-9 Whatsoever things are lovely
2 Pe. 3:11-18 Grow in grace
Re. 21:1-7 A new heaven and a new earth

Bed, *See* Rest

Beggar, *See* Poverty, Entreaty

Beginning
Ge. 1 In the beginning God created
Mat. 6:24-34 Seek ye first the kingdom
Mk. 1:1-15 The beginning of the gospel of Jesus Christ
Jn. 1:1-14 In the beginning was the Word
Jn. 8:51-59 Before Abraham was, I am
1 Co. 3:10-23 I have laid the foundation
Col. 1:1-19 He is the firstborn from the dead
Re. 21:1-7 I am Alpha and Omega

Behavior, *See* Character

Belief
Da. 3:8-30 We will not serve thy gods
Mat. 8:5-13 I have not found so great faith
Mat. 9:27-31 According to your faith be it unto you
Ac. 16:25-34 What must I do to be saved?

Belief *(cont.)*

Mk. 9:17-29 I believe; help thou mine unbelief

Jn. 6:24-59 He that believeth on me shall never thirst

Ro. 15:1-13 Peace in believing

2 Ti. 1:7-18 I know whom I have believed

He. 11:1-16 The substance of things hoped for

Benediction, *See* Beatitude

Beneficence, *See* Benevolence

Benefit, *See* Gain

Benevolence

Ge. 12:1-9 Thou shalt be a blessing

Ge. 13:1-12 Is not the whole land before thee?

2 S. 9 I will surely shew thee kindness

Pr. 11:24-31 There is that scattereth, yet increaseth

Is. 54:1-8 With kindness will I have mercy on thee

Lu. 10:25-37 The good Samaritan

Jn. 21:15-17 Feed my sheep

Ac. 3:1-10 Such as I have give I thee

Ac. 20:32-35 It is more blessed to give than to receive

Ep. 4:29-32 Be ye tenderhearted

Bequest, *See* Heritage

Bereavement, *See* Death

Best

Ps. 89:20-29 I will make him my firstborn

Pr. 4:1-13 Wisdom is the principal thing

Mat. 19:23-30 Many that are first shall be last

Mat. 20:20-29 Whosoever will be chief among you

1 Co. 12:27-31 Covet earnestly the best gifts

1 Co. 13 The greatest of these is charity

Ph. 4:1-9 Whatsoever things are pure

2 Ti. 4:1-8 A crown of righteousness

Bestowal, *See* Gift

Betrayal

Mal. 2:1-10 Why do we deal treacherously?

Mat. 26:17-25 One of you shall betray me

Lu. 22:31-48 Peter and Judas betray him

Ac. 7:44-53 Betrayers of the Just One

2 Ti. 3 In the last days men shall be traitors

Ja. 1:22-27 Deceive not your own selves

Betterment, *See* Advance

Bible

Ps. 19:7-14 The law of the Lord is perfect

Ps. 119:89-104 O Lord, thy word is settled in heaven

Ps. 119:161-168 I rejoice at thy word

Mat. 4:1-11 Jesus' use of the scriptures

Lu. 4:16-22 He found the place where it was written

Lu. 21:25-33 My words shall not pass away

Ac. 8:26-39 Philip began at the same scripture

Ac. 17:1-12 They searched the scriptures daily

Ro. 10:8-15 As it is written

Col. 3:12-17 Psalms and hymns and spiritual songs

1 Ti. 4:13-16 Give attendance to reading

2 Ti. 3:14-17 From a child thou hast known the scriptures

Bible Sunday, *See* Bible

Bigotry

Mat. 12:1-30 The Pharisees plot against Jesus

Mat. 23:23-33 Woe unto you, scribes and Pharisees

Mk. 2:23-28 The sabbath was made for man

Lu. 11:37-54 Ye make clean the outside of the cup

Lu. 18:10-14 I thank thee that I am not as other men

Ac. 23:1-6 I am a Pharisee, the son of a Pharisee

Birth

Ge. 2:1-7 The Lord God formed man of the dust

Jb. 3 Let the day perish wherein I was born

Is. 9:2-7 Unto us a child is born

Je. 20:14-18 Cursed be the day I was born

Mat. 2:1-15 Herod and the wise men

Lu. 1:5-25, 57-80 The birth of John

Jn. 1:6-14 The Word was made flesh

Jn. 16:21-33 Joy that a man is born into the world

1 Jn. 4:1-11 Every one that loveth is born of God

Birth, New

Eze. 36:16-38 A new heart will I give you

Eze. 37:1-14 The valley of dry bones

Lu. 2:1-7, 21-40 The birth of Jesus

Jn. 3:1-17 Ye must be born again

Jn. 6:47-59 He that eateth this bread shall live for ever

Ro. 6:1-13 Our old man is crucified with him

2 Co. 5 Any man in Christ is a new creature

1 Pe. 1:15-25 Being born again of incorruptible seed

1 Jn. 3:1-11 He cannot sin, because he is born of God

1 Jn. 5:1-6 Whatsoever is born of God overcometh

Re. 21:1-7 I make all things new

Birthright

Ge. 25:29-34 Sell me this day thy birthright

Bitterness

Ps. 69:1-21 They gave me gall and vinegar

La. 3:1-21 Remembering the wormwood and the gall

Mat. 27:29-38 They gave him vinegar to drink

Ro. 3:9-18 Their mouth is full of bitterness

Ep. 4:20-32 Let all bitterness be put away

He. 12:5-15 A root of bitterness

Blame, *See* Condemnation

Blamelessness, *See* Purity

Blasphemy, *See* Curse

Blessedness, *See* Beatitude

Blessing, *See* Beatitude

Blindness

Jb. 29 I was eyes to the blind

Is. 42:8-16 I will make darkness light before them

Mat. 15:1-14 If the blind lead the blind

Lu. 4:14-21 Recovering of sight to the blind

Lu. 7:19-23 Unto many that were blind he gave sight

Jn. 9 One thing I know, now I see

Jn. 20:19-29 Blessed are they that have not seen

Ac. 9:1-22 When his eyes were opened he saw no man

2 Co. 4:1-6 God commanded the light to shine

Ep. 4:1-21 Because of the blindness of their hearts

Blood

Ge. 4:1-15 The voice of thy brother's blood

Le. 17:1-11 Blood maketh atonement for the soul

Ps. 51 Deliver me from bloodguiltiness

Is. 1:10-15 Your hands are full of blood

Eze. 24:6-14 Woe to the bloody city!

Ac. 17:22-31 All nations are made of one blood

Ac. 20:17-27 Neither count I my life dear

He. 9:20-28 Without shedding of blood is no remission

He. 12:1-11 Ye have not yet resisted unto blood

Blossom, *See* Flower Sunday

Boasting, *See* Pride

Body

Jb. 19:21-27 Though worms destroy this body

Is. 40:1-8 All flesh is grass

Mi. 6:6-8 The fruit of my body for the sin of my soul

Mat. 6:24-34 Take no thought for your body

Mat. 10:24-33 Fear not them which kill the body

Jn. 1:1-18 The Word was made flesh

Ro. 8:1-17 The carnal mind is enmity against God

Ro. 12:1-8 Present your bodies a living sacrifice

Ro. 13 Make not provision for the flesh

1 Co. 6:12-20 Your body is the temple of the Holy Ghost

1 Co. 12:12-27 The body is one, and hath many members

2 Co. 5:1-8 If our earthly house be dissolved

Ga. 5:16-26 The flesh lusteth against the Spirit

Ga. 6 I bear in my body the marks of Jesus

Ep. 4:1-13 There is one body, and one Spirit

Ja. 2:14-26 The body without the spirit is dead

Boldness

1 S. 17:32-51 David fights Goliath

Ps. 3 I will not be afraid of ten thousands

Ps. 91 Thou shalt not be afraid

Boldness (*cont.*)

Pr. 28:1-10 The righteous are bold as a lion

Da. 3:13-18 They refused to worship the golden image

Ac. 4:1-22 When they saw their boldness

He. 4:9-16 Come boldly to the throne of grace

Bond

Ex. 1:8-14 They made their lives bitter with bondage

De. 15:12-15 Thou wast a bondman in the land of Egypt

Je. 5:19-29 Ye shall serve strangers

Mat. 11:25-30 My yoke is easy

Jn. 8:31-47 The truth shall make you free

Ro. 8:1-17 Ye have not received the spirit of bondage

Ga. 4:1-7 We were in bondage when we were children

Ep. 6:10-20 I am an ambassador in bonds

He. 13:1-14 Remember them that are in bonds

Bondage, *See* Captivity

Book

Ex. 31:12-18 Stone tables, written with the finger of God

Jb. 31:35-40 Oh that mine adversary had written a book

Ec. 12:8-14 Of making many books there is no end

Lu. 10:17-20 Your names are written in heaven

Jn. 21:18-25 Books that might have been written

Re. 20:11-15 The book of life was opened

Re. 21:1-7 Write: for these words are true

Boy

Ge. 21:1-21 The Lord heard the voice of Ishmael

1 S. 3:1-10 The Lord speaks to the boy Samuel

1 S. 17:32-51 The boy David fights with Goliath

Is. 11:1-9 A little child shall lead them

Zch. 8:1-8 The streets shall be full of boys

Lu. 2:41-52 When he was twelve years old

Jn. 6:1-14 The lad with the five barley loaves

1 Co. 13 When I was a child

Re. 12:1-5 She brought forth a man child

Boy Scout Sunday, *See* Scout

Branch

Le. 23:39-44 Ye shall dwell in booths seven days

Is. 11:1-9 A branch from the root of Jesse

Eze. 36:8-15 Yield your fruit to my people of Israel

Jn. 15:1-8 I am the vine, ye are the branches

Ro. 11:16-24 If the root be holy, so are the branches

Bravery, *See* Courage

Bread

Ex. 16:1-8 I will rain bread from heaven for you

Ex. 16:11-21 They said one to another, It is manna

2 K. 4:38-44 Thus saith the Lord, They shall eat

Jb. 28 Out of the earth cometh bread

Ps. 78:12-29 Man did eat angels' food

Ec. 11 Cast thy bread upon the waters

Da. 1:1-16 Daniel refuses the king's food

Mat. 4:1-11 Man shall not live by bread alone

Lu. 11:1-4 Give us day by day our daily bread

Lu. 24:13-35 He was known of them in breaking of bread

Jn. 6:1-14 Jesus feeds the five thousand

Jn. 6:30-51 I am the bread of life

Breadth

Jb. 11 Broader than the sea

Ps. 18:1-19 He brought me forth into a large place

Ps. 119:89-104 Thy commandment is exceeding broad

Mat. 7:13-14 Wide is the gate

Ep. 3 Breadth, length, depth, and height

Re. 21:10-27 The city lieth foursquare

Brevity

Ge. 47:1-10 Few and evil have my days been

Jb. 10 Are not my days few?

Jb. 14:1-14 Man is of few days

Ps. 90 A thousand years in thy sight

Jn. 16:7-16 A little while, and ye shall not see me

Ja. 4 Your life appeareth for a little time

Bribe

Ex. 23:1-8 The gift blindeth the wise

Ju. 16:1-20 The Philistines bribed Delilah

1 S. 8:1-5 The sons of Samuel took bribes

Is. 1:16-27 Every one followeth after rewards

Am. 5:11-20 They take a bribe

Mat. 28:11-15 The soldiers were bribed

Mk. 14:43-50 Judas betrays Jesus for money

Ac. 8:17-24 Simon seeks to purchase the gift of God

Bride, *See* Marriage

Bridegroom, *See* Marriage

Brotherhood

Ge. 4:1-15 Am I my brother's keeper?

Ge. 13:7-12 We be brethren

Ge. 44:18-34 Let thy servant abide instead of the lad

Mat. 23:8-12 All ye are brethren

Lu. 10:25-37 Which now of these three was neighbour?

Lu. 15:25-32 This thy brother was dead, and is alive

Ja. 2:14-16 What doth it profit?

Brute, *See* Beast

Builder

Ge. 11:1-9 Let us build us a city and a tower

2 Ch. 24:4-14 Joash repaired the house of the Lord

Ps. 127 Except the Lord build the house

Is. 65:17-25 They shall build houses and inhabit them

Mat. 7:24-27 The wise man built his house upon a rock

Mat. 16:13-20 I will build my church

Lu. 14:28-32 First he counteth the cost of the tower

1 Co. 3:10-15 As a wise master-builder

He. 11:1-10 He looked for a city whose builder is God

Bulwark, *See* Security

Burden

1 K. 12:1-11 I will add to your yoke

Is. 58:6-12 To undo the heavy burdens

Je. 23:33-40 The burden of the Lord

Mat. 11:25-30 My burden is light

Mat. 20:1-16 The burden and heat of the day

Mat. 23:1-12 They lay heavy burdens on men's shoulders

Lu. 23:26-33 They laid the cross on Simon

Ro. 15:1-7 Bear the infirmities of the weak

Ga. 6:1-10 Bear ye one another's burdens

1 Pe. 5:1-11 Casting all your care upon him

Burial, *See* Death

Burnt-Offering, *See* Sacrifice

Business

Pr. 22:17-29 He shall stand before kings

Mat. 6:19-24 Ye cannot serve God and mammon

Mat. 13:44-48 Like unto a merchant man

Mat. 25:14-30 The parable of the talents

Lu. 2:40-52 I must be about my Father's business

Lu. 19:1-10 Zacchaeus was rich and lost

Ro. 12:6-21 Not slothful in business

Ja. 4:10-17 Buying, selling, and getting gain

[C]

Calamity, *See* Adversity

Call

Ex. 3:1-10 I have heard their cry

1 S. 3:1-10 Speak, for thy servant heareth

1 K. 18:17-40 Elijah and the prophets of Baal

Ps. 91 He shall call, and I will answer

Mat. 3 The voice of one crying in the wilderness

Ac. 16:6-15 Come over into Macedonia

Calling

1 Ch. 28:1-8 The Lord God of Israel chose me

Is. 61 Men shall call you Ministers of our God

Calling *(cont.)*

Mk. 6:7-13   He called unto him the twelve

1 Co. 7:20-22   Abide in your calling

1 Co. 12:1-11   There are diversities of gifts

Ep. 4:1-7   Walk worthy of your vocation

Ep. 4:11-16   He gave some pastors and teachers

Callousness, *See* Indifference

Calm, *See* Peace

Calumny, *See* Slander

Calvary, *See* Good Friday

Candor

Jn. 10:22-42   If thou be the Christ, tell us plainly

Jn. 14:1-14   If it were not so I would have told you

Jn. 16:25-33   I shall shew you plainly of the Father

2 Co. 3   We use great plainness of speech

Canvass, Every Member

De. 16:16, 17   They shall not appear before the Lord empty

1 Ch. 29:10-19   Of thine own have we given thee

Ec. 11:1-6   In the morning sow thy seed

Mal. 3:7-12   Will a man rob God?

Mat. 7:1-12   With what measure ye mete

Lu. 21:1-4   The rich men and the poor widow

Ac. 2:41-47   They that believed had all things common

1 Co. 16:1-14   Let all things be done with charity

2 Co. 8:1-21   The riches of their liberality

2 Co. 9   God loveth a cheerful giver

Capacity, *See* Ability

Captivity

Ex. 1:8-14   They made them serve with rigour

Ps. 137:1-6   By the rivers of Babylon

Is. 61   Sent to proclaim liberty to the captives

Je. 29:20-23   Hear ye, all ye of the captivity

2 Co. 10:1-7   Bringing every thought into captivity

Ga. 5:1-6   Entangled with the yoke of bondage

Care, *See* Burden; Solicitude

Carelessness, *See* Indifference

Carpenter, *See* Builder

Catastrophe, *See* Adversity

Catholicity, *See* Universality

Cause

1 S. 24:9-15   The Lord plead my cause

Jb. 5   Unto God would I commit my cause

Ps. 140   The cause of the afflicted

Mat. 5:21-26   Angry without a cause

Jn. 18:28-40   For this cause came I into the world

Center

Ge. 2:1-9   The tree of life in the midst of the garden

Ex. 3:1-10   God called out of the midst of the bush

Is. 56:1-8   A house of prayer for all people

Da. 6:10-17   He opened his windows toward Jerusalem

Zch. 2   I will be the glory in the midst of her

Mat. 18:1-10   A little child in the midst of them

Jn. 4:1-26   Men ought to worship in Jerusalem

Jn. 12:23-36   I will draw all men unto me

Jn. 19:13-18   They crucified him, Jesus in the midst

1 Ti. 2:1-8   One God and one mediator

Ceremony

Le. 23:1-14   These are the feasts of the Lord

Nu. 9:1-5   Let Israel keep the passover

Is. 1:10-20   Bring no more vain oblations

Is. 58:1-7   The fast that I have chosen

Ho. 6   I desired mercy and not sacrifice

Am. 5:21-27   I despise your feast days

Lu. 11:37-44   Ye make clean the outside of the cup

Ro. 2:17-29   Circumcision is that of the heart

Ga. 4:1-11   Ye observe days, months, times, years

Certainty

Jb. 19:21-27   I know that my redeemer liveth

Ec. 8   It shall be well with them that fear God

Lu. 1:1-4   That thou mightest know the certainty

Jn. 6:66-69   We believe and are sure

2 Ti. 1   I know whom I have believed

He. 10:1-22 In full assurance of faith

Challenge

Nu. 23:1-13 How shall I defy whom God hath not defied?

1 S. 17:1-11 I defy the armies of Israel this day

2 S. 21:15-22 When he defied Israel, Jonathan slew him

2 S. 23:8-17 David's three mighty men

Jb. 41:1-10 Who is able to stand before me?

Chamber, *See* Room

Champion, *See* Challenge

Chance

Pr. 16:22-33 The lot is cast into the lap

Ec. 9:11-18 Time and chance happeneth to them all

Mat. 27:33-38 Upon my vesture did they cast lots

Lu. 10:30-37 By chance a certain priest came

Ac. 1:15-26 The lot fell upon Matthias

Chance, Second

Ju. 16:15-22 The hair of his head began to grow again

1 S. 3:1-10 The Lord called yet again, Samuel

Jb. 42 The Lord gave Job twice as much as before

Is. 55 Let the wicked forsake his way

Je. 1:11-19 The word of the Lord came a second time

Jon. 3 The word of the Lord came a second time

Mat. 11:1-6 Go and shew John again the things you see

Lu. 13:6-9 Let it alone this year also

He. 5 Ye have need that one teach you again

Change

Mat. 18:1-10 Be converted and become as little children

Ro. 1:14-17 The gospel is the power of God

Ro. 1:16-25 They changed the truth of God into a lie

Ro. 12 Transformed by the renewing of your mind

1 Co. 15:42-58 We shall be changed

2 Co. 3:12-18 Changed from glory to glory

2 Co. 5:17-21 In Christ he is a new creature

Ph. 3:13-21 Our vile body shall be changed

Ph. 4:4-9 Think on these things

Chaos, *See* Confusion

Character

1 Ch. 22:11-13 Be strong, and of good courage

Ps. 15 Who shall dwell in thy holy hill?

Ps. 19 Cleanse me from secret faults

Ps. 26:1-6 I have walked in mine integrity

Ps. 34:11-22 The righteous cry, the Lord heareth

Pr. 11 The integrity of the upright

Pr. 23:15-35 Look not upon the wine when it is red

Is. 33:13-24 He that walketh righteously

Da. 1 Children in whom was no blemish

Mi. 6:1-15 The Lord hath a controversy with his people

Mat. 5:1-16 Blessed are they which do hunger

Mat. 7:15-20 By their fruits ye shall know them

Mat. 12:1-13 It is lawful to do well on the sabbath

Mat. 19:16-22 There is none good but one

Lu. 6:39-49 A good tree bringeth forth good fruit

Ro. 10:5-11 The righteousness which is of faith

Ro. 12 Present your bodies a living sacrifice

2 Co. 7:1-4 We have not wronged, nor corrupted any man

Ga. 6:1-10 Not weary in well doing

Ep. 5 Walk as children of light

Ep. 6:13-17 Take unto you the whole armour of God

2 Ti. 2:22-26 Follow righteousness, faith, charity, peace

Tit. 3:1-8 These things are good and profitable

1 Pe. 2:11-25 Christ left us an example

2 Pe. 1:1-11 Add to your faith virtue

Charity

Mat. 6:1-4 Let thine alms be in secret

Mat. 19:16-22 Sell that thou hast and give to the poor

Lu. 10:25-37 The parable of the good Samaritan

Ac. 20:28-35 More blessed to give than to receive

Charity *(cont.)*

Ro. 15:1-7 The strong should help the weak
1 Co. 13 The greatest of these is charity
2 Co. 9:1-7 God loveth a cheerful giver
1 Pe. 4:7-10 Charity shall cover the multitude of sins
Charm, *See* Beauty
Chastisement, *See* Punishment
Chastity
Pr. 31:10-31 Who can find a virtuous woman?
Mat. 25:1-13 The parable of the ten virgins
Ro. 8:1-14 Mortify the deeds of the body
1 Co. 6:15-20 Your body is the temple of the Holy Ghost
1 Co. 7:25-40 The difference between a wife and a virgin
Ga. 5:13-26 Use not liberty for an occasion to the flesh
Tit. 2 Teach the young women to be chaste
Cheer, *See* Gayety
Chief
De. 7:6-11 God hath chosen thee to be a special people
Ps. 89:18-37 I will make him my firstborn
Mat. 18:1-10 Who is greatest in the kingdom of heaven?
Mat. 20:17-28 Whosoever will be great
Mat. 23:1-12 They love the uppermost rooms at feasts
Mk. 10:35-45 The chiefest shall be the servant of all
Lu. 19:1-10 Zacchaeus was chief among the publicans
1 Ti. 1:15-17 I am the chief of sinners
Child, *See* Children's Day
Children's Day
Ge. 33 The children are tender
De. 6:1-12 Thou shalt teach them unto thy children
Mat. 18:1-10 Despise not one of these little ones
Mat. 19:13-15 Of such is the kingdom of heaven
Mk. 9:33-37 He set a child in the midst of them
Lu. 2:41-52 They found him in the temple
Lu. 9:46-48 Jesus took a child, and set him by him

Choice
De. 7:6-11 The Lord chose you because he loved you
De. 11:8-12 Keep the commandments that ye may be strong
De. 11:26-32 I set before you a blessing and a curse
Jos. 24:14-25 Choose you this day whom ye will serve
1 S. 8 Israel demands a king
1 K. 18:30-39 The fire of the Lord fell
Ps. 89:18-37 I have exalted one chosen out of the people
Mat. 12:22-30 He that is not with me is against me
Lu. 23:34-38 If he be Christ, the chosen of God
Jn. 6:53-69 Many disciples walked no more with him
1 Co. 1:26-31 God hath chosen the weak things
2 Th. 2:13-17 God hath from the beginning chosen you
1 Pe. 2:1-10 Ye are a chosen generation
Christ
Mat. 17:1-9 This is my beloved Son
Mat. 26:57-68 The high priest questioned him
Mk. 8:27-29 Peter answered, Thou art the Christ
Lu. 2:7-16 A Saviour, which is Christ the Lord
Lu. 4:40-44 The devils cried, Thou art Christ
Jn. 1:15-28 I am not the Christ
Christ, Abiding in, *See* Christ, Communion with
Christ, the Accusing of, *See* Christ, Condemnation of
Christ, Adoration of
Mat. 8:1-4 There came a leper and worshipped him
Mat. 9:18-26 A certain ruler worshipped him
Mat. 28:16-20 When they saw him, they worshipped him
Mk. 5:1-17 He ran and worshipped him
Ph. 2:1-11 At the name of Jesus every knee should bow
He. 1 Let all the angels of God worship him
Christ, the Advocate
Is. 53 He made intercession for the transgressors
Lu. 22:31-38 I have prayed for thee
Ga. 3:13-29 A mediator is not a mediator of one

He. 7:22-28 He ever liveth to make intercession

He. 8 He is the mediator of a better covenant

He. 9:19-28 Now to appear in the presence of God for us

1 Jn. 2:1-11 If any man sin, we have an advocate

Christ, Agony of, *See* Christ, Suffering of

Christ, Antagonism to, *See* Christ, Denial of

Christ, Appeal of, *See* Christ, Call of

Christ, Appearance of

Mk. 16:1-15 He appeared first to Mary Magdalene

Lu. 1:67-80 The dayspring from on high hath visited us

Lu. 9:28-36 The fashion of his countenance was altered

Jn. 2:1-11 He manifested forth his glory

1 Co. 15:1-8 He was seen of above five hundred brethren

2 Co. 4:1-6 The glory of God in the face of Jesus Christ

2 Ti. 1:1-11 Life and immortality to light

2 Ti. 4:1-8 Unto all them that love his appearing

Tit. 2 Looking for the glorious appearance of Jesus

1 Pe. 1:1-13 At the appearing of Jesus Christ

1 Pe. 5:1-11 When the chief Shepherd shall appear

1 Jn. 3:1-11 He was manifested to take away our sins

Re. 1:10-18 One like unto the Son of man

Re. 22:1-4 They shall see his face

Christ, Ascension of

Ps. 68:1-20 Thou hast ascended

Lu. 24:36-53 He was carried up into heaven

Jn. 16:1-16 It is expedient for you that I go away

Jn. 20:11-18 I ascend unto my Father, and your Father

Ac. 1:1-11 A cloud received him out of their sight

He. 4:9-16 Our high priest has passed into heaven

Christ, Authority of

Mat. 8:18-27 Even the winds and the sea obey him

Mat. 21:23-32 By what authority doest thou these things?

Mat. 28:16-20 All power is given unto me

Mk. 1:14-22 He taught them as one with authority

Mk. 1:23-28 He commandeth even the unclean spirits

Mk. 2:1-12 The Son of man hath power to forgive sins

Jn. 2:1-11 Whatsoever he saith unto you, do it

Jn. 5:17-27 The Father hath given him authority

Jn. 17:1-10 Thou hast given him power over all flesh

1 Pe. 3:8-22 Authorities and powers are subject to him

Christ, Beauty of, *See* Christ, Grace of

Christ, Belief in

Mat. 14:22-33 O thou of little faith

Jn. 11:19-27 He that believeth in me shall live

Jn. 14:1-14 Ye believe in God, believe also in me

Ac. 8:26-40 I believe that Jesus is the Son of God

Ac. 16:25-34 Believe and thou shalt be saved

Ro. 10:1-13 Whosoever believeth shall not be ashamed

He. 12:1-14 Looking unto Jesus the author of our faith

1 Pe. 1:3-9 Ye believe, though now ye see him not

Christ, Betrayal of

Mat. 17:22-23 The Son of man shall be betrayed

Jn. 18:1-14 Judas betrays Jesus

Christ, Birth of, *See* Christmas

Christ, Blood of

Mat. 27:24-32 I am innocent of the blood of this just man

Mat. 27:33-50 They crucified him

Jn. 6:47-60 Except ye drink my blood

Ac. 3:12-26 Ye killed the Prince of life

Ro. 3:20-31 A propitiation through faith in his blood

1 Co. 5 Christ our passover is sacrificed for us

He. 10:19-25 Let us draw near with a true heart

He. 13:7-21 Through the blood of the everlasting covenant

1 Pe. 1:13-25 The precious blood of Christ

1 Jn. 1 The blood of Jesus Christ cleanseth us

1 Jn. 5:1-12 This is he that came by water and blood

Re. 7:9-17 Washed in the blood of the Lamb

Christ, Body of
Jn. 1:1-14 The Word was made flesh
Jn. 2:18-25 He spake of the temple of his body
Ro. 8:1-17 Christ came in the likeness of sinful flesh
1 Co. 11:20-34 This is my body, which is broken for you
1 Co. 12 Ye are the body of Christ
Ep. 5:15-32 We are members of his body
He. 10:1-14 Through the offering of the body of Jesus
1 Pe. 4:1-11 Christ hath suffered for us in the flesh

Christ, the Bread of Life
Mat. 26:26-30 Take, eat, this is my body
Lu. 24:13-36 He was known of them in breaking of bread
Jn. 6:24-35 I am the bread of life
Jn. 6:47-58 The bread that cometh down from heaven
1 Co. 10:16-33 We are all partakers of one bread

Christ, Call of
Mat. 11:25-30 Come unto me, all ye that labour
Mat. 20:1-16 Many are called, but few chosen
Mk. 1:14-20 Come, and I will make you fishers of men
Lu. 19:1-10 Zacchaeus, make haste
1 Th. 5:1-24 Faithful is he that calleth you
1 Pe. 2:1-12 He hath called you into his marvellous light
2 Pe. 1:1-8 He hath called us to glory and virtue
Re. 22:17-21 The Spirit and the bride say, Come

Christ, the Captain, *See* Christ, the Master

Christ, Centrality of, *See* Christ, Authority of

Christ, the Changeless
Mat. 28:16-20 Lo, I am with you alway
Lu. 1:26-38 Of his kingdom there shall be no end
Lu. 21:25-33 My words shall not pass away
Jn. 8:31-59 Before Abraham was, I am
Jn. 12:23-36 Christ abideth for ever
He. 6:13-20 Jesus, an high priest for ever
He. 13:1-8 The same yesterday, and today, and for ever

Re. 1:8-20 Behold, I am alive for evermore

Christ, the Chosen of, *See* Christ, Disciple of

Christ, the Comforter, *See* Christ, Compassion of

Christ, Coming to
Mat. 22:1-10 Come unto the marriage
Mk. 10:13-16 Suffer the little children to come unto me
Lu. 14:15-24 They began to make excuse
Jn. 1:35-49 They heard him speak and followed
Jn. 6:28-40 I will not cast out him that cometh to me
Jn. 10:1-16 I am the door of the sheep
Jn. 14:1-14 I am the way
He. 10:19-25 Let us draw near with a true heart
1 Pe. 2:1-10 To whom coming
Re. 3:14-22 I stand at the door, and knock

Christ, Commandments of
Mat. 8:18-27 Even the winds and the sea obey him
Mat. 21:1-11 The disciples did as Jesus commanded
Mat. 28:16-20 Observe all things I have commanded you
Lu. 8:22-25 He commandeth even the winds and water
Jn. 13:31-37 A new commandment I give unto you
Jn. 15:1-17 I command you, that ye love one another
2 Th. 3 We command you in the name of our Lord
1 Jn. 2:3-8 If we keep his commandments

Christ, Communion with
Jn. 6:47-58 He that dwelleth in me
Jn. 15:1-8 I am the vine
Ro. 8:28-39 Who shall separate us from the love of Christ?
1 Co. 10:14-33 The communion of the blood of Christ
2 Co. 5:14-20 If any man be in Christ
2 Co. 12:1-15 I knew a man in Christ
Ep. 2:4-9 In heavenly places in Christ Jesus
Ph. 3:7-14 That I may be found in him
Col. 3:1-15 Your life is hid with Christ

1 Jn. 4:4-15 That we might live through him

Jude 1-5 Preserved in Jesus Christ

Christ, Companionship of, *See* Christ, Communion with

Christ, Compassion of

Mat. 9:1-8 Son, be of good cheer thy sins be forgiven thee

Mat. 9:18-26 Be of good comfort

Mat. 9:32-36 He was moved with compassion on them

Mat. 15:29-39 I have compassion on the multitude

Mk. 1:33-45 Jesus was moved with compassion

Lu. 19:28-44 He beheld the city, and wept over it

Jn. 6:5-14 Jesus feeds five thousand

Jn. 11:11-36 Jesus wept

Jn. 14:1-14 Let not your heart be troubled

Jn. 14:15-31 I will not leave you comfortless

Jn. 16:16-20 Your sorrow shall be turned to joy

2 Co. 1:1-7 Our consolation abound- eth by Christ

Ph. 2:1-11 If there be any consola- tion in Christ

Christ, Compulsion of, *See* Christ, Authority of

Christ, Condemnation of

Lu. 6:27-38 Condemn not, and ye shall not be condemned

Lu. 19:12-26 Out of thine own mouth will I judge thee

Jn. 3:19-21 This is the condem- nation

Jn. 8:1-11 Being convicted by their own conscience

Ro. 8:1-17 No condemnation to them in Christ Jesus

Christ, the Contemporary, *See* Christ, the Changeless

Christ, Courage of

Mat. 26:57-68 They spit in his face, and buffeted him

Mk. 15:1-25 At the third hour they crucified him

Lu. 12:49-53 I have a baptism to be baptized with

He. 12:1-14 Jesus endured the cross

Christ, the Creator

Jn. 1:1-14 All things were made by him

Ep. 3:8-21 God created all things by Jesus Christ

Col. 1:1-19 By him were all things created

He. 1 By his Son he made the worlds

Christ, Cross of, *See* Good Friday

Christ, Crown of, *See* Christ, Reign of

Christ, Crucifixion of, *See* Good Friday

Christ, Cup of, *See* Christ, Suffering of

Christ, Day of, *See* Christ, the Judge

Christ, Death of, *See* Good Friday

Christ, Defiance of, *See* Christ, Denial of

Christ, the Deliverer, *See* Christ, the Saviour

Christ, Denial of

Is. 53 He is despised and rejected of men

Mat. 8:28-34 What have we to do with thee, Jesus?

Mat. 10:16-42 If he denies me, him will I also deny

Mat. 21:33-46 The stone which the builders rejected

Mk. 8:27-38 He who shall be ashamed of me

Mk. 14:66-72 Peter's denial

Lu. 20:9-20 They cast him out of the vineyard

1 Jn. 2:15-29 The liar denieth that Jesus is the Christ

Jude 1-6 Denying the only Lord God

Christ, Devotion to, *See* Christ, Love of

Christ, Dignity of, *See* Christ, Authority of

Christ, Disciple of

Mat. 4:18-25 I will make you fishers of men

Lu. 10:1-12 The Lord appointed other seventy also

Lu. 14:25-35 The disciple must bear his cross

Jn. 15:1-16 If ye bear fruit ye shall be my disciples

Jn. 15:18-27 I have chosen you out of this world

Jn. 17:6-19 Sanctify them through thy truth

Ac. 11:19-26 The disciples were called Christians in Antioch

1 Co. 7:17-24 He that is called is the Lord's freeman

Christ, Divinity of

Mat. 1:18-25 They shall call his name Emmanuel

Jn. 1:1-14 The Word was made flesh

Jn. 10:22-38 I and my Father are one

Jn. 17:1-19 Jesus Christ, whom thou hast sent

Jn. 20:24-29 My Lord and my God

Ph. 2:1-11 It was not robbery to be equal to God

Christ, Divinity of (*cont.*)

Col. 2:1-13 All the fulness of the Godhead

1 Ti. 3 God was manifest in the flesh

1 Jn. 5 This is the true God, and eternal life

Christ, the Door, *See* Christ, Coming to

Christ, Doubt of

Mat. 14:22-33 Wherefore didst thou doubt?

Mat. 28:9-18 Some doubted

Mk. 9:14-29 Lord, I believe: help thou mine unbelief

Jn. 10:22-42 If thou be the Christ, tell us plainly

Jn. 12:23-36 Who is this Son of man?

Jn. 12:37-41 They believed not on him

Jn. 20:24-29 Except I shall see the print of the nails

Christ, Encouragement of, *See* Christ, Compassion of

Christ, Enemy of, *See* Christ, Denial of

Christ, the Eternal, *See* Christ, the Changeless

Christ, Evidence of, *See* Christ, Witness of

Christ, Exaltation of, *See* Christ, Authority of

Christ, Example of

Mat. 8:1-22 Master, I will follow thee

Jn. 13:1-17 I have given you an example

Jn. 14:1-14 I am the way, the truth, and the life

Ep. 5:1-17 Walk in love, as Christ also hath loved us

Ph. 2:1-11 Let this mind be in you

1 Ti. 1:5-17 A pattern to them that should believe

He. 12:1-14 Looking unto Jesus, the author of our faith

1 Pe. 2:20-25 Christ left us an example

Christ, Face of, *See* Christ, Appearance of

Christ, Faith in, *See* Christ, Belief in

Christ, Faith of

Jn. 16:1-15 All things that t Father hath are mine

Jn. 16:21-33 I leave the world, and go to the Father

Jn. 17 O righteous Father, I have known thee

Ga. 2:11-21 By the faith of the Son of God

He. 12:1-14 Jesus the author and finisher of our faith

Re. 14:1-13 The faith of Jesus

Christ, Faithfulness of

Mat. 28 Lo, I am with you alway

Jn. 13:1-17 He loved them unto the end

Jn. 14:1-21 I will not leave you comfortless

2 Co. 1:14-24 All the promises of God in him are yea

He. 3:1-14 Christ Jesus was faithful

He. 13:1-14 The same yesterday, today, and for ever

Re. 1:4-20 Jesus Christ, who is the faithful witness

Christ, Fellowship with, *See* Christ, Communion with

Christ, Fidelity to, *See* Christ, Love of

Christ, Finality of, *See* Christ, the Changeless

Christ, Finding, *See* Christ, Coming to

Christ, Follower of, *See* Christ, Disciple of

Christ, Foreknowledge of

Mk. 8:27-38 The Son of man must suffer many things

Lu. 12:49-57 I have a baptism to be baptized with

Jn. 6:47-65 Jesus knew those that believed not

Jn. 7:32-53 I go unto him that sent me

Jn. 13:1-17 He knew who should betray him

Jn. 18:1-14 Jesus knew all things that should come

Christ, Forgiveness of

Mat. 9:1-8 The Son of Man hath power to forgive sins

Mk. 2:1-12 Son, thy sins be forgiven thee

Lu. 7:36-50 Her sins, which are many, are forgiven

Lu. 23:27-38 Father, forgive them

Ep. 1:1-14 In whom we have forgiveness of sins

Col. 3:1-17 Even as Christ forgave you, so also do ye

Christ, the Foundation

Ps. 118 The stone which the builders refused

1 Co. 3 Jesus Christ is the only foundation

Ep. 2 Jesus Christ being the chief corner stone

Col. 2:1-14 Rooted and built up in him

1 Pe. 1:13-25 Before the foundation of the world

1 Pe. 2:1-10 I lay in Sion a chief corner stone

Re. 13:1-9 The Lamb slain from the foundation

Christ, the Friend

Lu. 7:24-35 A friend of publicans and sinners

Jn. 10:1-16 He calleth his own sheep by name

Jn. 14:15-27 I will not leave you comfortless

Jn. 15:12-16 Ye are my friends

1 Co. 1:1-10 The fellowship of his Son Jesus Christ

Christ, Fullness of

Jn. 1:1-18 Of his fulness have all we received

Ro. 15:13-33 The fulness of the blessing of the gospel

Ep. 1:15-23 The fulness of him that filleth all in all

Ep. 4:1-13 The stature of the fulness of Christ

Col. 1:9-19 In him all fulness dwells

Col. 2:6-10 The fulness of the Godhead dwelleth in him

1 Ti. 1 The grace of our Lord was exceeding abundant

Christ, Gentleness of, *See* Christ, Goodness of

Christ, Gift of, *See* Christ, Help of

Christ, Glory of

Mat. 6:1-14 Thine is the glory

Mat. 17:1-9 He was transfigured before them

Jn. 13:18-35 Now is the Son of man glorified

Jn. 17:1-5 Glorify thou me

Jn. 17:6-26 That they may behold my glory

1 Co. 1:20-31 Let him glory in the Lord

He. 3 Worthy of more glory than Moses

Ja. 2:1-13 The Lord of glory

2 Pe. 1:16-18 He received from God honour and glory

Christ, the Goal

Mat. 28 Even unto the end of the world

Jn. 6:47-69 Thou hast the words of eternal life

Ro. 10 Christ is the end of the law

He. 12:1-14 Looking to Jesus, the finisher of our faith

Re. 21:1-7 I am the beginning and the end

Christ, God in, *See* Christ, Divinity of

Christ, Goodness of

Mat. 19:16-26 Why callest thou me good?

Jn. 10:1-18 I am the good shepherd

Ac. 10:34-48 Jesus of Nazareth went about doing good

2 Co. 12:1-9 My grace is sufficient for thee

Ep. 2 He showed kindness toward us through Christ

Ep. 3 The love of Christ, which passeth knowledge

Ep. 4:1-16 He gave gifts unto men

Christ, the Gospel of

Na.1:1-15 The feet of him that bringeth good tidings

Mat. 13:24-35 All these things spake Jesus in parables

Mat. 24:1-14 This gospel of the kingdom shall be preached

Mk. 1:1-15 The beginning of the gospel of Jesus Christ

Lu. 2:1-14 I bring you good tidings of great joy

Jn. 17:1-8 I have given unto them the words

Ro. 1:1-17 I am not ashamed of the gospel of Christ

Ro. 15:13-33 The fulness of the blessing of the gospel

1 Co. 1:1-23 Christ sent me to preach the gospel

Christ, Grace of

Ps. 45 Grace is poured into thy lips

Lu. 4:1-22 They wondered at his gracious words

Jn. 1:1-18 Grace and truth came by Jesus Christ

Ro. 5 The gift of grace is by one man, Jesus Christ

Ep. 2 By grace are ye saved through faith

2 Ti. 2:1-15 Be strong in the grace that is in Christ

Tit. 3:1-8 Justified by his grace

2 Pe. 3 Grow in grace

Christ, Gratitude to

Mat. 14:22-36 They that were in the ship worshipped him

Mat. 15:21-31 Then came she and worshipped him

Mat. 20:30-34 Their eyes received sight, and they followed

Mk. 1:38-45 He began to blaze abroad the matter

Lu. 7:36-50 This woman hath not ceased to kiss my feet

Christ, Gratitude to (*cont.*)

Lu. 17:1-19 One of the ten lepers returned to give thanks

1 Ti. 1:1-14 I thank Christ Jesus our Lord

Christ, Greatness of, *See* Christ, Authority of

Christ, Grief of, *See* Christ, Suffering of

Christ, the Guide, *See* Christ, the Master

Christ, Hand of

Mk. 8:22-37 They besought him to touch him

Mk. 9:14-29 Jesus took him by the hand, and lifted him

Lu. 24:13-40 Behold my hands

Jn. 5:1-17 My Father worketh hitherto, and I work

Jn. 8:1-11 Jesus wrote with his finger on the ground

Jn. 20:24-31 The print of the nails in his hands

Christ, Hatred of, *See* Christ, Denial of

Christ, the Healing

Mat. 8:1-17 Thou canst make me clean

Mat. 9:1-13 The whole need not a physician

Mk. 7:31-37 He maketh the deaf to hear, the dumb to speak

Lu. 4:16-37 He hath sent me to heal the brokenhearted

Lu. 8:41-56 Thy faith hath made thee whole

Jn. 5:2-9 Take up thy bed, and walk

Ac. 3:1-10 Such as I have give I thee

1 Pe. 2 By whose stripes ye were healed

Christ, Help of

Mat. 15:21-39 She came and said, Lord, help me

Mat. 20:20-34 The Son of man came to minister

Mk. 5:1-20 Jesus had done great things for him

Jn. 21:1-13 The right side of the ship

Ga. 6 Help each other, and so fulfil his law

He. 2:1-18 He is able to succour them that are tempted

Christ, the Hidden, *See* Christ, Loneliness of

Christ, Holiness of, *See* Christ, Goodness of

Christ, Hope in, *See* Christ, Belief in

Christ, Humanity of, *See* Christ, the Son of Man

Christ, Humiliation of, *See* Christ, Humility of

Christ, Humility of

Is. 53 He is despised and rejected of men

Mat. 3 Jesus is baptized by John

Mat. 11:25-30 I am meek and lowly in heart

Mat. 19:16-26 Why callest thou me good?

Lu. 22:31-38 He was reckoned among the transgressors

Jn. 13:1-15 Jesus washes the disciples' feet

Ga. 3:1-13 Christ was made a curse for us

Ph. 2:1-13 He took upon him the form of a servant

Christ, Imitation of, *See* Christ, Example of

Christ, Impotence of, *See* Christ, Humility of

Christ, the Indwelling, *See* Christ, Communion with

Christ, Influence of, *See* Christ, Authority of

Christ, the Inimitable, *See* Christ, Supremacy of

Christ, Innocence of, *See* Christ, Goodness of

Christ, Isolation of, *See* Christ, Loneliness of

Christ, Joy in, *See* Christ, Communion with

Christ, Joy of

Mat. 25:14-30 Enter thou into the joy of thy lord

Lu. 10:17-24 Jesus rejoiced in spirit

Jn. 16:21-33 That your joy may be full

He. 12:1-14 For joy he endured the cross

Christ, the Judge

Mat. 19:27-30 When the Son of man shall sit on the throne

Lu. 21:8-36 Worthy to stand before the Son of man

Jn. 5:17-38 My judgment is just

Jn. 8:1-19 I judge no man

Jn. 9:39-41 For judgment I am come into this world

Jn. 12:44-50 My word shall judge him in the last day

Ro. 2:1-16 God shall judge men by Jesus Christ

2 Co. 5 We must all appear before the judgment seat

Christ, the King, *See* Christ, Reign of

Christ, Knowledge of, *See* Christ, Wisdom of

Christ, the Lamb of God, *See* Christ, Suffering of

Christ, the Leader, *See* Christ, the Master

Christ, the Liberator, *See* Christ the Saviour

Christ, Liberty of
Is. 61 Sent to proclaim liberty to the captives
Jn. 8:21-32 The truth shall make you free
Jn. 8:33-59 Freed by the Son ye shall be free indeed
Ro. 8:1-17 Christ Jesus hath made me free
1 Co. 7:20-24 The servant in the Lord is a freeman
Ga. 5:1-6 Stand fast in the liberty of Christ

Christ, Life in, *See* Christ, Communion with

Christ, the Light
Is. 9:1-7 The people have seen a great light
Jn. 1:1-14 That was the true light
Jn. 8:12-20 My follower shall not walk in darkness
Jn. 9:1-11 I am the light of the world
Jn. 12:35-50 I am come a light into the world
Ep. 5:1-14 Christ shall give thee light
1 Jn. 2:1-11 The true light now shineth
Re. 21:9-27 The Lamb is the light thereof

Christ, the Living
Jn. 5:17-31 The Son hath life in himself
Jn. 14:1-20 Because I live, ye shall live also
Ro. 6 Christ being raised dieth no more
1 Co. 15:1-22 In Christ shall all be made alive
Col. 3:1-11 Christ is all, and in all
He. 13:1-14 Christ the same yesterday, and to day, and for ever
1 Jn. 4 That we might live through him
Re. 1 I am he that liveth, and was dead

Christ, Loneliness of
Mat. 8:18-20 The Son of man hath not where to lay his head
Mat. 27:35-50 My God, why hast thou forsaken me?
Lu. 9:18-27 He was alone praying

Jn. 6:15-21 He departed into a mountain himself alone
Jn. 16 I am not alone, for the Father is with me

Christ, the Lord
Lu. 2:1-14 A Saviour, which is Christ the Lord
Jn. 13:1-17 Ye call me Master and Lord, and so I am
Ep. 1 All things are under his feet
Ep. 4:1-13 One Lord, one faith, one baptism
Ph. 2:1-13 Confess that Jesus Christ is Lord
Col. 3 Do all in the name of the Lord Jesus
1 Ti. 6 The King of kings, and Lord of lords

Christ, Love of
Jn. 13:1-17 He loved his own unto the end
Jn. 14:15-31 If ye love me, keep my commandments
Jn. 21 Thou knowest that I love thee
2 Co. 5 The love of Christ constraineth us
Ep. 3:14-21 The love of Christ which passeth knowledge
Ep. 5:1-17 Walk in love, as Christ hath loved us
1 Jn. 4 We love him, because he first loved us

Christ, Loyalty to, *See* Christ, Love of

Christ, Majesty of, *See* Christ, Authority of

Christ, Manliness of, *See* Christ, the Son of Man

Christ, the Master
Mat. 23:1-12 One is your Master, even Christ
Mk. 9:38-50 Ye belong to Christ
Mk. 10:17-27 Good Master, what shall I do?
Lu. 6:27-49 The disciple is not above his master
Jn. 11:20-36 The Master is come, and calleth for thee

Christ, the Mediator, *see* Advocate

Christ, Meekness of, *See* Christ, Humility of

Christ, Mercy of, *See* Christ, Compassion of

Christ, Message of, *See* Christ, Gospel of

Christ, the Messiah
Mat. 16:13-20 Thou art the Son of the living God
Mk. 14:53-65 Art thou the Christ, the Son of the Blessed?

Christ, the Messiah *(cont.)*

Jn. 1:29-42 We have found the Messias

Jn. 4:1-26 I that speak unto thee am Messias

Jn. 6:53-71 Thou art Christ, the Son of the living God

Ac. 17:1-9 This Jesus, whom I preach unto you, is Christ

Ac. 18:24-28 Showing that Jesus was Christ

1 Th. 5 Unto the coming of our Lord

Christ, Mind of, *See* Christ, Wisdom of

Christ, Ministry of

Mat. 20:20-34 The Son of man came to minister

Lu. 4:1-21 Anointed to preach the gospel to the poor

Lu. 19:1-10 To seek and to save that which was lost

Jn. 13:1-15 Your Master has washed your feet

Ro. 15:1-16 Jesus was a minister of the circumcision

He. 4:12-16 We have a great high priest

He. 7 This man hath an unchangeable priesthood

Christ, Mission of, *See* Christ, Work of

Christ, Mystery of, *See* Christ, Loneliness of

Christ, Name of

Mat. 1:18-25 Thou shalt call his name Jesus

Mat. 28 In the name of Father, Son, and Holy Ghost

Jn. 20:19-31 Ye might have life through his name

Ac. 4:1-12 No other name whereby we must be saved

Ac. 8:1-17 They were baptized in the name of Jesus

Ph. 2:1-11 At the name of Jesus every knee should bow

Re. 19:1-16 His name is called The Word of God

Re. 22 His name shall be in their foreheads

Christ, Nature of

Mat. 3:16-17 This is my beloved Son

Mat. 16:13-27 Thou art the Christ

Mat. 22:34-46 What think ye of Christ?

Mk. 8:22-29 Whom do men say that I am?

Lu. 22:66-70 Art thou then the Son of God?

Jn. 6:22-42 Is not this Jesus, the son of Joseph

Jn. 14:1-14 He that hath seen me hath seen the Father

Jn. 19:1-12 Whence art thou?

Ac. 8:26-39 Philip baptizes the eunuch

Ac. 22:1-10 Who art thou, Lord?

He. 2 He took on him the seed of Abraham

2 Pe. 1:16-21 He received from God honour and glory

Christ, Nearness of, *See* Christ, Communion with

Christ, Obedience of, *See* Christ, Humility of

Christ, Obedience to, *See* Christ, Commandments of

Christ, Oneness with God, *See* Christ, Divinity of

Christ, Partnership with, *See* Christ, Communion with

Christ, Passion of, *See* Christ, Suffering of

Christ, the Passover, *See* Christ, Suffering of

Christ, Peace of

Is. 9:1-7 The Prince of Peace

Mat. 11 I will give you rest

Jn. 14 My peace I give unto you

Jn. 16 That in me ye might have peace

Jn. 20:19-31 Jesus saith unto them, Peace be unto you

Ep. 2 Christ came and preached peace to you

Christ, Perfection of, *See* Christ, Goodness of

Christ, Permanence of, *See* Christ, the Changeless

Christ, the Physician, *See* Christ, the Healing

Christ, Power of

Lu. 4:16-32 His word was with power

Lu. 7:11-23 He cured many of their infirmities

Ac. 9:36-42 The raising of Dorcas

Ac. 10:34-48 Anointed with the Holy Ghost and with power

1 Co. 1 Christ the power of God

2 Co. 12 That the power of Christ may rest upon me

Ep. 3 Able to do exceeding abundantly

Ph. 2:1-11 It was not robbery to be equal to God

Ph. 4:8-13 I can do all things through Christ

1 Ti. 6:13-16 The blessed and only Potentate

He. 7 He is able to save to the uttermost

1 Pe. 4 To whom be praise and dominion for ever

Christ, Praise of, *See* Christ, Devotion to

Christ, Preaching of, *See* Christ, Gospel of

Christ, Pre-eminence of, *See* Christ, Authority of

Christ, Pre-existence of, *See* Christ, the Changeless

Christ, Presence of, *See* Christ, Communion with

Christ, Priesthood of, *See* Christ, Ministry of

Christ, Promise of, *See* Christ, Gospel of

Christ, Purpose of, *See* Christ, Work of

Christ, Quest for, *See* Christ, Coming to

Christ, Recognition of, *See* Christ, Nature of

Christ, the Redeemer, *See* Christ, the Saviour

Christ, Reign of

Is. 9:1-7 The government shall be upon his shoulder

Mat. 24:3-42 Coming in the clouds of heaven with power

Mat. 28 All power is given unto me in heaven and earth

Jn. 3:22-36 The Father hath given all things unto him

Ro. 9:1-26 Christ is over all, God blessed for ever

Ro. 14 Lord both of the dead and the living

1 Co. 15:1-28 He hath put all things under his feet

Re. 11:1-15 He shall reign for ever and ever

Christ, Rejection of, *See* Christ, Denial of

Christ, Resurrection of, *See* Easter

Christ, Revelation of

Mk. 7:24-37 He could not be hid

Lu. 17:20-37 In the day when the Son of man is revealed

Jn. 14 He that hath seen me hath seen the Father

2 Th. 1 When Jesus shall be revealed from heaven

1 Pe. 4 When his glory shall be revealed

Christ, Riches of, *See* Christ, Fullness of

Christ, Righteousness of, *See* Christ, Goodness of

Christ, the Risen, *See* Easter

Christ, the Rock, *See* Christ, the Changeless

Christ, Sacrifice of, *See* Christ, Suffering of

Christ, Salvation of, *See* Christ, the Saviour

Christ, the Saviour

Mat. 1:18-25 He shall save his people from their sins

Lu. 2:1-14 A Saviour, which is Christ the Lord

Lu. 19:1-10 Jesus and Zacchaeus

Jn. 1:29-42 Behold the Lamb of God

Jn. 4:27-42 This is the Christ, the Saviour

Ac. 4:1-12 Neither is there salvation in any other

Ac. 16:25-40 Believe, and thou shalt be saved

Ro. 1:1-17 The gospel is the power of God unto salvation

Col. 1:1-17 We have redemption through his blood

1 Th. 5 Appointed to obtain salvation

Tit. 3 The washing of regeneration

He. 2 The captain of their salvation

Re. 15 They sing the song of the Lamb

Christ, Second Coming of

Mat. 16:21-28 Some shall not taste of death

Mat. 25:31-46 When the Son of man shall come

Lu. 12:31-40 He cometh at an hour when ye think not

Lu. 21:8-38 They shall see the Son of man coming

Jn. 14 I go away, and come again unto you

Ac. 1:1-14 In like manner as ye have seen him go

1 Co. 1 Waiting for the coming of the Lord

1 Co. 4 Until the Lord come

Col. 3:1-17 Ye shall also appear with him in glory

He. 9:10-28 He shall appear the second time

Ja. 5 The coming of the Lord draweth nigh

Jude Behold, the Lord with his saints

Re. 1 Behold, he cometh with clouds

Re. 22 Surely I come quickly. Amen

Christ, the Servant, *See* Christ, Ministry of

Christ, the Shepherd
Jn. 10:1-16 Jesus, the good shepherd
Jn. 10:22-42 My sheep hear my voice
Jn. 21:15-25 Feed my sheep
He. 13 Jesus, that great Shepherd of the sheep
1 Pe. 5 When the chief Shepherd shall appear
Christ, Silence of
Mat. 15:21-28 He answered her not a word
Mat. 16:13-20 They should tell no man that he was the Christ
Mat. 26:57-75 Jesus held his peace
Lu. 23:1-11 He answered him nothing
Jn. 8:1-11 With his finger Jesus wrote on the ground
Ac. 8:26-40 He opened not his mouth
Christ, Simplicity of, See Christ, Humility of
Christ, Sinlessness of, See Christ, Goodness of
Christ, the Son of God
Ps. 2 This day have I begotten thee
Mat. 11:25-30 No man knoweth the Father, save the Son
Mat. 16:13-20 Thou art the Christ, the Son of God
Mat. 27:50-66 Truly this was the Son of God
Mk. 14:53-65 Art thou the Christ, the Son of the Blessed?
Jn. 3:14-21 God gave his only begotten Son
Jn. 14:8-14 I am in the Father, and the Father in me
Ga. 4:1-18 God sent forth his Son
Col. 1:9-19 Christ, the image of the invisible God
He. 1 This day have I begotten thee
1 Jn. 4 Confess that Jesus is the Son of God
2 Jn. Jesus Christ, the Son of the Father
Christ, the Son of Man
Is. 7:10-16 A virgin shall conceive, and bear a son
Is. 9:1-7 Unto us a son is given
Mat. 11:7-19 The Son of man came eating and drinking
Mat. 16:13-20 Whom do men say that I the Son of man am?
Mat. 16:21-28 The Son of man shall come in glory

Mat. 22:34-46 What think ye of Christ? Whose son is he?
Lu. 4:14-27 Is not this Joseph's son?
He. 4 In all points tempted like as we are
Christ, Sorrow of, See Christ, Suffering of
Christ, Spirit of
Lu. 4:14-30 Jesus returned in the power of the Spirit
Ro. 8:1-17 If any man have not the Spirit of Christ
2 Co. 3 Where the Spirit of the Lord is
Ga. 4:1-7 God hath sent forth the Spirit of his Son
Ep. 3 Strengthened with might by his Spirit
Ph. 1:1-21 The supply of the Spirit of Jesus Christ
Ph. 2:1-11 Let this mind be in you
Christ, Strength of, See Christ, Power of
Christ, Suffering for
Mat. 20:17-29 Ye shall drink indeed of my cup
Mk. 8:34-38 Let him deny himself, and take up his cross
Lu. 5:1-11 They forsook all, and followed him
2 Co. 1 The sufferings of Christ abound in us
Ph. 3 The fellowship of his sufferings
1 Pe. 4 Ye are partakers of Christ's suffering
Christ, Suffering of
Is. 53 A man of sorrows, acquainted with grief
Is. 63 In all their affliction he was afflicted
Mat. 26:36-46 Let this cup pass from me
Lu. 22:31-46 Great drops of blood fell down to the ground
Lu. 24:13-29 Ought not Christ to have suffered?
Jn. 1:29-36 Behold the Lamb of God!
Jn. 10:1-18 I lay down my life for the sheep
1 Co. 5:6-13 Christ our passover is sacrificed for us
He. 5 He learned obedience by the things he suffered
He. 9:11-28 Christ offered himself without spot to God
1 Pe. 3:8-22 Christ also hath once suffered for sins

Christ, Supremacy of, *See* Christ, Authority of

Christ, Sympathy of, *See* Christ, Compassion of

Christ, Table of, *See* Christ, Communion with

Christ, the Teacher, *See* Christ, Gospel of

Christ, Temptation of
Mat. 4:1-11 The temptation of Jesus
Mat. 16:1-12 The Pharisees and the Sadducees tempted him
Lu. 10:25-37 A certain lawyer tempted him
Lu. 22:19-30 Ye have continued with me in my temptations
He. 2 He himself hath suffered being tempted
He. 4 In all points tempted as we are

Christ, Touch of, *See* Christ, the Healing

Christ, Transfiguration of
Mat. 17:1-9 Jesus was transfigured before them
Mk. 9:2-10 Master, it is good for us to be here
2 Pe. 1:16-18 A voice from the excellent glory

Christ, Triumph of
Mat. 21:1-11 The multitudes cried, Hosanna
Mat. 21:33-42 The rejected stone has become the corner stone
Jn. 16:21-33 I have overcome the world
1 Co. 15:35-58 God giveth us the victory through Christ
2 Co. 2 God causeth to triumph in Christ
Col. 2 He triumphed over principalities and powers
1 Pe. 3:10-22 He is on the right hand of God
Re. 1 I am alive for evermore, Amen

Christ, Trust in, *See* Christ, Belief in

Christ, Trustworthiness of, *See* Christ, Faithfulness of

Christ, the Truth
Mat. 22:15-46 Thou teachest the way of God in truth
Jn. 1:15-28 Grace and truth came by Jesus Christ
Jn. 8:32-47 I tell you the truth, and ye believe not
Jn. 14:1-14 I am the way, the truth and the life

Jn. 18:28-40 I bear witness unto the truth
Ep. 4 As the truth is in Jesus
1 Ti. 2 I speak the truth in Christ

Christ, Union with, *See* Christ, Communion with

Christ, Uniqueness of
Mat. 23:1-12 One is your Master, even Christ
Ac. 4:1-12 Neither is there salvation in any other
Ep. 4:1-14 There is one Lord
Ph. 2:1-11 God gave him a name above every name
Col. 1:1-18 In all things he hath preeminence

Christ, Unity of
Jn. 10:19-30 I and my Father are one
1 Co. 1:1-13 Is Christ divided?
1 Co. 12:1-14 Many members in one body: so also is Christ
1 Jn. 5 The Father, the Word, and the Holy Ghost are one

Christ, Universality of
Mat. 13:24-43 The field is the world
Mat. 28 Go ye, and teach all nations
Jn. 1:1-18 The Light which lighteth every man
Jn. 4:1-42 This is the Christ, the Saviour of the world
Jn. 6:22-65 I will give my flesh for the life of the world
Jn. 8:12-32 I am the light of the world
Ep. 3 The Gentiles are fellowheirs
Col. 3:1-16 Christ is all, and in all

Christ, Vision of
Lu. 24:13-31 Their eyes were opened and they knew him
Jn. 12:20-36 Sir, we would see Jesus
He. 2 We see Jesus crowned with glory and honor
He. 9 To them that look for him he shall appear

Christ, Watchfulness of, *See* Christ, the Shepherd

Christ, the Way, *See* Christ, Coming to

Christ, Wisdom of
Lu. 2:40-52 Jesus increased in wisdom
Lu. 4:33-39 What a word is this!
Jn. 6:47-65 The words I speak are spirit and life
Jn. 16 We are sure that thou knowest all things
1 Co. 1 Christ, the wisdom of God

Christ, Wisdom of *(cont.)*

1 Co. 2 We have the mind of Christ
Ph. 2:5-11 The mind that was in Christ Jesus

Christ, Witness of
Jn. 3:1-13 We testify that we have seen
Jn. 5:31-47 The scriptures testify of me
Jn. 15 The Comforter shall testify of me
Ac. 2:14-40 We are all witnesses
Ac. 10:34-48 All the prophets give witness to him
1 Ti. 6 Christ Jesus witnessed a good confession
1 Pe. 1 Christ was manifest in these last times
1 Pe. 5 I am a witness of the sufferings of Christ
2 Pe. 1 We were eyewitnesses of his majesty

Christ, The Word
Lu. 24:13-27 He expounded unto them the scriptures
Jn. 1:1-14 In the beginning was the Word
1 Jn. 5 The Father, the Word, and the Holy Ghost
Re. 19:1-16 His name is called The Word of God

Christ, Word of, *See* Christ, Gospel of
Christ, Work of
Is. 61 The Lord hath anointed me to proclaim liberty
Lu. 2:41-52 I must be about my Father's business
Lu. 4:16-30 He hath anointed me to preach
Jn. 4:31-54 My meat is to finish his work
Jn. 5:17-31 My Father worketh hitherto, and I work
Jn. 5:32-38 My works bear witness of me
Jn. 9:1-11 I must work the works of him that sent me
Jn. 17 I have finished the work

Christ, Worship of, *See* Christ, Adoration of
Christening, *See* Baptism
Christian
Ac. 11:19-26 The disciples called Christians in Antioch
Ac. 16:22-34 Believe on the Lord Jesus Christ
Ac. 26 Almost thou persuadest me to be a Christian

Ep. 4:1-24 Walk not as other Gentiles walk
Ph. 3:7-14 That I may win Christ
Ja. 2 The worthy name by which ye are called
1 Pe. 4 If any man suffer as a Christian

Christmas
Is. 9:6,7 Unto us a child is born
Is. 42:1-9 Behold my servant
Is. 49:7-13 The Lord hath comforted his people
Is. 53 A man of sorrows, acquainted with grief
Is. 61 The spirit of the Lord is upon me
Mi. 4:1-7 We will walk in the name of the Lord
Mat. 1:18-25 She was found with child
Mat. 2:1-11 There came wise men
Lu. 1:26-35, 38 The annunciation
Lu. 1:39-56 The magnificat
Lu. 2:1-20 There were shepherds
Ga. 4:1-7 When the fulness of time was come
1 Jn. 4:7-21 God sent his Son to be a propitiation

Church
2 S. 7:25-29 Bless the house of thy servant
Ps. 50:1-15 Gather my saints together
Ps. 73:1-17 I went into the sanctuary of God
Ps. 84 How amiable are thy tabernacles!
Ps. 100 Enter into his gates with thanksgiving
Ps. 122 Our feet shall stand within thy gates
Mat. 5:13-16 Ye are the light of the world
Mat. 16:13-19 Upon this rock I will build my church
Mat. 18:19-20 Where two or three are gathered together
Mat. 21:12-17 The den of thieves
Lu. 4:16-22 As his custom was, he went into the synagogue
Ac. 2:41-47 The Lord added to the church daily
Ac. 4:31-35 Of one heart and of one soul
Ep. 1 The church is his body
Ep. 4:1-7 One Lord, one faith, one baptism
Ep. 4:11-16 Apostles, prophets, evangelists, pastors

Ep. 5:15-33 The church is subject unto Christ

Col. 1:9-19 He is the head of the body, the church

Col. 3:12-17 Psalms and hymns and spiritual songs

He. 10:23-25 Not forsaking the assembling of ourselves

1 Pe. 2:11-25 Love the brotherhood

1 Pe. 5 Feed the flock of God among you

Re. 2:1-7 What the Spirit saith unto the churches

Circumcision

Ge. 17:1-14 Circumcize the flesh of your foreskin

Je. 4:1-18 Circumcize yourselves unto the Lord

Ro. 2:17-29 Circumcision is that of the heart

Ro. 3 There is much profit of circumcision

Ga. 6 Neither circumcision nor uncircumcision

Citizenship, *See* City

City

De. 28:1-24 Blessed or cursed shalt thou be in the city

1 S. 5 The hand of God was very heavy on the city

Ps. 107:1-22 They found no city to dwell in

Ps. 127 Except the Lord keep the city

Eze. 22:1-12 The city sheddeth blood

Zph. 3:1-5 Woe to the oppressing city

Mat. 5:1-16 A city set on a hill cannot be hid

Lu. 4:16-32 They thrust him out of the city

Lu. 19:41-48 He beheld the city, and wept over it

Jn. 19:13-22 Jesus was crucified nigh to the city

Ac. 9:1-9 Arise, and go into the city

Ac. 20:17-27 The Holy Ghost witnesseth in every city

2 Co. 11:22-33 In perils in the city

He. 13 Here we have no continuing city

City, the Holy

Ps. 87 The Lord loveth the gates of Zion

Is. 26:1-13 We have a strong city

Is. 52:7-10 The Lord hath comforted Jerusalem

Is. 60:10-22 Thou shalt call thy walls salvation

Zph. 3:14-20 Sing, O daughter of Jerusalem

Zch. 8:1-15 I will dwell in the midst of Jerusalem

He. 11:1-10 A city whose builder and maker is God

He. 12:18-29 The city of the living God

Re. 21 I John saw the holy city

Re. 22 The city of God

Cleanness

Ps. 19 Cleanse thou me from secret faults

Ps. 24 He that hath clean hands

Ps. 51 Wash me, and I shall be whiter than snow

Ps. 73 God is good to such as are of a clean heart

Ps. 119:1-16 Wherewithal shall a young man cleanse his way?

Is. 1 Wash you, make you clean

Mat. 8:1-13 If thou wilt, thou canst make me clean

Mat. 23:23-39 Ye make clean the outside of the cup

Lu. 4:22-32 None was cleansed, saving Naaman

Lu. 11:37-54 All things are clean unto you

Ac. 10:1-18 What God hath cleansed

Ja. 4 Cleanse your hands, ye sinners

Climbing, *See* Mountain

Clothes

Ps. 102:26 All of them shall wax old like a garment

Ps. 104:1-14 Thou coverest thyself with light

Is. 61 Clothed with the garments of salvation

Jo. 2:1-13 Rend your heart, and not your garments

Mat. 6:24-34 Why take ye thought for raiment?

Mat. 25:31-46 I was naked, and ye clothed me

Mk. 12:35-44 The scribes love to go in long clothing

Lu. 19:28-40 They spread their clothes in the way

Jn. 15:17-27 Now they have no cloke for their sin

Jn. 19:23-24 The coat was without seam

1 Pe. 5 Be clothed with humility

Re. 7 A multitude clothed with white robes

Cold, *See* Winter

Collection, *See* Offering

Comfort

Jb. 16 Miserable comforters are ye all

Ps. 23 Thy rod and thy staff they comfort me

Is. 40:1-11 Comfort ye, comfort ye my people

Is. 61 Anointed to comfort all that mourn

Mat. 5:1-12 They that mourn shall be comforted

Jn. 16:20-33 Be of good cheer

2 Co. 1:1-12 Our consolation aboundeth by Christ

1 Th. 4 Comfort one another

Comforter, *See* Spirit, Holy

Commander, *See* Chief

Commandment

Ex. 20:1-17 The ten commandments

Le. 26:1-13 If ye walk in my statutes

Ps. 19 The law of the Lord is perfect

Mat. 5:17-20 I am not come to destroy the law

Mat. 22:15-21 Is it lawful to give tribute to Caesar?

Mk. 10:17-22 Thou knowest the commandments

Jn. 12:37-50 His commandment is life everlasting

Ro. 7:1-12 The law is holy, and the commandment holy

Ga. 3:1-13 The curse of the law

Ga. 3:15-24 The law was added because of transgressions

1 Ti. 1:5-17 The end of the commandment is charity

1 Jn. 2:1-17 A new commandment I write unto you

1 Jn. 4 This commandment have we from him

Commencement Day

Es. 4:1-17 For such a time as this

Pr. 3 Let thine heart keep my commandments

Is. 6:1-8 Whom shall I send, and who will go for us?

Is. 32:1-8 A man shall be as an hiding place

Mat. 28:9-20 Go ye therefore, and teach

Mk. 1:16-20 I will make you fishers of men

2 Co. 5 We are ambassadors for Christ

Ep. 2:13-22 The household of God

He. 12:1-3 Lay aside every weight

Commendation, *See* Praise

Commerce, *See* Business

Communion

Ps. 4 Commune with your own heart upon your bed

Jn. 15:1-17 Abide in me, and I in you

Ac. 2:41-47 Continuing in the apostles' fellowship

Ac. 20:28-38 He kneeled down, and prayed with them all

Ro. 12:3-21 Live peaceably with all men

Ro. 14 None of us liveth to himself

1 Co. 3 We are labourers together with God

2 Co. 6 What communion hath light with darkness?

2 Co. 13 The communion of the Holy Ghost

Ep. 2:1-19 Fellowcitizens with the saints

He. 12:22-24 An innumerable company of angels

1 Jn. 1:1-7 Our fellowship is with the Father

Re. 21:1-7 God himself shall be with them

Communion, Service of

Ex. 12:1-31 What mean ye by this service?

Ex. 24:9-18 They saw God, and did eat and drink

Ps. 19:7-14 Cleanse thou me from secret faults

Ps. 23 Thou preparest a table before me

Ps. 34 Taste and see that the Lord is good

Ps. 51 The sacrifices of God are a broken spirit

Ps. 107:1-9 He satisfieth the longing soul

Ps. 116 I will take the cup of salvation

Ps. 139:1-12 The darkness hideth not from thee

Is. 40:1-5, 9-11, 28-31 Comfort ye, comfort ye my people

Is. 53 Surely he hath borne our griefs

Mat. 26:17-30 Jesus took bread, and blessed it

Mk. 14:12-26 Jesus eats the passover with his disciples

Lu. 22:1-23 When the hour was come, he sat down

Lu. 23:13-49 The crucifixion

Jn. 6:27-58 My flesh is meat indeed, my blood is drink

Jn. 11:47-57   Will he not come to the feast?

Jn. 15:1-11   I am the vine, ye are the branches

1 Co. 11:17-34   To eat the Lord's supper

2 Ti. 2   Remember that Jesus was raised from the dead

He. 10:19-25   Let us draw near with a true heart

1 Pe. 1:1-21   Redeemed with the precious blood of Christ

Re. 21:10-27   The nations shall walk in the light of it

Community, Christian

Pr. 22   The rich and the poor meet together

Ec. 5:8-20   The profit of the earth is for all

Ec. 9   All things come alike to all

Mat. 20:1-16   I will give unto this last, even as unto thee

Ac. 4:31-37   There was none among them that lacked

1 Co. 10:21-33   Let every man seek another's wealth

2 Co. 8   That there may be equality

Ja. 1:1-11   Let the rich rejoice, in that he is made low

Companionship, *See* Communion

Compassion, *See* Solicitude

Compensation, *See* Reward

Competition, *See* Rivalry

Complaint

Jb. 23   Even to day is my complaint bitter

Ps. 38   I have roared by reason of disquietness

Ps. 77   I complained, and my spirit was overwhelmed

Pr. 19   His heart fretteth against the Lord

Pr. 27   The eyes of man are never satisfied

Jn. 6:37-59   Murmur not among yourselves

Ph. 2:12-30   Do all things without murmurings

Jude 16   These are murmurers

Completion

Ge. 2:1-7   The heavens and the earth were finished

Mat. 5:17-20   I am not come to destroy, but to fulfil

Jn. 17   I have finished the work thou gavest me to do

Jn. 19:13-37   Jesus said, It is finished

Ro. 13   He that loveth another fulfils the law

Ep. 4:1-13   Unto the perfect man

Col. 2:1-10   Ye are complete in him

2 Ti. 4:1-8   I have finished my course

He. 12:1-14   Jesus the author and finisher of our faith

Compulsion

Jb. 6   How forcible are right words!

Jb. 32   The spirit within me constraineth me

Pr. 10:1-12   Violence covereth the mouth of the wicked

Mat. 5:38-48   Whosoever shall compel thee

Mat. 11:1-15   The violent take the kingdom by force

Mk. 15:15-25   They compel Simon to bear his cross

Lu. 14:15-24   Compel them to come in

Ac. 4:1-20   We cannot but speak

2 Co. 5   The love of Christ constraineth us

Comradeship, *See* Communion

Concealment

Ge. 4:1-15   From thy face shall I be hid

Ps. 17   Hide me under the shadow of thy wings

Ps. 27   In the time of trouble he shall hide me

Ps. 32   Thou art my hiding place

Ps. 85   Thou hast covered all their sin

Pr. 25   It is the glory of God to conceal a thing

Pr. 28:1-13   He that covereth his sins shall not prosper

Mat. 5:1-16   A city set on a hill can not be hid

Mat. 13:44-52   Like unto a treasure hid in a field

1 Pe. 4   Charity covers a multitude of sins

Re. 6   Hide us from the wrath of the Lamb

Conceit, *See* Pride

Concord, *See* Peace

Condemnation

2 S. 12:1-14   Nathan said to David, Thou art the man

Is. 50:1-9   God will help; who shall condemn me?

Je. 22:1-9   I will make thee a wilderness

Lu. 6:36-49   Judge not, and ye shall not be judged

Condemnation (*cont.*)

Jn. 8:1-11 Neither do I condemn thee

Jn. 8:14-17 I judge no man

Ro. 2:1-11 Judging another, thou condemnest thyself

Ro. 8:1-17 No condemnation to them which are in Christ

Ja. 3 We shall receive the greater condemnation

Ja. 5 Ye have condemned the just

Conduct, *See* Character

Confession

Jos. 7:16-26 Achan's sin, confession, and stoning

Ps. 32 I will confess my transgressions

Ps. 51:1-12 Create in me a clean heart, O God

Mat. 3:1-6 They confessed their sins and were baptized

Mat. 16:13-20 Thou art the Christ

Lu. 15:11-32 Father, I have sinned against heaven and thee

Jn. 1:43-51 Rabbi, thou art the Son of God

Ph. 2:1-11 Confess that Jesus Christ is Lord

1 Ti. 6:1-14 Christ witnessed a good confession

Ja. 5 Confess your faults one to another

1 Jn. 1 If we confess our sins, he will forgive

Confidence, *See* Faith

Confirmation

Le. 19:1-18 Ye shall be holy

Ju. 13 Samson is dedicated to God

Is. 6:1-8 Here am I; send me

Jn. 17 For their sakes I sanctify myself

Ac. 14:19-28 Confirming the souls of the disciples

Ro. 12 A living sacrifice, holy, acceptable

1 Co. 1:1-10 Called to be saints

1 Co. 6:9-20 Your body is the temple of the Holy Ghost

1 Th. 4 God hath called us unto holiness

He. 10:16-26 By a new and living way

1 Pe. 1:13-25 Seeing ye have purified your souls

Conflict, *See* Strife

Confusion

Ge. 11:1-9 The confusion of tongues at Babel

Ps. 22 They trusted in thee, and were not confounded

Ps. 71:1-19 Let me never be put to confusion

Is. 19:1-10 Every one shall fight against his brother

Ac. 19:21-41 The whole city was filled with confusion

1 Co. 14 God is not the author of confusion

Ja. 3 Envying and strife bring confusion

1 Pe. 2:1-10 He that believeth shall not be confounded

Congregation, *See* Church

Conquest, *See* Victory

Conscience

Pr. 28 The wicked flee when no man pursueth

Jn. 8:1-11 Hath no man condemned thee?

Ac. 23:1-11 I have lived in all good conscience

Ac. 24:10-21 A conscience void of offence

1 Co. 8 Wound not the weak conscience of the brethren

1 Ti. 1:5-17 Charity out of a good conscience

1 Ti. 4 Their conscience seared with a hot iron

He. 13 We trust we have a good conscience

1 Pe. 3:8-22 A good conscience toward God

Consecration

Ex. 32 Consecrate yourselves today to the Lord

Nu. 32:6-19 They have wholly followed the Lord

Is. 6 Here am I; send me

Ro. 1:1-17 Separated unto the gospel of God

He. 7:19-28 The Son is consecrated for evermore

He. 10 He hath consecrated a new way for us

1 Jn. 3 We ought to lay down our lives for others

Consolation, *See* Comfort

Contemplation, *See* Meditation

Contention, *See* Strife

Contentment

Ps. 37:1-11 Rest in the Lord, and wait patiently for him

Ps. 107:1-9 He satisfieth the longing soul

Pr. 15:1-17 Better a dinner of herbs where love is

Pr. 16 Better is a little with right-eousness

Ec. 4 Better a handful with quiet-ness

Ph. 4:1-13 I have learned to be content

1 Ti. 6 Godliness with contentment is great gain

He. 13:1-21 Be content with what ye have

Contrition, *See* Repentance

Controversy, *See* Strife

Conversation

Jb. 11 Should a man full of talk be justified?

Ps. 19 Let the words of my mouth be acceptable

Pr. 18 The words of a man's mouth

Mat. 5:33-48 Let your communica-tion be Yea, yea; Nay, nay

Mat. 6:5-15 Use not vain repeti-tions

1 Co. 15:33-58 Evil communica-tions corrupt good manners

Ph. 3 Our conversation is in heaven

Col. 4:1-6 Let your speech be alway with grace

1 Ti. 4 Be thou an example in con-versation

Ja. 3 The tongue can no man tame

1 Pe. 1 Be ye holy in all manner of conversation

Conversion

Ps. 19 The law of the Lord con-verts the soul

Is. 1:16-20 Wash you, make you clean

Is. 55:6-13 Seek ye the Lord while he may be found

Mat. 18:1-6 Be converted, and be-come as little children

Lu. 14:16-24 They all began to make excuse

Lu. 19:1-10 The Son of man is come to save

Jn. 5:17-31 He passed from death unto life

Ac. 3:19-26 Repent, and be con-verted

Ac. 9:1-9 Lord, what wilt thou have me to do?

Ep. 4:17-32 Put on the new man

1 Ti. 1:12-14 I obtained mercy

Ja. 5 He which converteth the sinner

Conviction, *See* Belief

Cooperation, *See* Communion

Cornerstone, *See* Foundation

Coronation, *See* Crown

Correction, *See* Punishment

Corruption, *See* Sin

Cost

Jb. 28 The price of wisdom is above rubies

Je. 29:10-19 Ye shall search for me with all your heart

Mat. 19:16-26 What good thing shall I do?

Lu. 14:25-35 Which of you count-eth not the cost?

Ac. 8:18-24 The gift of God is not purchased with money

Ac. 22:24-30 With a great sum ob-tained I this freedom

1 Co. 6 Ye are bought with a price

Ph. 3 I count all things but loss

Counsel, *See* Instruction

Countenance, *See* Face

Country, *See* Nation

Country, the Better, *See* Kingdom, the Coming

Courage

De. 20:1-9 Let not your hearts be faint

Jos. 1:1-18 Be strong and of good courage

Ju. 6:11-17 Thou mighty man of valor

Ju. 6:11-23 An angel summons Gideon to save Israel

Ju. 7:1-22 The sword of the Lord, and of Gideon

1 K. 18:30-39 Elijah and the proph-ets of Baal

2 Ch. 32:1-8 There be more with us than with him

Ne. 6:1-14 Should such a man as I flee?

Es. 4 So will I go in unto the king

Ps. 91 Thou shalt not be afraid

Is. 41:10-20 Fear thou not; for I am with thee

Da. 6:10-28 Daniel is cast into the lions' den

Lu. 5:1-11 Launch out into the deep

Ac. 27:1-25 I exhort you to be of good cheer

2 Co. 4:8-18 Persecuted, but not forsaken

Ep. 6:10-24 The whole armour of God

Ph. 1 In nothing terrified by your adversaries

Covenant

Ge. 9:8-17 The covenant with Noah

Ge. 17:1-8 The covenant with Abraham

Ge. 26:17-29 Let us make a cove-nant

Covenant *(cont.)*

Ge. 28:10-22 The covenant with Jacob
Ex. 6:1-8 The covenant with Israel
Ps. 89:1-4 The covenant with David
Je. 31:31-34 The new covenant
Je. 50:1-8 A perpetual covenant with the Lord
He. 8 This is the covenant that I will make
He. 12:18-29 Ye are come unto mount Sion

Covetousness, *See* Greed

Creation

Ge. 1:1-31 In the beginning God created
Ge. 2:4-7 God formed man of the dust
Ge. 2:18-24 The rib made he a woman
Ps. 8 When I consider thy heavens
Ps. 100 It is he that hath made us
Ps. 104 O Lord, how manifold are thy works!
Je. 18:1-17 I went down to the potter's house
Ep. 2 We are his workmanship

Creator, *See* Creation

Creature, *See* Beast

Creed, *See* Belief

Crime, *See* Sin

Cross

Mk. 8:34-38 Let him deny himself
Lu. 14:25-33 Counting the cost
Lu. 23:13-33 They laid the cross on Simon of Cyrene
Ga. 2 I am crucified with Christ
Ga. 6 I glory in the cross
Ph. 2:1-17 He became obedient unto death
1 Pe. 4 Ye are partakers of Christ's sufferings

Crowd

Mat. 9:27-38 Compassion for the multitude
Mat. 14:1-14 He feared the multitude
Mat. 21:1-11 The multitudes that went before cried Hosanna
Mk. 1:28-45 All the city was gathered at the door
Lu. 2:1-7 There was no room in the inn
Lu. 23:12-26 They cried, Crucify him, crucify him

Jn. 6:1-14 Feeding the five thousand

Crown

Ps. 65 Thou crownest the year with thy goodness
Is. 62 A royal diadem in the hand of thy God
Mat. 5:1-12 Great is your reward in heaven
1 Co. 9 We do it to obtain an incorruptible crown
2 Ti. 4:1-8 There is laid up for me a crown
Re. 2:1-11 I will give thee a crown of life
Re. 3:7-13 Hold fast thy crown

Crucifixion, *See* Good Friday

Cruelty

Ex. 1:7-14 The Egyptians made them serve with rigour
Pr. 12:1-10 The tender mercies of the wicked are cruel
Is. 3:1-15 Ye beat my people to pieces
Mat. 18:23-35 He delivered him to the tormentors
He. 11:32-40 Trial of cruel mockings and scourgings

Cry

Jos. 6:1-20 When the people shouted, the wall fell down
Jb. 34:1-28 He heareth the cry of the afflicted
Pr. 8 Wisdom crieth at the gates
Pr. 21:1-13 He shall cry, but shall not be heard
Mat. 3 The voice of one crying in the wilderness
Lu. 19:28-40 The stones would immediately cry out
1 Th. 4 The Lord shall descend with a shout

Cup

Ps. 23 My cup runneth over
Ps. 116 I will take the cup of salvation
Is. 51:17-23 The cup of the Lord's fury
Mat. 23:13-33 Cleanse first that which is within the cup
Mat. 25:31-46 I was thirsty, and ye gave me drink
Jn. 7:32-39 Let him come unto me and drink
1 Co. 12 All made to drink into one Spirit

Cure, *See* Healing

Curse

Nu. 23:1-26 Balaam refuses to curse Jacob and Israel

De. 11:26-32 I set before you a blessing and a curse

Mat. 5:33-48 Bless them that curse you

Mat. 26:69-75 He began to curse

Mk. 11:12-21 Jesus curseth the fig tree

1 Co. 16 If he love not, let him be Anathema Maran-atha

Ga. 3:1-14 Christ hath redeemed us from the curse

Re. 22 There shall be no more curse

[D]

Damnation, *See* Hell

Danger

2 S. 23:13-17 David's three mighty men

Ps. 91 Thou shalt not be afraid

Ac. 15:24-41 Men that have hazarded their lives

Ac. 27 Paul suffers shipwreck

Ro. 8:31-39 We are killed all day long

2 Co. 11:22-33 In perils everywhere

2 Ti. 2:1-10 Endure hardness as a good soldier

2 Ti. 3 Perilous times shall come

Darkness

Ge. 1:1-8 Darkness was upon the face of the deep

Ps. 42 In the night his song shall be with me

Ps. 139:1-12 The darkness hideth not from thee

Ec. 2:1-17 The fool walketh in darkness

Is. 21:1-12 Watchman, what of the night?

Lu. 23:33-45 There was a darkness over all the earth

Jn. 8:12-20 He shall not walk in darkness

Ep. 6:10-20 Rulers of the darkness of this world

Col 1:3-19 He hath delivered us from darkness

1 Jn. 2:7-17 He that hateth is in darkness

Daughter, *See* Girl

Dawn, *See* Morning

Day

Ge. 1:1-8 God called the light Day

Ex. 13:17-22 The Lord went before them by day

Ps. 19 Day unto day uttereth speech

Ps. 84 A day in thy courts is better than a thousand

Pr. 27 Thou knowest not what a day may bring forth

Jn. 9:1-38 I must work while it is day

2 Pe. 3:1-13 One day is with the Lord as a thousand years

Death

De. 34 No man knoweth of his sepulchre

Ps. 23 Though I walk through the valley

Mat. 16:21-28 Some here shall not taste of death

Lu. 8:41-56 She is not dead, but sleepeth

Jn. 8:51-58 If a man keep my saying, he shall not die

Jn. 11:23-45 Though he were dead, yet shall he live

Ro. 6 The wages of sin is death

1 Co. 15:12-26 The last enemy that shall be destroyed is death

Re. 14:1-13 Blessed are the dead which die in the Lord

Re. 21:1-7 There shall be no more death

Debt

Mat. 6:5-15 Forgive us our debts

Mat. 18:23-35 The lord of that servant forgave him

Lu. 16:1-8 The parable of the unjust steward

Ro. 1:1-17 I am debtor to Greeks and to the Barbarians

Ro. 8:1-17 We are not debtors to the flesh

Ro. 13 Owe no man anything but love

Decay

Ge. 3:8-19 Unto dust shalt thou return

Jb. 14 He cometh forth like a flower, and is cut down

Ps. 90 In the evening it is cut down, and withereth

Decay *(cont.)*

Ec. 10 By slothfulness the building decayeth
Is. 14:4-23 Thy pomp is brought down to the grave
Is. 64 We all do fade as a leaf
Deceit, *See* Lie
Declaration, *See* Proclamation
Dedication, *See* Consecration
Deed

Pr. 20 Even a child is known by his doings
Lu. 10:38-42 My sister hath left me to serve alone
Jn. 3:16-21 Their deeds were evil
Jn. 10:37-42 Though ye believe not me, believe the works
Ro. 7 What I would, that do I not
Ja. 1:19-27 Not a forgetful hearer, but a doer
1 Jn. 3:18-24 In deed and in truth
Re. 20 The dead were judged according to their works
Deep

Ge. 1:1-9 The Spirit of God moved on the waters
Ex. 49:22-26 Blessings of the deep that lieth under
Ps. 36 Thy judgments are a great deep
Ps. 42 Deep calleth unto deep
Ps. 92 Thy thoughts are very deep
Mat. 8:23-27 Even the winds and the sea obey him!
Mk. 4:1-20 It sprang up, because it had no depth of earth
Lu. 5:1-11 Launch out into the deep
1 Co. 2 The Spirit searcheth the deep things of God
Re. 14:1-7 Worship him that made the sea
Defeat

1 S. 4:1-11 The ark of God was taken
2 S. 1:17-27 How are the mighty fallen!
Ps. 22 Why hast thou forsaken me?
Pr. 24:1-16 A just man falleth seven times, and riseth
Pr. 24:17-34 Rejoice not when thine enemy falleth
Is. 37:1-7 There is not strength to bring forth
Lu. 5:1-11 We have toiled all night, and taken nothing
Lu. 14:25-33 This man was not able to finish
Defence, *See* Security

Defiance, *See* Challenge
Delight, *See* Joy
Deliverance

Ex. 5:1-9 Let my people go
Ps. 18:1-24 He brought me forth into a large place
Ps. 43 Send out thy light
Ps. 116 Thou hast delivered my soul
Da. 6:16-28 My God hath shut the lions' mouths
Lu. 11:1-13 Deliver us from evil
Ac. 5:17-28 The angel of the Lord brought them forth
Ac. 12:1-17 Peter delivered from prison
Ac. 16:19-34 Immediately all the doors were opened
Democracy

Le. 25:10-19 Proclaim liberty throughout all the land
1 S. 8:1-9 Hearken unto the voice of the people
Pr. 22 The Lord is the maker of them all
Is. 62 Prepare ye the way of the people
1 Co. 12 All the members suffer with one member
Col. 3:1-17 Where there is neither bond nor free
Ja. 2:1-12 They shall be judged by the law of liberty
Denial

Lu. 9:23-27 Let him deny himself
Lu. 12:1-12 He that denieth shall be denied
Lu. 20:27-38 The Sadducees deny the resurrection
1 Co. 15:1-14 Some say there is no resurrection
Re. 2:1-13 Thou hast not denied my faith
Departure

Ju. 16:1-20 He wist not that the Lord was departed
2 S. 12:18-23 I shall go to him, but he shall not return
Ps. 31:1-16 Into thine hand I commit my spirit
Ec. 12 The spirit shall return unto God who gave it
Lu. 2:25-35 Now lettest thou thy servant depart in peace
Lu. 24:13-31 He vanished out of their sight
Lu. 24:36-53 While he blessed them, he was parted from them
Jn. 16:7-11 If I go away the Comforter will come

2 Ti. 4:1-8 The time of my departure is at hand

He. 13:1-21 I will never leave thee, nor forsake thee

Dependence, *See* Reliance

Depravity, *See* Sin

Depression, *See* Sorrow

Desert, *See* Solitude

Desertion

Je. 13:15-25 Thou hast forgotten me

Zch. 13:1-6 I was wounded in the house of my friends

Jn. 6:51-66 Many of the disciples walked no more with him

Jn. 16:21-33 The hour cometh when ye shall leave me alone

2 Ti. 4:1-11 Demas hath deserted me

Desire

Ps. 63 My soul thirsteth for thee

Ps. 107:1-9 He satisfieth the longing soul

Ps. 145 Thou satisfiest the desire of every living thing

Pr. 13 Desire accomplished is sweet to the soul

Ec. 6 Sight is better than the wandering of desire

1 Co. 14:1-15 Desire spiritual gifts

He. 11:1-16 Now they desire a better country

Desolation

Ps. 34 None that trust in him shall be desolate

Is. 64 Thy holy cities are a wilderness

La. 5 Thou hast utterly rejected us

Ho. 9 Thorns shall be in their tabernacles

Jo. 1:1-13 The field is wasted, the land mourneth

Jo. 1:13-20 Alas for the day!

Mat. 12:22-30 A kingdom divided is brought to desolation

Despair

1 K. 19:1-8 Now, O Lord, take away my life

Jb. 10 My soul is weary of my life

Ps. 42 My soul is cast down within me

Ps. 80 Thou feedest them with the bread of tears

Hab. 1 How long shall I cry, and thou wilt not hear?

Mk. 15:24-38 My God, why hast thou forsaken me?

2 Co. 4 We are perplexed, but not in despair

Destiny

Es. 4 Thou art come to the kingdom for such a time

Ec. 3 All turn to dust again

Is. 65:17-25 They shall build houses, and inhabit them

Lu. 22:7-23 The Son of man goeth, as it was determined

Lu. 23:33-45 Christ, the chosen of God

Ro. 1:1-7 Called to be saints

1 Co. 13 Then shall I know even as also I am known

1 Pe. 2:1-10 A royal priesthood, an holy nation

Destitution, *See* Poverty

Destruction

Ps. 91 The destruction that wasteth at noonday

Ps. 103 He redeemeth thy life from destruction

Is. 11:1-9 They shall not destroy in all my holy mountain

Eze. 21:18-32 I will overturn, overturn, overturn, it

Ho. 10 They shall say to the hills, Fall on us

Ho. 13 O grave, I will be thy destruction

Mat. 7:6-14 Broad is the way which leadeth to destruction

Mat. 10:16-28 He is able to destroy both soul and body

Lu. 11:14-26 A house divided against a house falleth

1 Co. 15:12-26 The last enemy to be destroyed is death

Devil, *See* Satan

Difficulty

Ps. 137 How shall we sing the Lord's song?

Pr. 4 When thou runnest, thou shalt not stumble

Pr. 13 The way of transgressors is hard

Je. 32:16-27 Is there any thing too hard for me?

Mat. 7 Narrow is the way which leadeth unto life

Lu. 8:4-15 Some fell among thorns

2 Co. 11:21-30 I will glory in mine infirmities

2 Co. 12:7-10 There was given to me a thorn in the flesh

1 Th. 2 Satan hindered us

He. 5 Many things are hard to be uttered

Diligence, *See* Ardor

Disappointment
De. 28:15-48 The locust shall consume thy trees
De. 34 Thou shalt not go over thither
1 Ch. 22:6-16 It was in my mind to build an house
Pr. 15 Without counsel purposes are disappointed
Is. 5:1-7 It brought forth wild grapes
Is. 55 Ye spend money for that which is not bread
Am. 5:1-17 In all vineyards shall be wailing
Hag. 1:1-11 Ye have sown much, and bring in little
Lu. 13:31-35 Jesus laments over Jerusalem
Lu. 24:13-35 We believed that he would redeem Israel
Jn. 1:14 His own received him not

Disarmament, See Armistice Sunday

Disaster, See Adversity

Disciple
Mat. 4:18-22 Follow me
Mat. 9:35-38; 10:1-8 Jesus calls the twelve apostles
Lu. 5:27-39 He left all, rose up, and followed him
Lu. 9:57-62 I will follow thee whithersoever thou goest
Lu. 10:1-11,17 Jesus sends out the seventy
Lu. 10:38-42 One thing is needful
Lu. 14:25-33 He cannot be my disciple
Jn. 1:35-51 Jesus findeth the disciples
Jn. 15:1-8 So shall ye be my disciples
Ph. 3 Brethren, be followers together of me
Col. 1:9-17 That ye might walk worthy of the Lord
Re. 14:1-7 These are they which follow the Lamb

Discipline, See Punishment

Discord, See Strife

Discouragement
Nu. 14:1-10 Would God that we had died in Egypt
1 K. 19:9-18 I, even I only, am left
Ps. 42 My soul is cast down within me
Is. 42:1-16 He shall not fail nor be discouraged
Is. 49:1-15 The Lord hath forsaken me
Lu. 5:1-11 We have toiled all night, and taken nothing

Col. 3:12-25 Do not discourage your children
1 Th. 5 Quench not the Spirit

Discovery
De. 3:18-29 Let me see the good land beyond Jordan
Ps. 107 These see his wonders in the deep
Je. 2:1-7 I brought you into a plentiful country
Je. 29:10-14 Ye shall seek me, and find me
Mk. 5:1-20 They come to Jesus
Lu. 15:11-32 He came to himself
He. 11:1-16 They desire a better country

Disease
Ps. 103 He healeth all thy diseases
Je. 8:18-22 Is there no balm in Gilead?
Mat. 10:1-23 Heal the sick, cleanse the lepers
Mk. 2:15-28 They that are sick need the physician
Lu. 4:16-30 Physician, heal thyself
Lu. 9:1-17 He healed them that had need of healing
Ro. 15:1-7 We ought to bear the infirmities of the weak
2 Co. 12:1-10 I take pleasure in infirmities
Ja. 5:1-15 The prayer of faith shall save the sick

Disgrace, See Dishonor

Dishonesty, See Lie

Dishonor
Ps. 119:17-32 O Lord, put me not to shame
Je. 14:7-22 Do not abhor us, for thy name's sake
Jn. 8:31-59 I honour my Father, and ye do dishonour me
Ac. 5:17-42 They were counted worthy to suffer shame
2 Ti. 2:20-26 Vessels to honour and to dishonour
He. 6:1-12 They put the Son of God to open shame
He. 11:23-40 Choosing to suffer affliction

Disobedience
1 S. 13:1-14 Thou hast not kept the commandment
Je. 7:21-28 A nation that obeyeth not the voice of God
Ac. 5:25-32 We ought to obey God rather than men
Ac. 26:1-20 I was not disobedient unto the vision

Ga. 3:1-14 O foolish Galatians, ye obey not the truth

Ep. 5:1-17 The children of disobedience

Tit. 3 We ourselves were sometimes disobedient

He. 2 Every disobedience receives a just reward

Disorder, *See* Confusion

Dispersion, *See* Captivity

Dispute, *See* Strife

Distinction, *See* Best

Distress, *See* Adversity

Disturbance, *See* Confusion

Diversity

De. 25:13-16 Thou shalt not have divers measures

Mat. 13:47-58 The net gathered of every kind

1 Co. 12 There are diversities of gifts

1 Co. 14:1-15 There are many kinds of voices in the world

Ja. 1 Be glad when ye fall into divers temptations

Ja. 3 Every kind of beast hath been tamed

Divinity

Ps. 97 Worship him, all ye gods

Ro. 1:15-21 His eternal power and Godhead

1 Co. 8 One God, the Father; one Lord Jesus Christ

Ga. 4 God sent forth his Son

Col. 2:1-12 In him dwelleth the fulness of the Godhead

3 Jn. He that doeth good is of God

Division

1 K. 12:1-24 The kingdom divided

Ho. 10:1-4 Their heart is divided

Mat. 6:24-34 No man can serve two masters

Mat. 12:22-30 A divided house shall not stand

Lu. 12:49-57 I am come to give division

1 Co. 1:1-13 Is Christ divided?

1 Co. 12:1-11 The Spirit divides to every man

Divorce

Mat. 5:27-32 The writing of divorcement

Mk. 10:2-12 They twain shall be one flesh

1 Co. 7:25-40 Seek not to be loosed from a wife

Doctrine

De. 32:1-14 My doctrine shall drop as the rain

Mat. 7:21-29 The people were astonished at his doctrine

Jn. 7:14-31 If ye do his will, ye shall know the doctrine

Ac. 24:1-16 After the way which they call heresy

1 Co. 14:26-40 Every one of you hath a doctrine

Ep. 4:1-16 One Lord, one faith, one baptism

2 Ti. 3 All scripture is profitable for doctrine

Tit. 2:1-8 The things which become sound doctrine

1 Jn. 5:1-5 Our faith is the victory that overcometh

Dogma, *See* Doctrine

Dominion

Ps. 22:22-31 He is the governor among the nations

Ps. 93 The Lord reigneth

Ps. 138 All the kings of the earth shall praise thee

Lu. 19:28-40 Blessed be the King that cometh

Ro. 6:1-18 Sin shall not have dominion over you

Ro. 13:1-7 Let every soul be subject to the higher powers

Re. 22:1-7 They shall reign for ever and ever

Doom, *See* Destiny

Door

Ps. 24 Lift up your heads, ye everlasting doors

Ps. 84 A doorkeeper in the house of my God

Mat. 6:1-18 Enter into thy closet and shut the door

Mat. 19:23-26 A rich man shall hardly enter the kingdom

Mat. 25:1-13 The parable of the ten virgins

Lu. 11:5-13 Knock, and it shall be opened unto you

Jn. 10:1-16 I am the door

Re. 3:14-22 Behold, I stand at the door and knock

Doubt

Ju. 6:11-24 If God be with us, why has this befallen us?

Mat. 21:7-22 If ye have faith, and doubt not

Mk. 4:35-41 Why are ye so fearful?

Mk. 9:14-24 Lord, I believe; help thou mine unbelief

Lu. 7:19-28 Art thou he that should come?

Doubt *(cont.)*

Lu. 12:22-31 Neither be ye of doubtful mind

Jn. 20:19-29 Except I see the print of the nails

Ac. 17:22-34 TO THE UNKNOWN GOD

Ja. 1:5-8 A double minded man is unstable

Dream

Ge. 28:10-17 He dreamed, and behold a ladder

Ge. 37:1-11 I have dreamed a dream

Ge. 37:1-22 Behold, this dreamer cometh

Ps. 126 We were like them that dream

Jo. 2:21-32 Your old men shall dream dreams

Mat. 1:8-25 The angel appeared unto him in a dream

Ac. 18:7-11 The Lord spoke to Paul in the night

Drought

Ps. 63 My soul thirsteth for thee in a dry land

Ps. 107:31-43 He turneth rivers into a wilderness

Is. 35 The parched ground shall become a pool

Is. 44:1-8 I will pour water on him that is thirsty

Is. 53 As a root out of a dry ground

Is. 58:1-12 The Lord shall satisfy thy soul in drought

Drunkenness, *See* Temperance Sunday

Dust

Ge. 2:4-7 God formed man out of the dust of the ground

Ge. 3:8-21 Dust thou art, and unto dust shalt thou return

Jb. 30 I am become like dust and ashes

Ps. 103 He remembereth that we are dust

Ec. 12 Then shall the dust return to the earth

Duty

1 Ch. 16:7-36 Give unto the Lord the glory due his name

Ec. 12 This is the whole duty of man

Eze. 33:7-16 I have set thee a watchman

Lu. 2:40-52 I must be about my father's business

Lu. 12:49-59 I have a baptism to be baptized with

Lu. 17:1-10 We have done that which was our duty to do

Jn. 9:1-7 I must work the works of him that sent me

Ro. 13 Owe no man any thing, but to love one another

Ep. 6:1-9 Children, obey your parents

Dwelling, *See* House

[E]

Eagerness, *See* Ardor

Ear, *See* Hearing

Earnestness, *See* Ardor

Earth

Nu. 14:15-21 The earth filled with the Lord's glory

Ps. 24 The earth is the Lord's

Ps. 65:9 Thou visitest the earth, and waterest it

Ps. 95 In his hand are the deep places of the earth

Ec. 1:1-11 The earth abideth for ever

Is. 11:1-9 The earth shall be full of the knowledge of God

Mat. 6:5-15 Thy will be done on earth

Re. 21:1-7 I saw a new heaven and a new earth

Earthquake, *See* Adversity

Ease, *See* Rest

Easter

Mat. 16:13-24 Raised again the third day

Mat. 28:1-10 He is not here, he is risen

Mk. 16:1-8 The stone was rolled away

Mk. 16:9-20 The appearances of Jesus

Lu. 24:13-35 The road to Emmaus

Lu. 24:36-53 Why are ye troubled?

Jn. 20:1-10 The first day of the week

Jn. 20:11-18 She knew not that it was Jesus

Jn. 20:19-23 Jesus stood in the midst

Jn. 20:24-31 Thomas will not believe

1 Co. 15:1-10 He was seen of me also

1 Co. 15:12-23 If in this life only we have hope in Christ

1 Co. 15:24-40 The last enemy that shall be destroyed is death

1 Co. 15:41-52 Sown in corruption, raised in incorruption

1 Cor. 15:53-58 O death, where is thy sting?

Ep. 2:1-10 Sitting together in heavenly places

Col. 3:1-17 If ye are risen with Christ

Eden

Ge. 2:8-17 The Lord God planted a garden in Eden

Is. 51:1-6 He will make her wilderness like Eden

Eze. 28:11-19 Thou hast been in Eden the garden of God

Jo. 2:1-11 The land is as the garden of Eden before them

Edification

Ac. 9:23-31 The churches were edified

Ro. 2:17-29 Instructed out of the law

1 Co. 8 Charity edifieth

1 Co. 10:23-33 Lawful but not edifying

2 Co. 12 We do all things for your edifying

Education

De. 6:1-12 Thou shalt teach them unto thy children

Ps. 32 I will instruct thee and teach thee

Is. 28:9-13 Precept upon precept

Mat. 11:25-30 Learn of me

Mat. 28:16-20 Go ye therefore, and teach all nations

Lu. 2:41-52 Jesus increased in wisdom

1 Ti. 4 These things command and teach

2 Ti. 2:15-26 Apt to teach

2 Pe. 2:1-3 Beware of false teachers

Egotism, *See* Pride

Egypt

Ge. 46:1-7 I will go down with thee to Egypt

Ex. 7:1-13 The Egyptians shall know that I am the Lord

Ex. 20 I brought thee out of the land of Egypt

Is. 31 The Egyptians are men, and not God

He. 11:23-29 Greater riches than the treasures in Egypt

Elder

De. 27:1-10 Moses and the elders commanded

Mat. 15:1-9 Thy disciples transgress the elders' tradition

1 Ti. 5 Elders worthy of double honor

Tit. 1 Ordain elders in every city

Re. 4 The four and twenty elders

Election, *See* Choice

Eloquence, *See* Conversation

Emancipation, *See* Liberty

Eminence, *See* Best

Emotion

Jb. 38 When the morning stars sang together

Lu. 22:39-45 Being in an agony he prayed more earnestly

Jn. 21:15-25 Lovest thou me?

He. 4 Touched with the feeling of our infirmities

1 Pe. 1:13-25 Love one another fervently

Re. 2:1-7 Thou hast left thy first love

Employee

Ex. 20:1-11 Six days shalt thou labour

Ps. 104:1-24 Man goeth to his labour until the evening

Mat. 9:32-38 The harvest is plenteous, the labourers few

Mat. 20:1-16 The labourers in the vineyard

Lu. 10:1-16 The labourer is worthy of his hire

Jn. 10:1-18 The hireling fleeth, because he is an hireling

1 Th. 4 Work with your own hands

Employer, *See* Business; Employee

Emptiness

Pr. 12 He is void of understanding

Ho. 10 Israel is an empty vine

Lu. 1:46-56 The rich he hath sent empty away

1 Co. 13 If I have not charity, I am nothing

Encouragement, *See* Courage

End

Ps. 22:22-31 All the ends of the world shall remember

Ps. 37:27-40 The end of the perfect man is peace

Ps. 39 Lord, make me to know mine end

Ps. 119:33-40 I shall keep it unto the end

Ec. 7:1-10 Better is the end than the beginning

Mat. 24:1-13 He that shall endure shall be saved

Lu. 1:26-38 Of his kingdom there shall be no end

End *(cont.)*

1 Co. 9:13-27   So run, that ye may obtain
2 Ti. 4:6-18   I am now ready to be offered
1 Pe. 4:7-19   The end of all things is at hand

Endeavor

Lu. 13:24-30   Strive to enter in at the strait gate
Ro. 15:13-25   I have strived to preach the gospel
Ep. 4:1-13   Endeavouring to keep the unity of the Spirit
1 Ti. 4   Exercise thyself unto godliness

Endowment, *See* Ability

Endurance

Jb. 2   Shall we not receive evil?
Mat. 24:1-28   He that shall endure unto the end
Lu. 14:25-33   Bearing his cross
Lu. 21:1-19   In your patience possess ye your souls
1 Co. 3   Hitherto ye were not able to bear it
1 Co. 13   Charity endureth all things
2 Co. 4   We faint not
Ph. 1:15-30   To suffer for his sake
2 Ti. 2:1-12   Endure hardness as a good soldier
He. 6   He patiently endured and obtained the promise
Ja. 5:1-11   We count them happy which endure
1 Pe. 4:12-19   The fiery trial that is to try you
Re. 2:1-11   Be thou faithful unto death

Enemy

Ps. 23   In the presence of mine enemies
Ps. 59   Deliver me from mine enemies, O my God
Pr. 24:1-20   Rejoice not when thine enemy falleth
Mi. 7:1-13   A man's enemies are the men of his own house
Mat. 5:43-48   Love your enemies
Jn. 15:17-27   Ye know that the world hated me
Ro. 12:9-21   If thine enemy hunger, feed him
1 Co. 15:12-26   The last enemy to be destroyed is death
1 Th. 5   Let none render evil for evil

Energy, *See* Might

Enjoyment, *See* Joy

Enthusiasm, *See* Ardor

Enticement, *See* Temptation

Entrance, *See* Door

Entreaty

Ru. 1:6-18   Intreat me not to leave thee
Ps. 38   All my desire is before thee
Ps. 130   Out of the depths have I cried unto thee
Is. 55   Seek ye the Lord while he may be found
Is. 65:17-25   Before they call, I will answer
Ep. 6:10-18   Praying always with all prayer
Ph. 4:4-13   Let your requests be made known unto God
Ja. 3   Wisdom easy to be intreated
Ja. 5:13-20   Is any afflicted? Let him pray

Envy, *See* Jealousy

Epistle

2 Co. 3   Ye are our epistle written in our hearts
2 Th. 2   Whether by word, or our epistle
1 Jn. 2:1-17   These things I write unto you

Equality

Pr. 22   The Lord is the maker of them all
Pr. 24:17-23   It is not good to have respect of persons
Is. 40:1-8   Every valley shall be exalted
Mat. 20:1-16   I will give unto this last as unto thee
Mat. 23:1-12   All ye are brethren
2 Co. 8:9-15   That there may be equality
Ga. 3:21-29   Ye are all one in Christ Jesus
Ph. 2:1-11   It was not robbery to be equal with God

Era, *See* Time

Error

Ps. 95   It is a people that do err in their hearts
Pr. 10   He that refuseth reproof erreth
Is. 28:1-13   They err in vision, they stumble in judgment
Da. 6:1-9   No error nor fault was found in him
Mat. 22:23-33   Ye do err, not knowing the scriptures
Ga. 6   Restore a man overtaken in a fault

Escape

1 K. 19:1-18   Elijah flees to the wilderness

Jb. 1 I only am escaped

Ps. 55:1-8 Oh that I had wings like a dove!

Ps. 124 As a bird out of the snare of the fowlers

Jon. 1 Jonah rose up to flee

Mat. 2:7-23 Arise, and flee into Egypt

Mat. 23:23-33 How can ye escape the damnation of hell?

Ac. 27 They escaped all safe to land

He. 2 How shall we escape, if we neglect salvation

He. 11:23-40 By faith they escaped the edge of the sword

Eternity, *See* Immortality

Eucharist, *See* Communion, Service of

Eulogy, *See* Praise

Evangelism, *See* Gospel

Evening

Ge. 3:1-21 God walked in the garden in the cool of the day

De. 28:58-68 Would God it were even!

Ps. 104 Thou makest darkness, and it is night

Ec. 11 In the evening withhold not thine hand

Lu. 24:13-35 Abide with us: for it is toward evening

Evidence

Is. 55 An everlasting sign that shall not be cut off

Mat. 7:15-29 By their fruits ye shall know them.

Lu. 24:36-53 He showed them his hands and his feet

Jn. 1:43-51 Come and see

Ac. 4:13-30 That signs and wonders may be done

1 Co. 15:1-11 Last of all he was seen of me

2 Co. 12:1-12 The signs of an apostle were wrought

2 Ti. 4:1-8 Make full proof of thy ministry

He. 11:1-22 Faith is the evidence of things not seen

Evil, *See* Sin

Evolution, *See* Advance

Example

Ex. 23:1-9 Thou shalt not follow a multitude to do evil

Ho. 4:1-11 There shall be, like people, like priest

Mat. 5:13-17 Ye are the light of the world

Ro. 14 None of us liveth to himself

1 Co. 5 A little leaven leaveneth the whole lump

1 Th. 1 Ye were ensamples to all that believe

1 Ti. 4 Be thou an example of the believers

He. 12:1-14 Looking unto Jesus the author of our faith

Jude 1-13 Sodom and Gomorrha are an example

Excellence, *See* Best

Excuse

Je. 1:1-10 I cannot speak: for I am a child

Mat. 19:16-26 He went away sorrowful

Lu. 14:12-24 They all began to make excuse

Ac. 24:22-27 In a convenient season, I will call for thee

Ro. 2:1-11 Thou art inexcusable, O man

Exile

Ex. 2:11-22 I have been a stranger in a strange land

2 K. 17:6-23 So was Israel carried away to Assyria

Ps. 137 How shall we sing the Lord's song

Is. 5:1-25 My people are gone into captivity

Je. 22:1-10 He shall return no more, nor see his country

Eze. 36:16-24 I scattered them among the heathen

Re. 13 He that leadeth into captivity

Existence, *See* Life

Expectancy, *See* Hope

Experience

Ec. 1 My heart had great experience of wisdom

Jn. 3:1-13 We testify that we have seen

Jn. 9:1-25 Whereas I was blind, now I see

Jn. 20:24-31 Because thou hast seen me, thou hast believed

Ac. 14:19-28 They rehearsed all that God had done

Ro. 5:1-11 Experience worketh hope

1 Co. 9:1-16 Have I not seen Jesus Christ our Lord?

2 Pe. 1 We were eyewitnesses of his majesty

1 Jn. 1 We have seen it, and bear witness

Expert, *See* Ability

Eye, *See* Sight

Face
Ge. 3:14-19 In the sweat of thy face shalt thou eat
Ex. 34:29-35 The skin of Moses' face shone
2 Ch. 6:32-42 Turn not away the face of thine anointed
Jb. 11 Thou shall lift up thy face without spot
Ps. 4 Lift the light of thy countenance upon us
Pr. 15:1-17 A merry heart maketh a cheerful countenance
Is. 25:1-8 God will wipe away tears from off all faces
Ac. 6 They saw his face as the face of an angel
2 Co. 3 We all with open face beholding

Failure, *See Defeat*
Faintness, *See Weakness*
Fairness, *See Justice*
Faith
Ge. 12:1-9 Abram departed, as the Lord had spoken
Mat. 8:5-10 I have not found so great faith
Mat. 9:27-38 According to your faith be it unto you
Mat. 15:21-31 Great is thy faith
Mk. 2:1-12 One sick of the palsy
Mk. 10:46-52 Thy faith hath made thee whole
Ro. 4:1-5 Faith is counted for righteousness
Ro. 5:1-11 Being justified by faith
2 Co. 4:8-18 Troubled, yet not distressed
Ga. 3:23-29 Before faith was the law
Ep. 3:14-21 That Christ may dwell in your hearts
Ph. 1:21-26 Having this confidence
He. 11 The substance of things hoped for

Faithfulness
Mat. 25:14-30 Parable of the talents
Lu. 12:41-48 Who is that faithful and wise steward?
Lu. 19:12-26 The parable of the pounds
Jn. 13:1-17 He loved his own unto the end
Ac. 26:1-20 I was not disobedient unto the vision
1 Co. 4 A steward must be faithful

1 Co. 16:1-14 Stand fast in the faith
Tit. 2 Showing all good fidelity
Re. 2:1-11 Be thou faithful unto death
Re. 21:1-10 These words are true and faithful

Faithlessness, *See* Betrayal
Fall, *See* Defeat
Falsehood, *See* Lie
Fame, *See* Best
Family
De. 11:18-25 Ye shall teach them your children
Ps. 68:3-6 God setteth the solitary in families
Ps. 128 Thou shalt see thy children's children
Ps. 133 How good for brethren to dwell in unity
Ps. 144:11-15 That our sons may be as plants
Am. 3 You only have I known of all the families
Mat. 10:16-39 A man's foes shall be in his own household
Mat. 12:38-50 Behold my mother and my brethren!
Mk. 7:9-13 Ye let him do nothing for father and mother
Lu. 2:40-52 Jesus in the temple
Lu. 15:11-32 The prodigal son
Ep. 3:14-21 The whole family in heaven and earth
Col. 3:12-25 Forbearing one another
1 Jn. 3:1-11 We should love one another

Famine
Ge. 41:52-57 The famine was over all the face of the earth
Ps. 107:1-15 He filleth the hungry soul with goodness
Pr. 10:1-12 The soul of the righteous will not famish
Am. 8 A famine of hearing the words of the Lord
Mat. 24:1-28 There shall be famines
Lu. 6:20-31 Blessed are ye that hunger now
Ph. 4:8-13 I am instructed both to be full and hungry
Re. 7:9-17 They shall hunger no more

Fanaticism, *See* Bigotry
Fast
Ps. 35:1-13 I humbled my soul with fasting

Is. 58:1-7 Is not this the fast that I have chosen?

Mat. 6:16-34 When thou fastest, anoint thine head

Mk. 2:15-20 Can the children of the bridechamber fast?

2 Co. 11:18-30 In fastings often

Fate, *See* Destiny

Father's Day

1 K. 8:57-61 God be with us, as he was with our fathers

Pr. 4:1-13 Hear the instruction of a father

Pr. 10:1-13 A wise son maketh a glad father

Pr. 17 The glory of children are their fathers

Pr. 23:22-26 Hearken unto thy father that begat thee

Is. 9:1-7 His name shall be The everlasting Father

Mal. 4 He shall turn the heart of the fathers

Lu. 2:41-52 I must be about my Father's business

Lu. 15:11-32 His father saw him, and had compassion

Ep. 6:1-18 The first commandment with promise

Fault, *See* Imperfection

Fear

Ex. 14:10-15 Fear ye not, stand still

Jos. 1:1-9 Be strong and of a good courage

Ps. 34 He delivered me from all my fears

Ps. 56 What time I am afraid, I will trust in thee

Ps. 91 Thou shalt not be afraid

Is. 12 I will trust, and not be afraid

Mat. 14:22-33 It is I; be not afraid

2 Ti. 1 God hath not given us the spirit of fear

1 Pe. 1:13-25 Pass the time of your sojourning here in fear

1 Jn. 4 Perfect love casteth out fear

Fearlessness, *See* Courage

Feast

Pr. 15:1-17 Better a dinner of herbs where love is

Ec. 7:1-10 It is better to go to the house of mourning

Ec. 10:16-20 A feast is made for laughter

Is. 22:1-14 Eat and drink; for tomorrow we die

Ho. 9 The day of the feast of the Lord

Lu. 14:7-14 When thou makest a feast, call the poor

Jn. 21:1-14 Jesus saith unto them, Come and dine

Feebleness, *See* Weakness

Feeling, *See* Emotion

Fellowship, *See* Communion

Fervor, *See* Ardor

Festival, *See* Feast

Fickleness, *See* Change

Fidelity, *See* Loyalty

Fight, *See* Strife

Financial Canvass, *See* Canvass, Every Member

Fire

Ex. 3:1-5 Behold, the bush burned with fire

Ex. 13:17-22 The Lord went before them in a pillar of fire

1 K. 19:1-18 The Lord was not in the fire

Is. 43:1-7 The flame shall not kindle upon thee

Mat. 3 He shall baptize with the Holy Ghost and fire

Lu. 12:49-59 I am come to send fire on the earth

Ac. 2:1-21 Cloven tongues like as of fire

1 Co. 3 He shall be saved, but as by fire

Ja. 3 The tongue is a fire, a world of iniquity

Firmament, *See* Heaven

Firmness, *See* Steadfastness

First, *See* Beginning; Chief

Fisher

Ge. 1:26-31 Let them have dominion over the fish of the sea

Mat. 4:18-22 I will make you fishers of men

Mat. 13:47-52 The kingdom of heaven is like a net

Lu. 5:1-11 Jesus calls the fishermen

Jn. 21:1-14 I go a fishing

Flag Day, *See* Banner

Flame, *See* Fire

Flattery

Ps. 12 With flattering lips they speak

Pr. 20:11-30 Meddle not with him that flattereth

Pr. 25:16-28 It is not good to eat much honey

Pr. 26:20-28 A flattering mouth worketh ruin

Pr. 29:1-14 The flatterer spreadeth a net

Flattery (*cont.*)

Ep. 6:1-17 Not with eyeservice, as menpleasers

1 Th. 2 We never used flattering words

Flesh, *See* Body

Flight, *See* Escape

Flock, *See* Shepherd

Flood, *See* Adversity

Flower Sunday

Ge. 2:8-17 God put the man into the garden

S. of S. 2 The flowers appear on the earth

Is. 35 The desert shall blossom as the rose

Is. 40:1-11 The flower fadeth; the word of God standeth

Ho. 14 He shall grow as the lily

Mat. 6:28-34 Consider the lilies of the field

Ja. 1:9-11 As the flower of the grass he shall pass away

Foe, *See* Enemy

Folly

Ps. 14 The fool hath said, There is no God

Ec. 2:1-17 Wisdom excelleth folly

Mat. 7:24-29 The foolish man built his house on the sand

1 Co. 1:17-31 The foolishness of God is wiser than men

2 Co. 11:1-19 Suffer fools gladly, seeing ye are wise

Ep. 5:1-17 Walk circumspectly, not as fools, but as wise

Food, *See* Bread

Fool, *See* Folly

Foot

Ps. 40:1-11 He hath set my feet upon a rock

Ps. 115 Feet have they, but they walk not

Ps. 121 He will not suffer thy foot to be moved

Pr. 4 Ponder the path of thy feet

Is. 52 The feet of him that bringeth good tidings

Mat. 18:1-14 If thy foot offend thee, cut it off

Lu. 24:36-53 He showed them his hands and his feet

Ep. 6 Your feet shod with the gospel of peace

Force, *See* Compulsion

Forefathers Day, *See* Ancestor

Foreigner, *See* Stranger

Foreordination, *See* Predestination

Forerunner, *See* Ambassador

Forest, *See* Tree

Forgetfulness

Ge. 41:46-57 God hath made me forget all my toil

De. 6:1-15 Beware lest thou forget the Lord

Ps. 51 Blot out all mine iniquities

Ps. 103 Forget not all his benefits

Ps. 137:1-6 If I forget thee, O Jerusalem

Am. 1:9-15 They remembered not the brotherly covenant

Ph. 3:1-13 Forgetting those things which are behind

He. 13 Be not forgetful to entertain strangers

Forgiveness

Ge. 50:15-21 Forgive, I pray thee

Nu. 14:1-24 Pardon, I beseech thee, the iniquity

1 S. 26:7-21 David spares the life of Saul

Is. 55 He will abundantly pardon

Mat. 18-21-35 How oft shall I forgive?

Lu. 7:36-50 The alabaster box of ointment

Lu. 11:1-13 Forgive us our sins

Jn. 8:1-11 Neither do I condemn thee

1 Jn. 2:1-12 Your sins are forgiven you

Formalism, *See* Ceremony

Fornication, *See* Lust

Fortitude, *See* Endurance

Fortress, *See* Security

Fortune, *See* Chance

Foundation

Ezr. 3:8-13 The foundation of the house of the Lord

Is. 48:12-19 I have laid the foundation of the earth

Mat. 7:24-29 The house built on a rock

Mat. 16:13-23 Upon this rock I will build my church

Ac. 4:1-12 The head of the corner

1 Co. 3 Other foundation can no man lay

1 Pe. 2:1-10 I lay in Sion a chief corner stone

Frankness, *See* Candor

Fraternal Orders

Ge. 1:14-23 God made two great lights

Ge. 4:1-9 Am I my brother's keeper?

1 K. 7:1-13 Solomon finished his house

Ps. 96   The trees of the wood rejoice
Ps. 136:1-9   The sun to rule by day
Pr. 28:14-28   He that tilleth shall have plenty
Je. 13:1-11   Get thee a linen girdle
1 Co. 3:10-17   As a wise master-builder
1 Co. 13   Though I understand all mysteries
2 Co. 3   The letter killeth, the spirit giveth life

Fraternity, *See* Brotherhood

Fraud, *See* Lie

Freedom, *See* Liberty

Friendship

1 S. 18:1-4   Jonathan loved him
Pr. 17:1-17   A friend loveth at all times
Pr. 18   To have friends a man must be friendly
Pr. 27   Faithful are the wounds of a friend
Ec. 4:9-16   Woe to him that is alone when he falleth
Lu. 16:1-12   Make to yourselves friends
Jn. 15:10-15   Ye are my friends

Fruit

Ge. 1:9-13   The fruit tree yielding fruit
Ps. 92   They shall bring forth fruit in old age
Mat. 3   Bring forth fruits meet for repentance
Mat. 7:1-20   By their fruits ye shall know them
Mk. 4:26-29   First the blade, then the ear, then the corn
Jn. 15   Ye should go and bring forth fruit
Ja. 3   Wisdom from above if full of good fruits
Re. 22   The tree of life bare twelve manner of fruit

Fruitfulness, *See* Abundance

Fruitlessness, *See* Barrenness

Fulfillment, *See* Completion

Fullness, *See* Life, the Full

Funeral, *See* Death

Future

Ex. 14:10-22   Speak unto Israel that they go forward
2 K. 6:1-7   Let us go, we pray thee, unto Jordan
Pr. 27   Boast not thyself of to-morrow
Is. 33:13-24   Thine eyes shall behold the land far off
Zph. 1   The great day of the Lord is near
Jn. 14:1-14   Greater works than these shall he do
1 Co. 13   Then shall we see face to face
He. 6   Let us go on to perfection
He. 13   We seek a city to come
Ja. 4:8-17   Ye know not what shall be on the morrow

[G]

Gain

Jb. 1:6-12   Doth Job fear God for nought
Pr. 3:13-26   Wisdom is better than fine gold
Pr. 15   Greedy of gain he troubleth his own house
Mi. 3   The priests teach for hire
Mat. 6:19-34   Lay up treasures in heaven
Mat. 16:24-28   What profit if he gain the whole world
Mat. 25:14-29   Parable of the talents
Lu. 12:16-21   I will build greater barns
Ac. 5:1-11   Ananias and Sapphira
Ph. 1   For me to die is gain
Ph. 3:7-14   What things were gain I counted loss
1 Ti. 6   Godliness with contentment is great gain

Galilee

Mat. 26:17-35   I will go before you into Galilee
Mat. 26:69-75   Thou also wast with Jesus of Galilee
Jn. 7:40-53   Out of Galilee ariseth no prophet
Ac. 10:34-43   The word God sent began from Galilee

Gambling, *See* Chance

Garden

Ge. 2:1-9   The Lord God planted a garden
Ec. 2:1-11   I made me gardens and orchards
Is. 51:1-6   The Lord will make her wilderness like Eden
Is. 58:8-12   Thou shalt be like a watered garden
Eze. 28:11-19   Thou hast been in Eden the garden of God

Garden, *(cont.)*

Mat. 26:36-46 Jesus cometh to Gethsemane
Jn. 19:38-42 There was in the garden a new sepulchre
Re. 22:1-5 The tree of life

Garment, *See* Clothes

Gayety

Ge. 21:1-8 God hath made me to laugh
Pr. 14:1-13 Even in laughter the heart is sorrowful
Pr. 17 A merry heart doeth good like a medicine
Ec. 2:1-11 I will prove thee with mirth
Ec. 3:1-15 A time to weep, and a time to laugh
Lu. 15:11-32 It was meet that we should make merry

Generation

Ps. 90 Our dwelling place in all generations
Ps. 145 One generation shall praise thee to another
Is. 51:1-8 My salvation is from generation to generation
Lu. 1:46-55 All generations shall call me blessed
1 Pe. 2:1-10 Ye are a chosen generation

Generosity, *See* Benevolence

Genesis, *See* Beginning

Gentile, *See* Stranger

Gentleness

Ps. 37:1-11 The meek shall inherit the earth
Is. 40:1-11 He shall gently lead those with young
Is. 42:1-4 A bruised reed shall he not break
2 Co. 10:1-7 By the meekness and gentleness of Christ
Ga. 5 The fruit of the Spirit is gentleness
Ep. 4:25-32 Be ye kind, tender-hearted, forgiving
Ja. 3 Peaceable, gentle, easy to be intreated
1 Pe. 3:1-11 Love as brethren, be pitiful, be courteous

Gethsemane

Mat. 26:36-56 Then cometh Jesus unto Gethsemane
Mk. 14:26-52 They went out into the mount of Olives
Lu. 22:39-46 Not my will, but thine, be done

Jn. 18:1-14 Over the brook Cedron was a garden

Ghost, Holy, *See* Spirit, Holy

Gift

Mat. 2:1-15 They presented unto him gifts
Mat. 6:5-15 Give us this day our daily bread
Mat. 7:1-12 Your Father in heaven shall give good things
Ac. 20:28-38 It is more blessed to give than to receive
Ro. 12 Present your bodies a living sacrifice

Girl

Pr. 30:1-19 The way of a man with a maid
Jo. 3:1-8 They have sold a girl for wine
Zch. 8:1-8 The streets shall be full of boys and girls
2 Co. 6 Ye shall be my sons and daughters

Girl Scout Sunday, *See* Scout

Gladness, *See* Joy

Gloom, *See* Discouragement

Glory

Ex. 34:28-35 The skin of his face shone
Ps. 24 Who is the King of glory?
Pr. 4 The path of the just is as the shining light
Je. 9:23-24 Let him that glorieth glory in this
Mat. 6:24-34 Solomon in all his glory was not arrayed
1 Co. 6 Glorify God in your body, and in your spirit
2 Co. 3 We are changed from glory to glory
2 Co. 10 He that glorieth, let him glory in the Lord
2 Co. 11:16-33 I will also glory after the flesh
Ga. 1 They glorified God in me
1 Th. 2 Ye are our glory and joy
1 Pe. 1:13-25 The glory of man is as the flower of grass

Gluttony, *See* Greed

Goal, *See* End

God, Access to, *See* God, Finding

God, Adoration of, *See* God, Worship of

God, Anger of

De. 4:14-24 The Lord thy God is a consuming fire
Ps. 6 Chasten me not in thy hot displeasure
Ps. 7 God is angry with the wicked every day

Ps. 78:40-62 God was wroth with his inheritance

Ps. 103 The Lord is slow to anger

Is. 54:1-8 In a little wrath I hid my face from thee

Mi. 7:16-20 He retaineth not his anger for ever

Jn. 3:25-36 The wrath of God abideth on him

Re. 19:11-15 The fierceness and wrath of Almighty God

God, Antagonism to, See God, Denial of

God, Aspiration for, See God, Longing for

God, Belief in, See God, Faith in

God, Beneficence of, See God, Benevolence of

God, Benevolence of

Ge. 13:14-18 To thee will I give the land

Ge. 45:1-15 God did send me before you to preserve life

Ex. 16:1-15 They said, It is manna

De. 8:1-18 Thou shalt remember the Lord thy God

1 K. 17:1-6 The ravens fed him

Ps. 23 The Lord is my shepherd

Ps. 46 God is our refuge and strength

Ps. 84 No good thing will he withhold

Ps. 103:1-18 Forget not all his benefits

Ps. 104:24-34 Thou openest thine hand

Is. 40:1-11 He shall feed his flock like a shepherd

Ho. 6:1-7 He hath torn, and he will heal us

Ho. 11:1-4 I drew them with bands of love

Jon. 4 Should not I spare Nineveh

Zph. 3:14-20 He will rest in his love

Lu. 19:1-10 He also is a son of Abraham

Jn. 3:1-21 God so loved the world

Jn. 15:1-16 My Father is the husbandman

Ja. 1:1-17 Every perfect gift is from above

1 Jn. 4 Love is of God

Re. 21:1-7 God shall wipe away all tears

God, Blessing of, See God, Benevolence of

God, the Builder, See God the Creator

God, Call of, See God, Voice of

God, Care of, See God, Benevolence of

God, Certainty of

Ex. 3:1-14 Certainly I will be with thee

Ps. 19 The testimony of the Lord is sure

Mal. 3:1-6 I am the Lord, I change not

2 Ti. 2:15-26 The foundation of God standeth sure

He. 6 The immutability of his counsel

Ja. 1:17-27 With whom is no variableness

God, Chastisement of

Jb. 5 Happy is the man whom God correcteth

Ps. 94 Blessed is the man whom thou chasteneth

Is. 13:6-13 I will punish the world for their evil

Ho. 9 The days of recompense are come

Am. 3 Therefore will I punish you for iniquity

He. 10:30-39 Vengeance belongeth unto me

He. 12:1-11 Whom the Lord loveth he chasteneth

Re. 3:14-22 As many as I love, I rebuke and chasten

God, Children of

Ps. 100 We are his people

Ps. 103 Like as a father pitieth his children

Mat. 5:1-12 The peacemakers are the children of God

Mat. 19:13-15 Of such is the kingdom of heaven

Ac. 17:24-28 We are also his offspring

Ro. 8:1-17 We are the children of God

Ro. 9:25-33 They shall be called children of God

1 Jn. 3 Beloved, now are we the sons of God

God, City of, See God, Kingdom of

God, Comfort of, See God, Compassion of

God, Commandment of, See God, Law of

God, Communion with, See God, Fellowship with

God, Companionship of, See God, Fellowship with

God, Compassion of

Ex. 20 Showing mercy unto thousands that love me

Ex. 34:1-6 The Lord God, merciful and gracious

God, Compassion of *(cont.)*

Ne. 9:6-31 Thou didst not utterly consume them

Ps. 36 Thy mercy is in the heavens

Ps. 51 Create in me a clean heart

Ps. 103:8-13 He hath not dealt with us after our sins

Is. 40:1-11 Comfort ye my people

La. 3:22-36 His compassions fail not

Ho. 11 I drew them with bands of love

Jon. 3 God repented of the evil

Jon. 4 Thou art gracious, merciful, of great kindness

Mi. 7:8-20 He will have compassion upon us

Ja. 4 God will draw nigh to you

God, Confidence in, *See* God, Faith in

God, Consciousness of

Ge. 32:24-30 I have seen God face to face

Ex. 3:1-12 Certainly I will be with thee

Ex. 33:12-23 My presence shall go with thee

2 Ch. 17:1-6 The Lord was with Jehoshaphat

Jb. 36 God is great, and we know him not

Ps. 23 He leadeth me

Ps. 139:1-12 Whither shall I flee from thy presence?

Mat. 6:24-34 Your heavenly Father knoweth

Ac. 17:22-31 In him we live and move

Col. 1 That ye might be filled with his knowledge

God, the Creator

Ge. 2:1-7 God ended his work which he had made

Ps. 100 It is he that hath made us

Is. 40:18-31 The Creator of the ends of the earth

Is. 65:17-25 I create new heavens and a new earth

Ac. 14:8-18 The living God, which made heaven and earth

2 Ti. 2 The foundation of God standeth sure

He. 3 He that built all things is God

He. 11:1-16 The worlds were framed by the word of God

God, Day of

Jo. 2:21-32 The great and terrible day of the Lord

Zph. 1:7-18 The great day of the Lord is near, it is near

Tit. 1 In hope of eternal life

2 Pe. 3 Hasting unto the coming of the day of God

God, Deliverance of, *See* God, Salvation of

God, Denial of

Ex. 5:1-9 I know not the Lord

Jb. 2:1-10 Curse God, and die

Ps. 53 The fool hath said, There is no God

Pr. 30:1-9 Lest I be full and deny thee

Je. 2:26-32 My people have forgotten me

Je. 5:10-18 They have belied the Lord

Je. 5:21-29 This people hath a revolting heart

Ho. 13:9-16 She hath rebelled against God

Jo. 2:15-17 Where is their God?

Ro. 8:1-14 The carnal mind is enmity against God

Jude 1:1-13 Denying the only Lord God

God, Dominion of, *See* God, Kingdom of

God, Duty to

Nu. 23 All that the Lord speaketh, that must I do

1 Ch. 16:23-36 Give unto the Lord the glory due him

Ec. 12 This is the whole duty of man

Lu. 2:40-52 I must be about my Father's business

Lu. 20:19-26 Render unto God the things that are God's

Jn. 9:1-12 I must work the works of him that sent me

Ac. 5:29-42 We ought to obey God rather than men

1 Pe. 2:11-25 Fear God

God, the Eternal

De. 32:36-43 I live for ever

Ps. 48 This God is our God for ever and ever

Ps. 111 His righteousness endureth for ever

Ps. 146 The Lord shall reign for ever

Ps. 147 His understanding is infinite

Is. 9:1-7 The everlasting Father

Is. 57:12-21 The lofty One that inhabiteth eternity

1 Ti. 1:12-17 Now unto the King eternal, immortal

God, Evidence of, *See* God, Proof of
God, Existence of
Ex. 3:1-14 God said, I AM THAT I AM
2 S. 22:33-51 The Lord liveth
Mal. 3:1-6 I am the Lord, I change not
Mat. 5:1-12 The pure in heart shall see God
2 Co. 5 We walk by faith, not by sight
He. 11:1-16 He that cometh to God must believe that he is
Re. 1:4-18 From him which is, and was, and is to come
God, Face of
Ge. 32:24-32 I have seen God face to face
Nu. 6:22-27 The Lord lift up his countenance
Ps. 27 Thy face, Lord, will I seek
Ps. 67 God cause his face to shine upon us
Ps. 89:1-16 Mercy and truth shall go before thy face
Ps. 90 Our sins are in the light of thy countenance
Is. 33:13-24 Thine eyes shall see the king in his beauty
Mat. 18:1-14 Their angels do always behold the face of God
Re. 22 They shall see his face
God, Faith in
Ge. 12:1-9 Abram departed as the Lord had spoken
Jb. 13 Though he slay me, yet will I trust in him
Ps. 16 In thee do I put my trust
Ps. 31 Thou hast set my feet in a large room
Ps. 36 Their trust is under the shadow of thy wings
Ps. 37:1-18 Trust in the Lord, and do good
Ps. 40 Blessed the man that maketh the Lord his trust
Ps. 55 Cast thy burden upon the Lord
Ps. 91 He shall give his angels charge over thee
Is. 26:1-11 Trust ye in the Lord for ever
Mat. 6:25-30 Your heavenly Father feedeth them
Mk. 11:20-26 Have faith in God
Lu. 7:1-10 I have not found so great faith
He. 11:1-16 He went out, not knowing whither he went

God, Faithfulness of
Ps. 103 His mercy is from everlasting to everlasting
Ps. 119:89-112 Thy faithfulness is unto all generations
Is. 25 Thy counsels of old are faithfulness
1 Co. 1:1-9 God is faithful, by whom ye were called
He. 10:23-39 He is faithful that promised
Re. 15 Just and true are thy ways
God, Fatherhood of
Mat. 5:38-48 Be ye perfect, even as your Father
Mat. 6:1-15 Your Father knoweth the things ye need
Lu. 11:1-13 When ye pray, say, Our Father
Jn. 14:6-13 He that hath seen me hath seen the Father
Jn. 14:15-31 My Father is greater than I
Jn. 15:1-13 I am the vine, my Father the husbandman
Ac. 17:24-31 For we are also his offspring
Ep. 4:1-16 One God and Father of all
He. 1 I will be to him a Father
Ja. 1:17-27 Every perfect gift cometh from the Father
1 Jn. 1 Our fellowship is with the Father
Re. 21:1-7 He that overcometh shall be my son
God, Fear of
Ex. 33:12-23 There shall no man see me, and live
Ps. 19 The fear of the Lord is clean
Pr. 14:26-35 The fear of the Lord is the fountain of life
Pr. 23:1-17 Be thou in the fear of the Lord all day long
Ec. 12 Fear God, and keep his commandments
Jon. 1 I fear the Lord, the God of heaven
1 Pe. 2:11-25 Fear God
God, Fellowship with
Jos. 1:1-9 I will not fail thee, nor forsake thee
Jn. 16:20-33 I am not alone, for the Father is with me
Jn. 17 Thou, Father, art in me and I in thee
2 Co. 6:1-10 As workers together with him

God, Fellowship with *(cont.)*

Ep. 2 Ye are of the household of God

1 Jn. 1 Our fellowship is with the Father

Re. 3:1-6 They shall walk with me in white

God, Finding

1 Ch. 28:1-10 If thou seek him, he will be found of thee

Jb. 23 Oh that I knew where I might find him!

Is. 2:2, 3 Let us go up to the mountain of the Lord

Je. 29:10-14 Ye shall seek me, and find me

Ho. 10 It is time to seek the Lord

Ac. 17:24-28 In him we live, and move, and have our being

He. 11:1-16 He is a rewarder of them that seek him

Ja. 4 Draw nigh to God, and he will draw nigh

God, Foreknowledge of, *See* God, Omniscience of

God, Forgetfulness of, *See* God, Denial of

God, Forgiveness of, *See* God, Compassion of

God, the Friend, *See* God, Fellowship with

God, Fullness of

Ps. 50 The world is mine, and the fulness thereof

Is. 6 The whole earth is full of his glory

Ep. 3 Filled with the fulness of God

God, Gentleness of, *See* God, Compassion of

God, Gift of, *See* God, Benevolence of

God, Glory of

Ex. 33:12-23 While my glory passeth by

1 K. 8:1-11 The glory of the Lord filled the house

Ps. 8 Thy glory is above the heavens

Ps. 19:1-6 The heavens declare the glory of God

Ps. 24 Who is this King of glory?

Ps. 77 Thou art the God that doest wonders

Ps. 89:1-17 The heavens shall praise thy wonders

Ps. 104:1-24 Thou art clothed with honor and majesty

Ps. 105:1-8 Talk ye of all his wondrous works

Is. 2:10-17 The Lord alone shall be exalted

Is. 6 The whole earth is full of his glory

Is. 40:1-9 The glory of the Lord shall be revealed

Lu. 2:1-14 Glory to God in the highest

Re. 5 Blessing, and honor, and glory, and power

God, Goodness of, *See* God, Benevolence of

God, Grace of

Nu. 6:22-27 The Lord be gracious unto thee

Ps. 77 Hath God forgotten to be gracious?

Je. 31:1-9 With lovingkindness have I drawn thee

Ho. 14 I will be as the dew unto Israel

Lu. 1:26-35 Thou hast found favor with God

1 Co. 1:1-9 The grace of God is given you by Jesus

1 Co. 15:1-11 By the grace of God I am what I am

2 Co. 1:1-12 Not with fleshly wisdom, but by grace

Ep. 2:1-10 The exceeding riches of his grace

Tit. 2:11-14 The grace of God bringeth salvation

He. 4 Let us come boldly unto the throne of grace

God, Gratitude to, *See* God, Thankfulness to

God, Greatness of, *See* God, Omnipotence of

God, Guidance of

Ps. 23 He leadeth me beside the still waters

Ps. 48 He will be our guide even unto death

Ps. 61 Lead me to the rock that is higher than I

Ps. 139 Lead me in the way everlasting

Is. 42:1-16 I will bring the blind by a way they knew not

Is. 49:1-12 Even by springs of water shall he guide them

Mat. 6:1-13 Lead us not into temptation

Lu. 1:67-80 To guide our feet into the way of peace

2 Th. 3 The Lord direct your hearts

God, Hand of, *See* God, Guidance of

God, the Healer
Ex. 15:22-27 I am the Lord that healeth thee
De. 32:39-43 I wound, and I heal
Ps. 147 He healeth the broken in heart
Je. 3:12-25 I will heal your backslidings
Je. 33:1-8 I will cure them
Ho. 6 He hath torn, and he will heal us
Mal. 4 With healing in his wings

God, Heirs of
Ps. 16 The Lord is the portion of mine inheritance
Mat. 25:31-46 Inherit the kingdom prepared for you
Ro. 8:15-17 Ye have received the spirit of adoption
Ga. 4:1-7 An heir of God through Christ
Col. 1:1-17 Partakers of the inheritance of the saints
Tit. 3 Heirs according to the hope of eternal life
He. 9 The promise of eternal inheritance
1 Pe. 1:1-13 An inheritance incorruptible

God, Help of, *See* God, Benevolence of
God, the Hiding, *See* God, the Unseen
God, Holiness of
1 Ch. 16:7-36 Worship the Lord in the beauty of holiness
Ps. 47 God sitteth upon the throne of his holiness
Is. 8:9-18 He shall be for a sanctuary
Is. 43:1-7 I am the Holy One of Israel
Is. 57:13-21 I dwell in the high and holy place
Ho. 11 The Holy One in the midst of thee
Mat. 6:5-15 Hallowed be thy name
He. 12:1-11 That we might be partakers of his holiness
1 Pe. 1:1-16 Be ye holy; for I am holy
Re. 15 Thou only art holy

God, Hope in, *See* God, Faith in
God, House of
Ge. 28:10-19 Surely the Lord is in this place
Ps. 26 I have loved the habitation of thy house
Ps. 122 Let us go into the house of the Lord
Hag. 1:2-12 The Lord's house should be built

Hag. 2:1-9 I will fill this house with glory
Mk. 11:15-19 My house shall be called the house of prayer
Ep. 2 An habitation of God through the Spirit
1 Ti. 3 The house of God is the church of God
1 Pe. 4 Judgment must begin at the house of God

God, Image of
Ge. 1:26-31 Let us make man in our image
Ps. 17 When I awake with thy likeness
1 Co. 15:45-58 We shall also bear the image of the heavenly
2 Co. 4:1-7 The gospel of Christ, who is the image of God
Col. 1:1-17 Jesus is the image of the invisible God

God, Immanence of, *See* God, Consciousness of
God, Impartiality of
2 Ch. 19 There is no respect of persons with God
Ps. 139:1-12 The darkness and the light are both alike
Pr. 22:1-9 The Lord is the maker of them all
Ec. 9:1-10 All things come alike to all
Eze. 18:25-32 Are not my ways equal?
Mat. 5:38-48 He sendeth rain on the just and on the unjust
Col. 3:1-15 There is neither Greek nor Jew
Ja. 3 Wisdom that is without partiality
1 Pe. 1:13-25 The Father judgeth without respect of persons

God, Incarnation of
Mat. 1:18-25 They shall call his name Emmanuel
Jn. 1:1-18 The Word was made flesh
Ph. 2:1-11 He was made in the likeness of men
Col. 2:1-9 In him dwelleth all the fulness of the Godhead
1 Ti. 3:14-16 God was manifest in the flesh

God, the Infinite, *See* God, the Eternal
God, Joy in
Ps. 32 Be glad in the Lord and shout for joy
Ps. 35:1-9 My soul shall be joyful in the Lord

God, Joy in *(cont.)*

Ps. 37:1-11 Delight thyself also in the Lord

Is. 9:1-7 They joy before thee

Lu. 1:46-56 My spirit hath rejoiced in God

Ro. 5:1-11 We also joy in God through our Lord

Ph. 4:1-7 Rejoice in the Lord alway

God, the Judge

Ge. 18:23-33 Shall not the Judge of the earth do right?

Ps. 19 His judgments are sweeter than honey

Ps. 36 Thy judgments are a great deep

Ps. 98 With righteousness shall he judge the earth

Ps. 143 In thy sight shall no man living be justified

Ec. 12 God shall bring every work into judgment

Ho. 6 Thy judgments are as the light

Mal. 3:1-6 Who shall stand when he appeareth?

Ro. 11:22-36 How unsearchable are his judgments!

He. 10:21-39 It is a fearful thing to fall into his hands

1 Pe. 1:13-25 The Father judgeth according to the work

Re. 6 Who shall be able to stand?

God, the Keeper, *See* God, Faithfulness of

God, Kindness of, *See* God, Benevolence of

God, Kingdom of

Ps. 72:6-11 He shall have dominion from sea to sea

Ps. 103:18-22 His throne is in the heavens

Je. 10:1-13 The Lord is an everlasting king

Mat. 4:17-25 Repent: for the kingdom of heaven is at hand

Mat. 13:18-23 The parable of the sower

Mat. 13:24-30, 36-43 The wheat and the tares

Mat. 13:31-35 Like a grain of mustard seed

Mat. 13:44-52 Like a treasure hid in a field

Mk. 10:13-16 Of such is the kingdom of God

Lu. 8:1-15 Showing the glad tidings of the kingdom

Lu. 11:1-4 Thy kingdom come

Lu. 12:22-31 Seek ye the kingdom of God

Lu. 14:15-24 It is blessed to eat bread in God's kingdom

Lu. 17:20-25 The kingdom of God is within you

Jn. 3:1-10 A man must be born of the Spirit

1 Co. 4 The kingdom is not in word, but in power

He. 1 The sceptre of thy kingdom is righteous

Re. 19:1-9 The Lord God omnipotent reigneth

God, Knowledge of, *See* God, Consciousness of

God, Law of

Ps. 19 The law of the Lord is perfect

Ps. 119:1-24 The undefiled walk in the law of the Lord

Ps. 119:49-72 Thy law is better than gold and silver

Ps. 119:153-176 I do not forget thy commandments

Pr. 6:16-35 The commandment is a lamp; the law is light

Je. 31:31-40 I will put my law in their inward parts

Mi. 6:6-16 What doth the Lord require of thee?

Ro. 7 With the mind I serve the law of God

Ro. 16:24-27 The commandment of the everlasting God

1 Ti. 1:8-11 We know that the law is good

1 Jn. 5 His commandments are not grievous

Re. 22:1-14 Blessed are they that do his commandments

God, Leadership of, *See* God, Guidance of

God, Life in, *See* God, Fellowship with

God, the Light

Ps. 4 Lift thou up the light of thy countenance

Ps. 18:25-50 The Lord will enlighten my darkness

Ps. 36 In thy light shall we see light

Ps. 84 The Lord God is a sun

Ps. 104 Thou coverest thyself with light

Is. 60 The Lord shall be thine everlasting light

2 Co. 4 God hath shined in our hearts

Ja. 1 Every good gift cometh from the Father of lights

1 Jn. 1 God is light

God, the Living, *See* God, Existence of

God, Longing for
Ps. 27 Thy face, Lord, will I seek
Ps. 38 All my desire is before thee
Ps. 40:1-5 I waited patiently for God
Ps. 42 My soul panteth after thee, O God
Ps. 73 There is none I desire beside thee
Ps. 119:129-152 I cried unto thee
La. 3:37-58 Let us lift up our heart unto God

God, the Lord
Ex. 15:1-19 The Lord is his name
Ps. 100 Know ye that the Lord he is God
Is. 43:1-17 I am the Lord, your Holy One
Re. 4 Thou art worthy, O Lord, to receive glory
Re. 19:1-16 KING OF KINGS AND LORD OF LORDS

God, Loss of, *See* God, Denial of

God, Love of, *See* God, Benevolence of

God, Love to, *See* God, Faith in

God, Majesty of, *See* God, Kingdom of

God, Mercy of, *See* God, Compassion of

God, Messenger of
Is. 40:1-11 Prepare ye the way of the Lord
Is. 42:1-16 Behold my servant
Hag. 1:7-13 Then spake Haggai the Lord's messenger
Mal. 2:1-10 He is the messenger of the Lord
Mal. 3:1-6 Behold, I will send my messenger
Lu. 1:67-80 Thou shalt go before his face
Ga. 4:1-7 God hath sent forth the Spirit of his Son

God, Name of
Ex. 20:1-17 Thou shalt not take the name of God in vain
Ex. 34:10-17 The Lord, whose name is Jealous
Ps. 5 Let them that love thy name be joyful
Ps. 72 Blessed be his glorious name for ever
Ps. 135 Thy name, O Lord, endureth for ever
Mat. 6:5-15 Hallowed be thy name
Jn. 5:39-47 I am come in my Father's name
Jn. 12:20-36 Father, glorify thy name
Re. 3:7-13 I will write upon him my new name

God, in Nature
Nu. 14:15-21 All the earth shall be filled with the glory
Ps. 19 The heavens declare the glory of God
Ps. 104 The earth is full of thy riches
Ec. 3:1-15 He hath made every thing beautiful
Is. 11:1-9 The earth shall be full of the knowledge of God
Je. 23:9-32 Do not I fill heaven and earth?

God, Nature of
1 S. 2:1-11 The Lord is a God of knowledge
Ps. 147 His understanding is infinite
Is. 33:3-24 Judge, lawgiver, king
Is. 43:1-13 Before the day was I am he
Jn. 4:7-24 God is a Spirit
Ep. 4:1-13 He is above all, through all, in you all
1 Jn. 4 God is love

God, Nearness of, *See* God, Fellowship with

God, Obedience to
De. 5:22-33 Ye shall walk in all his ways
1 S. 15:10-23 I have obeyed the voice of the Lord
Ps. 119:1-16 Blessed those who walk in the law of the Lord
Je. 7:21-29 Obey my voice, and I will be your God
Re. 14:1-5 These are they which follow the Lamb

God, Omnipotence of
Ge. 18:1-14 Is any thing too hard for the Lord?
Ps. 27 The Lord is the strength of my life
Ps. 62 Power belongeth unto God
Ps. 89:1-16 Who is a strong Lord like unto thee?
Ps. 97 Thou art exalted far above all gods
Is. 26 In the Lord is everlasting strength
Is. 40:25-29 God giveth power to the faint
Is. 45:5-12 I am the Lord, there is none else
Je. 18:1-6 As clay in the potter's hand
Mat. 3:1-12 God is able of these stones to raise children
Ep. 6:10-18 Be strong in the Lord
Re. 19:1-10 The Lord God omnipotent reigneth

God, Omnipresence of
Ge. 28:10-19 Surely the Lord is in this place
Ps. 139:1-12 Whither shall I flee from thy presence?
Pr. 15:1-17 The eyes of the Lord are in every place
Je. 23:23-32 Can any hide himself in secret from me?
Ac. 17:16-28 In him we live, and move, and have our being

God, Omniscience of
1 S. 2:1-11 The Lord is a God of knowledge
Jb. 28 God seeth under the whole heaven
Ps. 44 He knoweth the secrets of the heart
Ps. 139 Thou art acquainted with all my ways
Ps. 147 His understanding is infinite
Pr. 15:1-17 The eyes of the Lord are in every place
Is. 40:25-31 There is no searching of his understanding
Ro. 8:18-28 He that searcheth the hearts knoweth
Ep. 3 The manifold wisdom of God
He. 4 All things are naked and opened unto him

God, Partnership with, *See* God, Fellowship with

God, Patience of
Je. 15:15-21 Take me not away in thy longsuffering
Jon. 3 The word of God came to Jonah the second time
Ro. 15:1-13 The God of patience and consolation
2 Pe. 3:1-9 The Lord is longsuffering to us-ward
Re. 3:1-13 The word of my patience

God, Peace of
Jb. 34:29-37 When he giveth quietness, who can make trouble?
Ps. 23 He maketh me to lie down in green pastures
Ps. 116 Return unto thy rest, O my soul
Is. 26:1-12 Lord, thou wilt ordain peace for us
Ro. 15:1-13 Now the God of hope fill you with peace
1 Co. 1:1-10 Grace be unto you, and peace
Ph. 4:1-8 The peace of God, which passeth understanding
Col. 3:1-15 Let the peace of God rule in your hearts

1 Th. 5 The very God of peace sanctify you

God, People of
De. 32:7-13 The Lord's portion is his people
Ps. 94 The Lord will not cast off his people
Ps. 100 We are his people
Ps. 125 The Lord is round about his people
Is. 49:13-23 The Lord hath comforted his people
Lu. 7:11-18 God hath visited his people
Ro. 9:20-33 I will call them my people
1 Jn. 3:1-6 Now are we the sons of God
Re. 21:1-7 They shall be his people

God, Perfection of, *See* God, Fullness of
God, Power of, *See* God, Omnipotence of
God, Praise of, *See* God, Thankfulness to

God, Prayer to
Pr. 15:1-17 The prayer of the upright is his delight
Is. 56 I will make them joyful in my house of prayer
Mk. 1:32-45 He went into a solitary place, and prayed
Ro. 12 Continuing instant in prayer
1 Ti. 2:1-8 I will that men pray everywhere

God, Preaching
Ps. 19 The heavens declare the glory of God
Is. 40:1-11 Say to the cities of Judah, Behold your God!
Is. 52 How beautiful the feet of him that preacheth
Mk. 16 Preach the gospel to every creature
Ac. 20:17-35 I have testified repentance toward God
Ac. 28:23-31 Paul preached the kingdom of God

God, Presence of, *See* God, Consciousness of

God, Promise of
De. 5:1-21 The Lord made a covenant with us
Jos. 23 He fighteth for you, as he promised
Lu. 24:36-49 I send the promise of my Father upon you
He. 10:16-39 He is faithful that promised
He. 11:1-16 These died, not having received the promises

2 Pe. 1:1-11 Exceeding great and precious promises

1 Jn. 2:15-29 He hath promised us eternal life

God, Proof of

Ps. 119:129-144 Thy testimonies are wonderful

Mat. 5:1-12 The pure in heart shall see God

Jn. 7:14-31 He that doeth his will knoweth the doctrine

2 Co. 5 We walk by faith, not by sight

He. 11:1-16 Faith is the evidence of things not seen

1 Jn. 3:14-24 We know that he is in us by the Spirit

1 Jn. 4 If we love one another, God dwelleth in us

God, Protection of, See God, Benevolence of

God, Providence of, See God, Benevolence of

God, Punishment of, See God, Chastisement of

God, Purpose of, See God, Will of

God, Quest for, See God, Longing for

God, Rebellion against, See God, Denial of

God, the Redeemer, See God, Salvation of

God, the Refuge, See God, Benevolence of

God, Rejection of, See God, Denial of

God, Reliance on, See God, Faith in

God, Rest in, See God, Peace of

God, the Restorer

Ps. 23 He restoreth my soul

Ps. 51 Restore unto me the joy of thy salvation

Is. 40:28-31 They shall renew their strength

Je. 30:1-17 I will restore health unto thee

Jo. 2:21-32 I will restore to you the locust-eaten years

God, Return to

De. 30:1-10 Thou shalt return and obey the Lord

Ec. 12 The spirit shall return unto God who gave it

Je. 3:12-22 Return, thou backsliding Israel

Ho. 6 Come, and let us return unto the Lord

Mal. 3:7-12 Return unto me, and I will return unto you

1 Pe. 2:19-25 Ye are now returned unto the shepherd

God, Revelation of

Is. 40:1-8 The glory of the Lord shall be revealed

Eze. 1 I saw visions of God

Da. 2:19-23 He revealeth the deep and secret things

Mat. 11:20-30 Thou hast revealed these things unto babes

Mat. 16:13-20 My Father hath revealed it unto you

Ro. 1:1-17 Therein is the righteousness of God revealed

1 Co. 2 God hath revealed them by his Spirit

God, Reward of

Jb. 42 The Lord gave Job twice as much as he had had

Je. 16:14-21 I will recompense their sin double

Mat. 6:1-4 Thy Father shall reward thee openly

Lu. 14:1-14 Thou shalt be recompensed at the resurrection

He. 11:1-16 God is a rewarder

God, Riches of, See God, Fullness of

God, Righteousness of, See God, Holiness of

God, the Rock

De. 32:1-18 Of the Rock that begat thee thou art unmindful

2 S. 22:1-18 The Lord is my rock, and my fortress

2 S. 22:47-51 Blessed be my rock

Ps. 18:25-36 Who is a rock save our God?

Ps. 28 Unto thee will I cry, O Lord my rock

Ps. 31 Be thou my strong rock

Ps. 61 Lead me to the rock that is higher than I

Ps. 95 The strength of the hills is his

God, Salvation of

Ps. 85 His salvation is nigh them that fear him

Ps. 91 I will deliver him and honor him

Ps. 119:153-176 I have longed for thy salvation

Is. 52:7-15 The ends of the earth shall see the salvation

Is. 62 Behold, thy salvation cometh

Lu. 2:25-32 Mine eyes have seen thy salvation

2 Pe. 2:1-9 The Lord knoweth how to deliver the godly

God, Search for, See God, Longing for

God, Servant of

Jos. 24:14-25 As for my house, we will serve the Lord

God, Servant of (*cont.*)

Ezr. 5:6-17 We are the servants of God

Ps. 90 Let thy work appear unto thy servants

Is. 42:1-16 Behold my servant, whom I uphold

Mat. 4:1-11 Him only shalt thou serve

Mat. 6:24-34 Ye cannot serve God and mammon

Lu. 2:25-35 Lettest thou thy servant depart in peace

Ac. 27:13-26 The angel of God, whom I serve

Ro. 6 Ye have become servants to God

Ep. 6:1-11 Doing service as to the Lord

God, the Shepherd, *See* God, Faithfulness of

God, Solicitude of, *See* God, Faithfulness of

God, Sons of, *See* God, People of

God, Sovereignty of, *See* God, Kingdom of

God, Spirit of

Ge. 1:1-8 The Spirit of God moved on the waters

Ps. 104 Thou sendest thy spirit, they are created

Ps. 139 Whither shall I go from thy spirit?

Is. 61 The Spirit of the Lord God is upon me

Jo. 2:21-32 I will pour out my spirit upon all flesh

Zch. 4 Not by might, but by my spirit

Jn. 4:3-26 God is a Spirit

Ro. 8:1-17 The Spirit itself beareth witness

1 Co. 2 The wisdom which the Holy Ghost teacheth

1 Co. 3 The Spirit of God dwelleth in you

1 Co. 6 Ye are sanctified by the Spirit of our God

Ep. 4:17-32 Grieve not the holy Spirit of God

1 Jn. 4 He hath given us of his Spirit

God, Splendor of, *See* God, Glory of

God, Strength of, *See* God, Omnipotence of

God, Sufficiency of, *See* God, Fullness of

God, Supremacy of, *See* God, Kingdom of

God, the Sustainer, *See* God, Benevolence of

God, Sympathy of, *See* God, Compassion of

God, the Teacher

1 K. 8:31-43 Teach them the good way

Jb. 34:29-37 That which I see not teach thou me

Ps. 12 The words of the Lord are pure words

Ps. 25 Teach me thy paths

Ps. 94 Blessed is the man whom thou teachest

Ps. 105:1-22 To teach his senators wisdom

Ps. 119:65-88 Teach me good judgment and knowledge

Ps. 143 Teach me to do thy will

Is. 25:1-8 Thy counsels of old are truth

God, Thankfulness to

Ps. 43:3-5 I shall yet praise him

Ps. 63 Thy lovingkindness is better than life

Ps. 92 It is a good thing to give thanks unto God

Ps. 100 Enter into his gates with thanksgiving

Ps. 113 From sunrise to sunset praise the Lord

Ps. 119:57-80 At midnight I will thank thee

1 Co. 15:39-58 Thank God which giveth us the victory

Ph. 4:1-13 With thanksgiving let your requests be made known

God, Thirst for, *See* God, Longing for

God, Thought of

Ps. 8 What is man, that thou art mindful of him?

Is. 14:24-32 As I have thought, so shall it come to pass

Is. 55 My thoughts are not your thoughts

Je. 29:1-14 I know the thoughts that I think toward you

Jon. 1 If so be that God will think upon us

God, Transcendence of, *See* God, the Eternal

God, Trust in, *See* God, Faith in

God, Truth of

Nu. 23:1-20 God is not a man that he should lie

Ps. 100 His truth endureth to all generations

Ps. 119:153-168 Thy word is true from the beginning

Jn. 3:25-36 God is true

Jn. 17 Thy word is truth

Ro. 2:1-11 The judgment of God is according to truth

He. 6 It was impossible for God to lie

Re. 19 He was called Faithful and True

Re. 22 These sayings are faithful and true

God, the Unchanging, *See* God, the Rock

God, Unity of

De. 6:4-9 The Lord our God is one Lord

Is. 43:1-13 Before me was no God, neither shall be after

Zch. 14:1-11 There shall be one Lord, and his name one

Mat. 23:1-12 One is your Father, which is in heaven

1 Co. 8 There is none other God but one

Ep. 4:1-16 One God and Father of all

1 Jn. 5 These three are one

God, Universality of

Ps. 22:23-31 The ends of the world shall turn unto him

Ps. 50 The world is mine

Is. 40:18-31 He sitteth upon the circle of the earth

Is. 66:1-13 Heaven is my throne, the earth my footstool

Zch. 9:9-17 His dominion shall be from sea to sea

Jn. 3:14-21 God so loved the world

Col. 3:1-15 Neither Greek nor Jew, Barbarian nor Scythian

Re. 14:1-7 To every nation, and kindred, and tongue

God, the Unseen

Ex. 33:12-23 My face shall not be seen

Ps. 77 Thy footsteps are not known

Jn. 5:32-47 Ye have not seen his shape at any time

Jn. 6:22-47 No man hath seen the Father save he which is of God

Ac. 17:22-31 TO THE UNKNOWN GOD

2 Co. 4 The things which are not seen are eternal

1 Ti. 1:1-17 The King eternal, immortal, invisible

He. 11:17-40 Seeing him who is invisible

1 Jn. 4 How can he love God whom he hath not seen?

God, Victory of

Ex. 15:1-19 The Lord hath triumphed gloriously

1 Ch. 29:10-20 Thine, O Lord, is the victory

Ps. 98 His holy arm hath gotten him the victory

Is. 25 He will swallow up death in victory

2 Co. 2 God causeth us to triumph in Christ

Re. 6 He went forth conquering, and to conquer

God, Vision of, *See* God, Revelation of

God, Voice of

1 S. 3 Here am I; for thou didst call me

1 K. 19:1-18 A still small voice

Ps. 29 The voice of the Lord is upon the waters

Ps. 106:1-27 They hearkened not unto the voice of the Lord

Is. 55:1-7 Come ye to the waters

Eze. 2 Son of man, stand upon thy feet

Eze. 43:1-6 His voice was like the noise of many waters

Am. 8 A famine of hearing the words of the Lord

Mat. 3 Lo a voice from heaven, saying, This is my Son

Mat. 10:16-39 The Spirit of your Father speaketh in you

He. 1 God spake in time past unto the fathers

God, Way of

Ps. 23 He leadeth me in paths of righteousness

Ps. 27 Teach me thy way, O Lord

Ps. 65 Thy paths drop fatness

Ps. 77 Thy way, O God, is in the sanctuary

Is. 55 Neither are your ways my ways, saith the Lord

Ho. 14 The ways of the Lord are right

Mat. 3:1-13 Prepare ye the way of the Lord

Mat. 22:15-22 Thou teachest the way of God in truth

Ro. 11:33-36 How unsearchable his ways

God, Wealth of, *See* God, Fullness of

God, Will of

1 S. 3:1-18 Let the Lord do what seemeth him good

Mat. 6:1-13 Thy will be done on earth, as it is in heaven

Mat. 26:36-46 Not as I will, but as thou wilt

Lu. 22:39-46 He went to the mount of Olives

God, Will of (cont.)

Jn. 1:1-14 Born of the will of God
Jn. 4:1-34 My meat is to do his will
Ac. 21:1-15 The will of the Lord be done
Ep. 5:1-21 Understand what the will of the Lord is
Col. 4 Perfect and complete in all the will of God
1 Th. 4 The will of God is your sanctification
Ja. 4:12-17 If the Lord will
1 Jn. 2:15-29 He that doeth the will of God abideth forever

God, Wisdom of, See God, Omniscience of

God, Witness of

Ju. 11:4-11 The Lord be witness between us
Jb. 16 Behold, my witness is in heaven
Ps. 119:24-48 Thy testimonies are my delight
Je. 29:10-29 I know, and am a witness, saith the Lord
Ro. 1:1-10 God is my witness
1 Jn. 5 There are three that bear witness in earth

God, Wonder of, See God, Glory of

God, Word of

De. 8 By the words of the Lord doth man live
1 K. 22:13-28 What the Lord saith, that will I speak
Ps. 119:129-144 The entrance of thy words giveth light
Pr. 30:1-9 Every word of God is pure
Is. 28:9-13 Precept upon precept
Lu. 8:1-15 The seed is the word of God
Ac. 19:8-20 The word of God prevailed
Ro. 10:1-17 The word is nigh thee
Ep. 6:1-17 The sword of the Spirit is the word of God
2 Ti. 2:1-10 The word of God is not bound
He. 11:1-16 The worlds were framed by the word of God
1 Pe. 1:13-25 The word of God liveth and abideth for ever

God, Work of

Ge. 2:1-7 God rested the seventh day from all his work
Jb. 37 Consider the wondrous works of God
Ps. 19:1-6 The heavens declare his glory

Ps. 66 Come and see the works of God
Ps. 104:24-35 O Lord, how manifold are thy works!
Ps. 139 Marvelous are thy works
Mat. 9:32-38 Pray God to send labourers into his harvest
Jn. 9:1-25 I must work the works of him that sent me
1 Co. 12:1-11 It is the same God which worketh all in all
Ep. 2 We are his workmanship
Ph. 2:1-13 It is God which worketh in you

God, Worship of

Ex. 34:1-17 Thou shalt worship no other God
Ps. 27 Wait on the Lord
Ps. 95 O come, let us worship and bow down
Ps. 96 Sing unto the Lord, bless his name
Ho. 6 I desire mercy, and not sacrifice
Mi. 6 What doth the Lord require of thee
Ac. 17:16-31 I declare to you him whom ye ignorantly worship
Ep. 3 I bow my knees unto the Father
Re. 5 The elders fell down and worshipped him

God, Wrath of, See God, Anger of
God, Yearning for, See God, Longing for
Godlessness, See God, Denial of
Godliness, See Holiness

Gods

Ex. 20 Ye shall not make gods of silver or gold
Ju. 2:8-17 They followed other gods
1 S. 7:1-8 Put away the strange gods
Is. 2:1-9 Their land is full of idols
Is. 44:9-17 He maketh a god, even his graven image
Ho. 13:1-4 Thou shalt know no god but me
2 Co. 6:14-18 What concord hath Christ with Belial?
1 Jn. 5 Little children, keep yourselves from idols

Gold, See Riches
Golgotha, See Good Friday
Good Friday

Mat. 21:33-42 The parable of the wicked husbandmen
Seven words from the cross
Lu. 23:13-49 When they were come to Calvary

Lu. 23:34 Father forgive them
Lu. 23:43 Today thou shalt be with me in paradise
Jn. 19:26-27 Woman, behold thy son!
Mk. 15:34 My God, my God
Jn. 19:28 I thirst
Jn. 19:30 It is finished
Lu. 23:46 I commend my spirit
Jn. 11:45-57 He prophesied that Jesus should die
Jn. 12:20-33 If it die, it bringeth forth much fruit
Jn. 19:17-37 The place of a skull
Ga. 6 Save in the cross
1 Pe. 2:20-25 Christ also suffered for us

Goodness, *See* Character
Goods, *See* Riches
Gospel
Pr. 25 Good news from a far country
Lu. 4:16-32 The Spirit of the Lord is upon me
Lu. 8:1-15 Shewing the glad tidings of the kingdom
Ro. 10:8-15 Glad tidings of good things
Ga. 2:11-21 They walked not according to the gospel
Col. 1:19-29 Be not moved from the hope of the gospel
1 Ti. 1:5-17 According to the glorious gospel
Re. 14:1-7 The everlasting gospel

Gossip, *See* Slander
Government
Ex. 18 Thou shalt provide able men to be rulers
Is. 9:1-7 The government shall be upon his shoulder
Mat. 2:1-10 Out of thee shall come a Governor
Mat. 10:16-39 Ye shall be brought before governors
Ro. 13 Render therefore to all their dues
1 Co. 4 It is required that stewards be faithful
1 Pe. 2:11-25 Submit yourselves to every ordinance of man
Re. 19:1-9 The Lord God omnipotent reigneth

Grace, *See* Beauty
Graces, Christian
Ga. 5:22-26 The fruit of the Spirit
Ph. 4:4-9 Whatsoever things are true
Col. 3:1-17 Put on therefore, as the elect of God

2 Pe. 1:1-14 Add to your faith virtue
Graduation, *See* Commencement Day
Gratitude, *See* Thanksgiving
Grave, *See* Death
Greatness, *See* Chief
Greed
2 S. 12:1-14 He took the poor man's lamb
1 K. 21:5-10 Ahab covets Naboth's vineyard
Pr. 15 He that is greedy of gain troubleth his house
Ec. 5:9-20 He shall not be satisfied with silver
Je. 17:5-11 He that getteth riches, and not by right
Mat. 26:14-25 The thirty pieces of silver
Lu. 12:13-21 Beware of covetousness
Ro. 1:18-32 Filled with all covetousness
1 Ti. 6 The love of money is the root of evil
Ja. 5 Ye have heaped treasure together

Grief, *See* Sorrow
Ground, *See* Earth
Growth, *See* Advance
Guidance
Ex. 13:17-22 God led them out
De. 32:7-14 The Lord alone did lead him
Ps. 16 Thou wilt show me the path of life
Ps. 31 For thy name's sake lead me, and guide me
Ps. 43 Let thy light and truth lead me
Mi. 7:1-7 Put ye not confidence in a guide
Mat. 15:1-20 If the blind lead the blind
Jn. 10:1-18 He leadeth out the sheep
Ro. 2:1-11 The goodness of God leadeth thee

Guilt
Ge. 3:1-13 Adam and his wife hid themselves
Ex. 20:1-17 The Lord will not hold him guiltless
Ezr. 9:5-15 I am ashamed and blush
Ps. 40 Mine iniquities have taken hold upon me
Ps. 51 Deliver me from blood-guiltiness

[H]

Half-Heartedness, *See* Indifference

Hand

Ex. 4:1-9 He put forth his hand

De. 16:13-20 God shall bless thee in the works of thine hands

Ps. 24 Clean hands and a pure heart

Ps. 90 The work of our hands, establish thou it

Ps. 115 They have hands, but they handle not

Ec. 9:10-18 Whatsoever thy hand findeth to do

Mat. 5:27-32 If thy right hand offend thee

Jn. 20:24-29 Behold my hands

1 Co. 12 The eye cannot say to the hand

1 Th. 4 Study to work with your own hands

Ja. 1:16-27 Be ye doers of the word, not hearers only

Ja. 4 Cleanse your hands, ye sinners

Happiness, *See* Joy

Hardness, *See* Cruelty

Hardship, *See* Endurance

Harm, *See* Injury

Harmony, *See* Agreement

Harshness, *See* Cruelty

Harvest

Ge. 41:46-49 Corn as the sand of the sea

Ps. 65 Thy paths drop fatness

Pr. 10:1-19 He that sleepeth in harvest causeth shame

Pr. 19:20-29 A slothful man hideth his hand

Je. 8:13-22 The harvest is past, and we are not saved

Ho. 8 Sowing the wind, reaping the whirlwind

Ho. 10 Sow in righteousness, reap in mercy

Mat. 7:13-20 Every good tree bringeth forth good fruit

Mat. 9:27-38 Pray that he will send forth harvest labourers

Mat. 13:18-30 Let both grow together until the harvest

Mat. 13:31-43 The harvest is the end of the world

Jn. 4:31-38 The fields are white already to harvest

1 Co. 3 Ye are God's husbandry

Ga. 6 We shall reap, if we faint not

Ep. 5:1-10 The fruit of the Spirit is in all goodness

Haste

1 S. 21:1-9 The king's business required haste

Ps. 70 Make haste unto me, O God

Pr. 28 He that hasteth to be rich hath an evil eye

Is. 28:9-22 He that believeth shall not make haste

Zch. 8:20-23 Let us go speedily to pray before the Lord

Mat. 28:1-8 They ran to bring the disciples word

Lu. 2:1-19 They came with haste and found the babe

Ac. 19:21-41 Ye ought to do nothing rashly

Hatred

Ge. 27:30-41 Esau hated Jacob because of the blessing

Ps. 97 Ye that love the Lord, hate evil

Ps. 119:97-112 I hate every false way

Ps. 139 I hate them, O Lord, that hate thee

Pr. 10:1-19 Hatred stirreth up strife

Mat. 5:38-48 Bless them that curse you

Lu. 6:20-35 Blessed are ye, when men shall hate you

Jn. 15 He that hateth me hateth my Father also

Ro. 12 Abhor that which is evil

1 Jn. 3 Whosoever hateth his brother is a murderer

1 Jn. 4 A man cannot love God and hate his brother

Re. 18 A cage of every unclean and hateful bird

Healing

De. 7:12-26 The Lord will take away from thee all sickness

Ps. 67 God cause his face to shine upon us

Ps. 147 He healeth the broken in heart

Je. 30:17-24 I will restore health unto thee

Mat. 12:1-13 It is lawful to heal on the sabbath

Mk. 2:1-12 They brought one sick of the palsy

Lu. 4:38-44 He rebuked the fever

Lu. 7:11-23 He cured many of their infirmities

Jn. 5:2-17 Wilt thou be made whole?

Ac. 3:1-11 Silver and gold have I none

Ac. 9:32-43 Jesus Christ maketh thee whole

1 Co. 12:1-12 To another the gifts of healing

Re. 22 The leaves of the tree were for healing

Health

Jos. 14:7-12 Even so is my strength now

Ps. 27 The Lord is the strength of my life

Pr. 13 A faithful ambassador is health

Eze. 47:1-9 The living waters that came from the temple

Ep. 6:10-18 Be strong in the Lord

3 Jn. That thou mayest be in health

Hearing

Ps. 5 My voice shalt thou hear in the morning

Ps. 115 They have ears, but they hear not

Pr. 20 The Lord hath made the hearing ear

Is. 40:18-31 Hast thou not known? Hast thou not heard?

Is. 42:17-25 Hear, ye deaf

Is. 65:17-25 While they are yet speaking, I will hear

Mat. 13:1-17 Blessed are your ears, for they hear

Jn. 5:17-31 They that hear shall live

Jn. 10:1-18 The sheep hear his voice

Ro. 10 Faith cometh by hearing

Ja. 1 Doers of the word, not hearers only

Heart

De. 6:1-15 Thou shalt love the Lord with all thine heart

1 S. 16:1-13 The Lord looketh on the heart

1 K. 3:5-15 I have given thee an understanding heart

1 K. 4:29-34 God gave Solomon largeness of heart

Ps. 73 God is the strength of my heart

Pr. 4 Keep thy heart with all diligence

Pr. 17:17-28 A merry heart doeth good

Ec. 3:1-15 He hath set the world in their heart

Je. 17:5-14 I the Lord search the heart

Mat. 11:20-30 I am meek and lowly in heart

Lu. 24:13-32 Did not our heart burn within us?

Ro. 10 With the heart man believeth

2 Co. 4 God hath shined in our hearts

He. 10:19-31 Let us draw near with a true heart

Heat, *See* Fire

Heathen

Ps. 46 I will be exalted among the heathen

Ps. 79 The heathen are come into thine inheritance

Is. 62 The Gentiles shall see thy righteousness

Zch. 9:1-11 He shall speak peace unto the heathen

Ro. 2:1-11 There is no respect of persons with God

Ro. 15:1-13 Praise the Lord, all ye Gentiles

Ep. 2:1-13 Aliens from the commonwealth of Israel

Heaven

Ge. 1:1-8 God created the heaven and the earth

Ge. 28:10-17 This is the gate of heaven

Ps. 8 When I consider thy heavens

Ps. 19:1-6 The heavens declare the glory of God

Ps. 73 Whom have I in heaven but thee?

Ps. 139 If I ascend into heaven, thou art there

Mat. 16:13-20 I will give thee the keys of the kingdom

Lu. 10:1-22 Your names are written in heaven

Jn. 3:1-15 I tell you of heavenly things

Ac. 26:1-20 I was not disobedient unto the heavenly vision

1 Co. 15:39-58 We shall bear the image of the heavenly

2 Co. 12 He was caught up into paradise

Ep. 1 Heavenly places in Christ

Col. 3:1-15 Seek those things which are above

He. 4 There remaineth a rest to God's people

Re. 21:1-7 I saw a new heaven and a new earth

Heaven, Kingdom of, *See* God, Kingdom of,

Hebrew

Ps. 73 Truly God is good to Israel

Ps. 125 Peace shall be upon Israel

Hebrew, *(cont.)*

Jn. 1:43-51 An Israelite in whom is no guile

Jn. 12:1-11 Many of the Jews believed on Jesus

Ro. 3:19-31 Is he the God of the Jews only?

Ro. 10 There is no difference between Jew and Greek

1 Co. 1:18-31 Unto the Jews a stumblingblock

1 Co. 9:19-27 Unto the Jews I became as a Jew

Ph. 3:1-14 A Hebrew of the Hebrews

Heed, *See* Solicitude

Heedlessness, *See* Indifference

Height

Ge. 28:10-22 The top of it reached to heaven

Jb. 22:1-21 Is not God in the height of heaven?

Ps. 24 Who shall ascend into the hill of the Lord?

Ps. 148 Praise him in the heights

Is. 2:1-5 The Lord's house shall be exalted

Lu. 2:41-52 Jesus increased in wisdom and stature

Re. 21:1-16 Length and breadth and height are equal

Heir, *See* Heritage

Hell

Ps. 139 If I make my bed in hell, thou art there

Mat. 16:13-23 Hell shall not prevail against it

Mat. 25:31-46 These shall go to everlasting punishment

Lu. 16:19-31 I am tormented in this flame

2 Th. 1 Punished with everlasting destruction

1 Pe. 3:15-22 He preached unto the spirits in prison

Jude 1-7 Suffering the vengeance of eternal fire

Re. 1:4-18 I have the keys of hell and of death

Re. 14 He shall be tormented

Re. 21:1-8 The lake which burneth with fire

Help

Ex. 2:16-20 Moses stood up and helped them

Ps. 121 My help cometh from the Lord

Is. 41:1-9 They helped every one his neighbour

Ac. 16:1-12 Come over into Macedonia, and help us

He. 13:5-14 The Lord is my helper

Herald, *See* Ambassador

Heresy

Mat. 22:23-40 Ye do err, not knowing the scriptures

Ac. 24:10-21 After the way they call heresy I worship

2 Co. 6 What part hath Christ with an infidel?

Ga. 5:16-26 The works of the flesh are heresies

Ep. 4:1-16 Carried about with every wind of doctrine

Ja. 4 The friend of the world is the enemy of God

Ja. 5:8-20 Convert the sinner from error

2 Pe. 2:1-11 False teachers bring damnable heresies

2 Pe. 3 They wrest the scriptures to their destruction

2 Jn. He that abideth not in the doctrine

Heritage

De. 18:1-14 The Lord is their inheritance

Ro. 8:1-17 Heirs of God, and joint-heirs with Christ

1 Co. 15:41-50 Flesh and blood cannot inherit the kingdom

Ga. 4:1-7 If a son, then a heir of God

Col. 1:1-17 The inheritance of the saints in light

He. 9:11-24 The promise of eternal inheritance

1 Pe. 1:1-9 An inheritance incorruptible

1 Pe. 3:1-11 Called to inherit a blessing

Heroism, *See* Courage

Hesitancy

1 K. 18:17-39 How long halt ye between two opinions?

Mat. 8:18-22 Suffer me first to bury my father

Lu. 9:51-62 No man looking back from the plow is fit

Jn. 6:53-69 Will ye also go away?

Ac. 26 Almost thou persuadest me

Ja. 1:1-17 Driven with the wind and tossed

Ja. 4 Purify your hearts, ye double minded

Highway

Ps. 37:1-8 Commit thy way unto the Lord

Ps. 139 Thou compassest my path

Pr. 4 The path of the just is as the shining light

Is. 35 A highway shall be there, and a way

Je. 31:18-26 Set thine heart toward the highway

Mat. 3 Prepare ye the way of the Lord

Mat. 7:1-14 Narrow is the way, which leadeth unto life

Mat. 22:1-14 Go ye into the highways

Hill, *See* Mountain

Hindrance, *See* Obstacle

History, *See* Past

Holiness

Ps. 1 The happiness of the godly

Ps. 29 Worship the Lord in the beauty of holiness

Ps. 119:9-16 I will delight in thy statutes

Jn. 17 For their sakes I sanctify myself

Ro. 8:1-18 To be spiritually minded is life

1 Co. 3 The temple of God is holy

1 Co. 6:15-20 Your body is the temple

Col. 3 Do all in the name of the Lord Jesus

1 Th. 4 God hath called us unto holiness

1 Ti. 3:15, 16 Great is the mystery of godliness

2 Ti. 2:19-26 The Lord knoweth them that are his

1 Pe. 1 Be ye holy; for I am holy

1 Pe. 3:8-17 Sanctify the Lord God in your hearts

Home Sunday

De. 6:1-12 Teach them unto thy children

De. 11:18-32 Write them upon the door posts of thine house

Ps. 133 How pleasant for brethren to dwell in unity!

Pr. 14:1-11 Every wise woman buildeth her house

S. of S. 1 Mine own vineyard have I not kept

Mat. 12:22-30 A divided house shall not stand

Jn. 2:1-11 The marriage in Cana

Ep. 6:1-4 Provoke not your children to wrath

Col. 3:18-21 Wives, husbands, children, fathers

Honesty, *See* Truth

Honor, *See* Character

Hope

Ro. 5:1-8 Hope maketh not ashamed

Ro. 8:18-28 Hope that is seen is not hope

Ro. 15:1-13 That ye may abound in hope

1 Co. 9:1-10 He that ploweth should plow in hope

1 Co. 13 Now abideth hope

1 Th. 5 For a helmet the hope of salvation

He. 6 Hope, the anchor of the soul

He. 11:1-16 Faith is the substance of things hoped for

1 Pe. 1:3-13 Be sober, and hope to the end

2 Pe. 3:13-18 We look for new heavens

Hospitality

Ge. 18:1-8 Abraham entertains the three strangers

De. 10:12-22 The Lord loveth the stranger

Is. 60:1-15 Thy gates shall be open continually

Mat. 25:31-46 I was a stranger, and ye took me in

Lu. 2:1-16 There was no room for them in the inn

Lu. 22:7-18 Where is the guest-chamber?

Ro. 15:1-13 Receive ye one another

Tit. 1 A lover of hospitality

He. 13 Be not forgetful to entertain strangers

1 Pe. 4 Use hospitality one to another

House

Ps. 84 The sparrow hath found a house

Pr. 3:21-35 He blesseth the habitation of the just

Pr. 12:1-7 The house of the righteous shall stand

Pr. 14:1-11 The house of the wicked shall be overthrown

Mat. 7:24-29 A wise man who built his house upon a rock

1 Pe. 2:1-10 Ye are built up a spiritual house

Humility

1 K. 3:3-14 Solomon asks not for riches or honour

Pr. 15:25-33 Before honour is humility

Is. 57:13-21 I dwell with him that is of a humble spirit

Mat. 3 He that cometh after me is mightier than I

Humility (*cont.*)

Mat. 5:1-12 The beatitudes
Mat. 23:1-12 The greatest shall be your servant
Lu. 14:1-14 Sit down in the lowest room
Lu. 15:11-32 The prodigal son
Lu. 18:1-14 God be merciful to me a sinner
Lu. 18:15-17 Receive the kingdom of God as a little child
Jn. 3:25-36 He must increase, but I must decrease
Jn. 13:1-17 Jesus washes the disciples' feet
1 Co. 4 We are made a spectacle unto the world
1 Ti. 1 I am the chief of sinners among men
1 Ti. 6 Be not highminded
Ja. 4 God giveth grace unto the humble

Hunger, *See* Famine
Hurt, *See* Injury
Husband, *See* Marriage
Hymn

Ps. 40 He hath put a new song in my mouth
Ps. 42 In the night his song shall be with me
Ps. 65 They shout for joy, they also sing
Ps. 137 How shall we sing in a strange land?
Is. 35 The ransomed shall return with songs
Mat. 26:17-30 When they had sung a hymn, they went out
1 Co. 14:1-15 I will sing with the spirit
Ep. 5:1-21 Singing and making melody to the Lord

Hypocrisy

Ps. 62 They bless with their mouth but curse inwardly
Pr. 11:1-14 The hypocrite destroyeth his neighbor
Is. 9:8-21 Every one is a hypocrite
Mat. 6:1-18 Be not as the hypocrites
Mat. 23:23-39 Woe unto you, scribes and Pharisees
Lu. 11:37-54 Woe unto you, hypocrites
2 Co. 11:1-15 Satan transformed into an angel of light
Re. 3:1-6 They say thou livest, but thou art dead

[I]

Ideal, *See* Perfection
Idleness

Ex. 5:15-23 Pharaoh said, Ye are idle, ye are idle
Pr. 6:1-15 How long wilt thou sleep, O sluggard?
Pr. 18 The slothful is brother to the waster
Pr. 31 She eateth not the bread of idleness
Ec. 10 By much slothfulness the building decayeth
Mat. 12:31-37 They shall give account of idle words
Mat. 20:1-16 Parable of the labourers in the vineyard
Ro. 12 Not slothful in business

Idolatry, *See* Gods
Ignorance

Ju. 2:1-10 Another generation which knew not the Lord
Jb. 38 Who darkeneth counsel by words without knowledge?
Pr. 1:1-23 Fools hate knowledge
Ec. 8:1-11 He knoweth not that which shall be
Ec. 11 Thou knowest not the works of God
Is. 56 His watchmen are blind, they are ignorant
Je. 4:19-31 Wise to do evil, no knowledge to do good
Ho. 4:1-9 My people are destroyed for lack of knowledge
Mi. 4 They know not the thoughts of the Lord
Mk. 13:24-37 No man knoweth the day and the hour
Lu. 23:27-34 They know not what they do
Jn. 1:1-14 The world knew him not
Jn. 14:1-14 We know not whither thou goest
Jn. 20:1-10 As yet they knew not the scripture
Ac. 17:22-34 The times of ignorance God winked at
Ac. 19:1-12 We have not heard whether there be any Holy Ghost
Ro. 10 Ignorant of God's righteousness
2 Co. 3 Their minds were blinded

Ep. 4:17-32 Having the understanding darkened
Illness, *See* Disease
Illumination, *See* Light
Image
Ps. 115 They have mouths, but they speak not
Is. 44:9-20 He maketh it a graven image
Mat. 22:15-22 Whose is this image?
Ac. 19:21-41 They be no gods, which are made with hands
1 Co. 15:47-58 We shall bear the image of the heavenly
2 Co. 3 We are changed into the same image
2 Co. 4 Christ is the image of God
Immersion, *See* Baptism
Immorality, *See* Sin
Immortality
Jb. 19:23-27 My redeemer liveth
Ps. 16:8-11 Pleasures for evermore
Ps. 17:5-8,15 When I awake with thy likeness
Ps. 22:22-31 Your heart shall live for ever
Ps. 23 The valley of the shadow
Ps. 90 Our dwellingplace in all generations
Je. 31:15-17 Thy children shall come again
Mk. 10:17-22 What shall I do to inherit eternal life
Jn. 4:5-29 The woman of Samaria
Jn. 12:23-36 Except a corn of wheat die
Jn. 14:1-19 The many mansions
Jn. 14:25-29 Peace I leave with you
1 Co. 15:12-26 Death shall be destroyed
1 Co. 15:35-49 We shall bear the image of the heavenly
1 Co. 15:50-58 Death, where is thy sting?
1 Ti. 6:11-19 That they may lay hold on eternal life
He. 13:12-15 Here have we no continuing city
Re. 7:9-17 God shall wipe away all tears
Re. 14:12-13 Blessed are the dead
Re. 19:6-9 The marriage of the Lamb
Re. 20:4-6,11-13 The great white throne
Re. 21:1-7,10,22-27 The new heaven and the new earth
Impatience, *See* Haste

Imperfection
Le. 5:15-19 If a soul sin through ignorance
Ps. 19 Cleanse thou me from secret faults
Mat. 5:27-37 If thy right eye offend thee, pluck it out
Jn. 18:28-40 I find in him no fault at all
1 Co. 1:1-8 That ye may be blameless
2 Co. 12:1-10 I will glory in mine infirmities
Ja. 2:1-12 He who offends in one point is guilty of all
Ja. 3 In many things we offend all
Ja. 5 Confess your faults one to another
Re. 3:1-6 I have not found thy works perfect
Importance, *See* Chief
Impossibility
Mat. 6:24-34 No man can serve two masters
Mat. 17:14-21 Nothing shall be impossible unto you
Lu. 1:26-38 With God nothing shall be impossible
Lu. 18:18-30 Things which are impossible with men
He. 6 It was impossible for God to lie
He. 11:1-16 Without faith it is impossible to please him
Imprisonment, *See* Captivity
Improvement, *See* Advance
Impurity, *See* Purity
Inauguration, *See* Beginning
Incarnation, *See* God, Incarnation of
Inclination
Jos. 24:14-25 Incline your heart unto the Lord God
1 K. 8:44-61 That he may incline our hearts unto him
Ps. 40 I delight to do thy will, O my God
Ps. 119:33-40 Incline my heart unto thy testimonies
Ps. 141 Incline not my heart to any evil thing
Je. 25:1-11 Ye have not inclined your ear to hear
Jn. 7:14-31 If any man will do his will
Inconstancy
Jb. 19 They whom I loved are turned against me
Ho. 6 Your goodness is as the early dew

Inconstancy *(cont.)*

Mk. 14:43-52 They all forsook him
Lu. 7:24-30 A reed shaken by the wind
1 Co. 4 We have no certain dwelling-place
Ep. 4:1-16 Tossed to and fro
Ja. 3 Doth a fountain have sweet and bitter water
2 Pe. 2:9-22 Beguiling unstable souls
2 Pe. 3 Unlearned and unstable

Increase

Ps. 62 If riches increase, set not your heart on them
Pr. 11 There is that scattereth, and yet increaseth
Lu. 8:1-18 Whosoever hath, to him shall be given
Jn. 3:22-36 He must increase, but I must decrease
1 Co. 3 God gave the increase
Col. 1:1-20 Increasing in the knowledge of God
2 Pe. 1 Add to your faith virtue; and to virtue knowledge
Jude 1-21 Mercy, peace, and love be multiplied

Independence Day

Ex. 1:6-14 Their lives were bitter with hard bondage
Ex. 2:23-25 They sighed by reason of the bondage
De. 6 That it may be well in the promised land
De. 30 I have set before thee life and death
Jos. 1:1-9 Be strong and of good courage
Jos. 23:1-5 Ye shall possess their land
1 S. 10:17-25 The people shouted, God save the king
1 S. 11:12-15 They made Saul king before the Lord
Ps. 16 I have a goodly heritage
Ps. 33 The nation whose God is the Lord
Ps. 85 Thou hast been favourable unto thy land
Ps. 122 Pray for the peace of Jerusalem
Ps. 137:1-6 If I forget thee, O Jerusalem
Is. 40 Her warfare is accomplished
Is. 62 They shall call them, The holy people
Ac. 21:33-40 Paul is bound with two chains

Ac. 22:24-30 I was free born
Ro. 13:1-7 Tribute to whom tribute is due
Re. 21:10-16 The city lieth four-square

Indifference

Nu. 32:1-22 Shall they go to war and ye sit here
Is. 5:1-12 They regard not the work of the Lord
Eze. 33:1-7, 30-33 They hear thy words, but do them not
Mat. 24:1-13 The love of many shall wax cold
Mat. 27:11-25 He washed his hands before the multitude
Mk. 6:46-56 Their heart was hardened
Ac. 18:12-17 Gallio cared for none of those things
Ep. 5:1-14 Awake thou that sleepest

Individual

Is. 27 Ye shall be gathered one by one
Lu. 8:41-56 Jesus said, Who touched me?
Lu. 12:1-12 Ye are of more value than many sparrows
Lu. 15:1-10 Joy shall be in heaven over one sinner
2 Co. 12:1-15 I seek not your's, but you

Indolence, *See* Idleness
Indulgence, *See* Body
Industry, *See* Business
Infallibility

Mat. 16:13-20 Upon this rock I will build my church
Mat. 22:23-33 Ye do err, not knowing the scriptures
Ac. 1 He showed himself by many infallible proofs
1 Ti. 3 The church is the pillar and ground of truth
2 Ti. 3 All scripture is given by inspiration of God
Tit. 1 God cannot lie

Infant, *See* Baby
Infidel, *See* Heresy
Infinity, *See* God, the Eternal
Infirmity, *See* Weakness
Influence, *See* Example
Ingratitude

Ge. 40 The chief butler forgot Joseph
Ec. 9:13-18 No man remembered that same poor man
Is. 17:1-11 Thou hast forgotten the God of thy salvation

Ho. 8 Israel hath forgotten his maker

Lu. 6:27-35 He is kind unto the unthankful

Lu. 17:11-19 Where are the nine?

Ro. 1:16-32 They glorified God not, neither were thankful

Inheritance, *See* Heritage
Inhumanity, *See* Cruelty
Iniquity, *See* Sin
Injury

Is. 11:1-9 They shall not hurt nor destroy

Is. 53 He was wounded for our transgressions

Je. 30:10-17 I will heal thee of thy wounds

Lu. 10:17-24 Nothing shall by any means hurt you

Lu. 10:30-37 He bound up his wounds

2 Co. 11:18-33 Five times I received forty stripes save one

He. 11:17-40 They were stoned, sawn asunder, slain

Injustice, *See* Justice
Injustice, Social, *See* Justice, Social
Innocence, *See* Purity
Insight, *See* Vision
Inspiration

Ex. 4:10-16 I will be with thy mouth

Nu. 11:24-29 When the spirit rested on them, they prophesied

Jb. 32 The inspiration of the Almighty

Je. 1:1-10 Behold, I have put my words in thy mouth

Zch. 4 Not by might, but by my spirit

Mk. 1:1-15 The Spirit like a dove descended on him

Jn. 3:1-8 That which is born of the Spirit is spirit

Ac. 2:1-8 Cloven tongues like as of fire

1 Co. 2 Words which the Holy Ghost teacheth

Ep. 5:1-21 Be filled with the Spirit

2 Ti. 3 All scripture is given by inspiration of God

2 Pe. 1 Holy men were moved by the Holy Ghost

Instruction

De. 6:1-12 Thou shalt talk of them in thine house

De. 11:18-25 Ye shall teach them your children

Ps. 71 O God, thou hast taught me from my youth

Mat. 5:1-16 He opened his mouth, and taught them

Jn. 6:44-59 They shall all be taught of God

Ro. 15:1-7 Things written aforetime were for our learning

1 Co. 4 Ten thousand instructors, not many fathers

Ph. 4:4-20 I am instructed in all things

Integration

Ps. 133 How pleasant for brethen to dwell in unity

Eze. 37:21-28 I will make them one nation

Am. 3 Can two walk together, except they be agreed

Ac. 10:19-35 God is no respecter of persons

Ac. 17:22-31 God hath made all men of one blood

1 Co. 1:1-24 Is Christ divided?

1 Co. 12 There should be no schism in the body

Ga. 3:13-29 Ye are all one in Christ Jesus

Col. 3:1-11 There is neither bond nor free

1 Th. 5 Be at peace among yourselves

Integrity, *See* Character
Intelligence, *See* Knowledge
Intemperance, *See* Temperance Sunday
Intercession, *See* Advocate
Internationalism, *See* Nations, United
Interpretation

Ge. 40:1-19 Do not interpretations belong to God?

Ec. 8 Who knoweth the interpretation of a thing

1 Co. 12 To one is given the interpretation of tongues

2 Pe. 1 No prophecy is of private interpretation

2 Pe. 3 There are some things hard to understand

Intolerance, *See* Bigotry
Intoxication, *See* Temperance Sunday
Invincibility, *See* Victory
Invitation

Is. 55:1-11 Ho, every one that thirsteth

Mat. 11:25-30 Come unto me, all ye that labour

Mat. 25:31-46 Come, ye blessed of my Father

Lu. 14:15-24 Come; for all things are now ready

Lu. 24:13-32 Abide with us, for it is toward evening

Invitation (cont.)

Jn. 1:35-39 He saith unto them, Come and see

[J]

Jealousy
Ge. 37:1-11 Jacob loved him, his brethren hated him
Ex. 20:1-17 I the Lord thy God am a jealous God
1 S. 18:1-9 Saul hath slain thousands, David ten thousands
1 K. 19 I have been very jealous for the Lord
Ps. 37:1-11 Be not envious against the workers of iniquity
Pr. 14:24-35 Envy is the rottenness of the bones
S. of S. 8 Jealousy is cruel as the grave
Zch. 1:12-17 I am jealous for Jerusalem
Lu. 22:24-30 Which of them should be accounted the greatest
Ro. 1:16-32 Full of envy
1 Co. 13 Charity envieth not
2 Co. 11 I am jealous over you with a godly jealousy
Ja. 5:1-9 Grudge not one against another
Jerusalem
Ps. 122 Pray for the peace of Jerusalem
Ps. 125 As the mountains are round about Jerusalem
Is. 40:1-11 Speak ye comfortably to Jerusalem
Is. 65:17-25 I create Jerusalem a rejoicing
Mat. 2:1-12 There came wise men to Jerusalem
Mat. 23:27-39 O Jerusalem that killest the prophets
He. 12:22-29 Ye are come unto the heavenly Jerusalem
Re. 21:1-7 I John saw the new Jerusalem
Re. 21:10-27 Jerusalem descending out of heaven
Jew, See Hebrew
Journey
Ex. 2:11-22 I have been a stranger in a strange land
Ho. 9 They shall be wanderers among the nations
Mk. 13:32-37 As a man taking a far journey

1 Co. 1:1-24 Ye were called
Re. 22 Whosoever will, let him take the water freely
Israel, See Hebrew

Lu. 9:1-6 Take nothing for your journey
Lu. 15:11-32 He took his journey into a far country
2 Co. 11:22-33 In journeyings often
Joy
De. 33:26-29 Happy art thou, O Israel
Ne. 8:9-18 The joy of the Lord
Ps. 63 My mouth shall praise thee with joyful lips
Ps. 100 Make a joyful noise unto the Lord
Pr. 3:13-18 Happy is the man that findeth wisdom
Is. 35:5-10 Everlasting joy upon their heads
Is. 61:1-3 The oil of joy for mourning
Mat. 5:1-12 Rejoice, and be exceeding glad
Jn. 16:1-20 Your sorrow shall be turned into joy
Jn. 17:1-13 That they might have my joy
Ac. 8:1-8 There was great joy in that city
Ph. 4:4-8 Rejoice in the Lord alway
1 Th. 5:15-23 Rejoice evermore
Re. 19:1-9 Alleluia: for the Lord God reigneth
Judgment
2 Ch. 19:4-7 Ye judge not for man, but for the Lord
Is. 11 He shall not judge after the sight of his eyes
Is. 26:12-21 Awake and sing, ye that dwell in dust
Am. 3 God's judgment against Israel
Mat. 7:1-12 Judge not that ye be not judged
Mat. 25:31-46 Then shall he sit upon the throne of his glory
Lu. 12:49-59 Why judge ye not yourselves what is right?
Jn. 7:1-24 Judge not according to the appearance
Jn. 12:23-36 Now is the judgment of this world
Ro. 14:1-13 We shall all stand before the judgment seat

1 Co. 4 He that judgeth me is the Lord

Ja. 4:8-17 Humble yourselves in the sight of God

Ja. 5:1-9 The judge standeth before the door

Re. 22:1-13 My reward is with me

Judgment, the Last

Jo. 2:1-14 The day of the Lord cometh

Mi. 4:1-7 In the last days it shall come to pass

Zph. 1 The great day of the Lord is near

Mat. 24:1-24 Then shall the end come

Mat. 25:31-46 When the Son of man shall come

Ac. 17:22-31 A day to judge the world

He. 9:23-28 After death the judgment

1 Jn. 4 Boldness in the day of judgment

Re. 14:1-7 The hour of his judgment is come

Re. 20:11-15 The books were opened

Justice

Le. 19:32-37 No unrighteousness in judgment

De. 24:10-22 Thou shall not pervert judgment

Ps. 94 They condemn the innocent

Pr. 4 The path of the just is as the shining light

Is. 5:1-7 He looked for righteousness, but behold a cry

Is. 10:1-4 Woe unto them that decree unrighteous decrees

Am. 5:4-15 Establish judgment in the gate

Am. 5:21-24 Let judgment run down as waters

Am. 7:7-17 The plumbline in the Lord's hand

Mi. 3 Is it not for you to know judgment?

Mi. 6 To do justly, and to love mercy

Mi. 7:1-7 The judge asketh for a reward

Mat. 12:1-9 Ye would not have condemned the guiltless

Mat. 18:21-35 Till he should pay all that was due

Lu. 18:1-8 The unjust judge

1 Pe. 3:8-22 Christ suffered, the just for the unjust

Justice, Social

Le. 19:9-18 Thou shalt not defraud

Pr. 22 The Lord will plead their cause

Pr. 29 The king that faithfully judgeth the poor

Ec. 5:1-12 The profit of the earth is for all

Is. 10:1-19 Woe unto them that rob the fatherless

Is. 65:11-25 They shall not build and another inhabit

2 Co. 8:1-15 That there may be equality

Col. 4:1-6 Give unto your servants that which is just

2 Ti. 2:1-15 The husbandman must be first partaker

Justification

Ro. 3:19-31 A man is justified by faith

Ro. 4 Jesus was raised for our justification

Ro. 5 Being justified by his blood

1 Co. 6 Ye are justified in the name of Jesus

Ga. 2 By the law shall no flesh be justified

[K]

Kindness, *See* Benevolence

King

1 S. 10:17-25 The people shouted, God save the king

Pr. 25:2-7 The heart of kings is unsearchable

Pr. 29 The king that faithfully judgeth the poor

Ec. 10:16, 17 When thy king is a child

Is. 33 Thine eyes shall see the king in his beauty

Mat. 22:15-22 Render unto Caesar the things that are Caesar's

Mat. 25:31-46 Inherit the kingdom prepared for you

Lu. 12:31-40 Seek ye the kingdom of God

Kingdom, the Coming

Is. 35 The desert shall rejoice

Kingdom, the Coming *(cont.)*

Is. 65:17-25 I create new heavens and a new earth

Zph. 1 The great day of the Lord is near

Mal. 3 The day when I make up my jewels

Mat. 3 The kingdom of heaven is at hand

Mat. 4:23-25 Jesus preached the gospel of the kingdom

Mat. 6:5-18 The kingdom come

Mat. 13:33-43 The kingdom of heaven is like unto leaven

Lu. 17:20-37 The kingdom cometh not with observation

He. 8 I will make a new covenant

2 Pe. 1 Until the day star arise in your hearts

Re. 7:9-17 The Lamb shall lead them

Re. 20 They reigned with Christ a thousand years

Knowledge

Ps. 90 That we may apply our hearts unto wisdom

Pr. 3:13-35 Happy is the man that findeth wisdom

Pr. 4:1-13 Wisdom is the principal thing

Pr. 8 Wisdom is better than rubies

Pr. 9 Wisdom hath hewn out her seven pillars

Ec. 1 In much wisdom is much grief

Ec. 10 The words of a wise man are gracious

Is. 45:20-25 They have no knowledge

Ho. 4:1-9 Thou hast rejected knowledge, I will reject thee

1 Co. 2 I know nothing save Christ crucified

1 Co. 3 Wisdom of this world is foolishness with God

1 Co. 8 Knowledge puffeth up

1 Co. 13 Then shall I know even as I also am known

[L]

Labor Day

Ex. 5:1-23 No more straw for the bricks

Ex. 18:13-24 This thing is too heavy for thee

Ne. 4:1-6 The people had a mind to work

Ps. 128 Thou shalt eat the labour of thine hands

Pr. 22 The diligent shall stand before kings

Ec. 1:1-11 All things are full of labour

Is. 41:1-13 They helped every one his neighbour

Mat. 9:35-38 The labourers are few

Mat. 13:44-58 Is not this the carpenter's son?

Mat. 20:1-16 The last shall be first

Mk. 6:1-6 Such mighty works are wrought

Mk. 9:14-27 After the transfiguration – work

Mk. 10:32-45 The Son of man came to minister

Mk. 13:32-37 To every man his work

Lu. 2:41-52 I must be about my Father's business

Lu. 5:1-11 We have toiled all the night

Ac. 18:1-5 He was of the same craft

Ac. 20:28-35 These hands have ministered

1 Co. 3:6-15 Every man's work shall be made manifest

Ga. 6 Let every man prove his own work

Ep. 6:5-8 Not with eyeservice, as menpleasers

Col. 3:22-25 Ye serve the Lord Christ

1 Th. 4:1-12 Work with your own hands

2 Th. 3 We wrought with labour and travail

Lamb, *See* Shepherd

Lamp, *See* Light

Land, *See* Earth

Land, the Promised

Ex. 3:1-10 A land flowing with milk and honey

De. 8 God bring thee to a good land

De. 19:1-14 The land which he promised

Jos. 24:1-13 A land for which ye did not labour

Ps. 143 Lead me into the land of uprightness

Je. 2:1-8 I brought you into a plentiful country

He. 11:1-16 They desire a better country

Language, *See* Conversation

Last, *See* End

Laughter, *See* Gayety

Law, *See* Commandment

Lawlessness, *See* Confusion

Laziness, *See* Idleness

Leadership

Ge. 41:33-44 A man in whom the spirit of God is

Ex. 3:1-12 I will send thee unto Pharaoh

Ex. 3:13-16 What shall I say unto them?

Ex. 13:17-22 The Lord went before them

Jos. 1:1-9 The Lord thy God is with thee

Ps. 43 Let them lead me

Is. 40:1-11 He shall gently lead those that are with young

Mat. 23:1-24 Ye blind guides

Jn. 1:35-51 The first disciples

2 Ti. 2:1-7 Be strong in grace

League

2 K. 6:1-17 They with us are more than they with them

Jb. 5 In league with the stones of the field

Ps. 20 Some trust in chariots, and some in horses

Is. 8:9-18 Say ye not, A confederacy

Learning, *See* Education

Least

Mat. 11:1-15 The least in heaven is greater than John

Mat. 13:31-32 The mustard is the least of all seeds

Mat. 25:31-46 Since ye have done it unto one of the least

Lu. 9:46-48 He that is least among you shall be great

Lu. 16:1-12 Faithful in least, faithful in much

Ep. 3 I am less than the least of all saints

Leisure. *See* Rest

Lent

Is. 43:1-13 Fear not, for I am with thee

Mat. 5:1-20 Blessed are the poor in spirit

Mat. 26:6-13 She did it for my burial

Mk. 6:7-13 He gave them power over unclean spirits

Jn. 12:20-26 If it die, it bringeth forth much fruit

Ro. 5:1-16 We joy in God through our Lord Jesus

Ro. 13:8-10 Love is the fulfilling of the law

2 Co. 3 Ye are our epistle

Ga. 5:16-26 Walk in the Spirit

Ph. 3 Our conversation is in heaven

Col. 1:23-29 I rejoice in my sufferings

Col. 3:5-10 Mortify your members

1 Pe. 4:12-16 Ye are partakers of Christ's sufferings

1 Jn. 2:1-6 He is the propitiation for our sins

Letter, *See* Epistle

Liberality, *See* Charity

Liberty

Le. 25:8-17 Proclaim liberty throughout the land

Ps. 68:17-35 Thou hast led captivity captive

Jn. 8:12-32 The truth shall make you free

Jn. 11:41-46 Loose him, and let him go

Ac. 16:25-31 Every one's bands were loosed

Ro. 8:18-39 The glorious liberty of the children of God

1 Co. 8 Let not your liberty become a stumblingblock

Ga. 5:13-26 Ye have been called unto liberty

Ja. 1:2-25 Whoso looketh into the perfect law of liberty

Ja. 2:1-12 They shall be judged by the law of liberty

1 Pe. 2:13-16 The free are servants of God

Lie

Ge. 27:1-29 Jacob deceives his father

Ps. 116 All men are liars

Ac. 5:1-11 Ananias and his wife

Ro. 1:16-32 They changed the truth of God into a lie

Tit. 1 God cannot lie

1 Jn. 2 No lie is of the truth

Re. 21:1-10 Liars shall have their part in the lake of fire

Life

Jb. 24 No man is sure of life

Lu. 10:25-37 This do, and thou shalt live

Lu. 12:22-31 The life is more than meat

Life *(cont.)*

Jn. 10:1-18 I am come that they might have life
Ro. 8:1-17 To be spiritually minded is life
1 Pe. 3:8-18 He that will love life, and see good days
1 Jn. 5 He that hath the Son hath life
Re. 3:1-6 Thou art dead
Re. 22 Take the water of life freely

Life, Book of, *See* Book
Life, Bread of, *See* Bread
Life, the Eternal, *See* Immortality
Life, the Full

Jn. 1:1-14 In him was life
Jn. 4:1-26 A well of water springing up into everlasting life
Jn. 10:1-18 That they might have life more abundantly
1 Co. 3 All things are yours
2 Co. 6 Be ye also enlarged

Life, the Long

Ps. 1 His leaf shall not wither
Ps. 34 What man is he that loveth many days?
Ps. 91 With long life will I satisfy him
Pr. 4:1-18 The years of thy life shall be many
Pr. 10 The fear of the Lord prolongeth days
Ep. 6 That thou mayest live long on the earth

Life, the New, *See* Birth, New
Life, the Short, *See* Brevity
Light

Ge. 1:1-8 God said, Let there be light
Pr. 4 The path of the just is as the shining light
Is. 9:2-7 The people have seen a great light
Mat. 4:1-16 The people which sat in darkness saw great light
Mat. 5:13-20 Ye are the salt of the earth
Mat. 25:1-13 Our lamps are gone out
Lu. 11:33-36 If thy whole body is full of light
Jn. 1:1-11 The light shineth in darkness
Jn. 3:18-21 He that doeth truth cometh to the light
Jn. 5:32-47 He was a burning and a shining light

Jn. 12:20-36 Walk while ye have the light
Ep. 5:6-21 Walk as children of light
Ph. 2:1-15 Ye shine as lights
1 Jn. 1 Walk in the light, as he is in the light

Likeness, *See* Image
Lincoln's Birthday

Ex. 18:17-27 Able men, such as fear God, men of truth
Nu. 14:1-10 Rebel not ye against the Lord
Pr. 8:14-36 By me kings reign
Pr. 10:1-12 The memory of the just is blessed
Mat. 20:20-28 The Son of man came to minister
Mk. 12:28-34 Thou shalt love thy neighbour as thyself
Jn. 13:1-17 Jesus washes the disciples' feet

Little, *See* Smallness
Liturgy, *See* Ceremony
Load. *See* Burden
Loaf, *See* Bread
Loan

Ps. 37 He is ever merciful, and lendeth
Ps. 112 A good man showeth favour, and lendeth
Pr. 22 The borrower is servant to the lender
Lu. 6:27-38 Lend, hoping for nothing again

Loneliness, *See* Solitude
Longing, *See* Desire
Long-Suffering, *See* Endurance
Lord, *See* Christ the Lord; *See* God the Lord
Lord, Day of, *See* Judgment, the Last
Love

1 S. 18:1-14 David and Jonathan
S. of S. 8 Many waters cannot quench love
Ho. 11:1-4,8,9 I drew them with bands of love
Ho. 14 I will heal their backsliding
Am. 5:1-20 Hate the evil, and love the good
Mat. 5:38-48 Love your enemies
Mat. 26:6-13 The alabaster box of precious ointment
Lu. 6:27-38 Bless them that curse you
Jn. 12:23-36 He that loveth his life shall lose it
Jn. 15 Love one another, as I have loved you

Jn. 15:9-19 Continue ye in my love
Jn. 21:15-24 Lovest thou me?
1 Co. 13 The greatest of these is charity
Ep. 3 The love of Christ passeth knowledge
Ph. 1:1-11 I have you in my heart
1 Jn. 4 There is no fear in love
Loveliness, *See* Beauty
Lovingkindness, *See* Benevolence
Loyalty
Ex. 20:1-6 Thou shalt have no other gods before me
Ru. 1 Ruth clave unto her
Ps. 31 The Lord preserveth the faithful

Pr. 27 Faithful are the wounds of a friend
Mat. 25:14-30 Thou hast been faithful over a few things
Lu. 14:25-27 A man must hate his own life
Lu. 16:13-15 No servant can serve two masters
Luck, *See* Chance
Lust
Ga. 5:13-21 The flesh lusteth against the Spirit
He. 11:17-40 Rather than enjoying the pleasures of sin
Ja. 4 Ye lust, and have not
Ja. 5 Ye have been wanton

[M]

Magnificence, *See* Glory
Majesty, *See* Glory
Maker, *See* Builder
Malice, *See* Hatred
Mammon
Ps. 73 These are the ungodly, who prosper
Mat. 6:19-24 Ye cannot serve God and mammon
Lu. 12:16-34 So is he that is not rich toward God
Lu. 16 No servant can serve two masters
Ro. 12 Be not conformed to this world
2 Co. 4 The god of this world hath blinded minds
1 Jn. 2:1-17 Love not the world
Man
Ge. 1:26-31 God said, Let us make man in our image
1 S. 16:1-13 The Lord seeth not as man seeth
Jb. 5 Man is born unto trouble
Ps. 1 Blessed is the man
Ps. 8 Thou hast crowned him with glory
Ps. 103 As for man, his days are as grass
Ps. 144 Man is like to vanity
Je. 17:5-14 Cursed be the man that trusteth in man
1 Co. 2 The natural man receiveth not the things of the Spirit
1 Co. 13 When I became a man
1 Co. 16 Quit you like men
He. 2:1-15 Not ashamed to call them brethren

Man, Divinity of
Ge. 3:1-21 Ye shall be as gods
Jn. 10:22-42 He called them gods, to whom the word came
Jn. 17 That they also may be one in us
Ac. 14:1-12 The gods are come in the likeness of men
Ac. 17:22-31 In him we have our being
1 Co. 11 A man is the image and glory of God
Ep. 3 According to the power that worketh in us
Ja. 3 Men are made after the similitude of God
2 Pe. 1 That ye might be partakers of the divine nature
Man, the New, *See* Birth, the New
Man, Son of
Mat. 13:33-43 The Son of man shall send forth his angels
Mat. 18:1-14 The Son of man is come to save that which was lost
Mat. 20:20-29 The Son of man came to minister
Jn. 12:23-36 The Son of man must be lifted up
Jn. 13:31-35 Now is the Son of man glorified
Ac. 7:54-60 I see the Son of man standing on the right hand of God
Man, Spirit of
Jb. 32 There is a spirit in man
Ps. 51 Take not thy holy spirit from me
Pr. 20 The spirit of man is the candle of the Lord

Man, Spirit of (cont.)

Lu. 1:67-80 The child waxed strong in spirit

Jn. 2:13-25 He knew what was in man

1 Co. 2 We have received the spirit which is of God

2 Co. 4 The inward man is renewed day by day

1 Pe. 3 The hidden man of the heart

Manifestation, See Revelation

Manna, See Bread

Market, See Business

Marriage

Ge. 2:18-25 It is not good that man should be alone

Pr. 18 Whoso findeth a wife findeth a good thing

Ho. 2:14-23 I will betroth thee unto me for ever

Mat. 19:1-9 What therefore God hath joined together

Mat. 22:23-33 In the resurrection they do not marry

Mat. 25:1-13 The ten virgins

Mk. 10:6-9 They twain shall be one flesh

Jn. 2:1-11 Jesus was called to the marriage

1 Co. 7 Let every man have his own wife

Col. 3:18-25 Husbands, love your wives

1 Pe. 3:1-9 On husbands and wives

Re. 19 The marriage supper of the Lamb

Martyr

Ac. 7:51-60 The martyrdom of Stephen

Ac. 15:13-35 Men that hazarded their lives for Jesus

Ro. 8:18-39 We are accounted as sheep for the slaughter

Ph. 3 I have suffered the loss of all things

He. 11:17-40 They were stoned, sawn asunder, slain

Re. 12 They loved not their lives unto death

Re. 17 The blood of the martyrs of Jesus

Re. 20 I saw the souls of them that were beheaded

Marvel

Ge. 9:8-17 I do set my bow in the cloud

Ex. 4:1-9 The signs given by Moses

Ps. 139 Marvellous are thy works

Mat. 16:1-12 A wicked generation seeketh after a sign

Mat. 22:15-22 They marvelled, and left him

Lu. 21:25-33 Signs in the sun, and moon, and stars

Ac. 15:6-12 God wrought miracles and wonders

Master

Mat. 6:19-34 No man can serve two masters

Mat. 23:1-12 One is your Master, even Christ

Lu. 6:39-45 The disciple is not above his master

Jn. 13:1-17 Ye call me Master, and ye say well

Ep. 6:1-9 Your Master is in heaven

Ja. 3 My brethren, be not many masters

Mastery

Pr. 16:19-33 He that ruleth his spirit

Pr. 25 He that hath no rule over his own spirit

1 Co. 9:24-27 The man that striveth for mastery

Col. 1 That he might have the pre-eminence

Materialism, See Mammon

Maundy Thursday, See Communion, Service of

Meaning, See Interpretation

Measure

Pr. 20 Divers measures are an abomination

Je. 33:19-26 The sand of the sea cannot be measured

Zch. 2 A man with a measuring line in his hand

Mat. 7 With what measure ye mete, it shall be measured

Lu. 6:27-38 Good measure, pressed down

Jn. 3:23-36 God giveth not the Spirit by measure unto him

2 Co. 10 They measure themselves by themselves

Meat

Mat. 6:24-34 Is not the life more than meat?

Jn. 4:27-38 My meat is to do his will

Jn. 6:22-35 Labour not for the meat which perisheth

1 Co. 8 If meat make my brother offend, I will eat no flesh

He. 5 Ye have need of milk, and not of strong meat

Medicine, *See* Healing
Mediation, *See* Advocate
Meditation
Jos. 1 Thou shalt meditate therein day and night
Ps. 19 Let the meditation of my heart be acceptable
Ps. 39 While I was musing the fire burned
Ps. 63 I meditate on thee in the night watches
Ps. 119:89-112 Thy law is my meditation all the day
Pr. 4 Ponder the path of thy feet
Pr. 23:1-24 As a man thinketh in his heart, so is he
Mat. 22:41-46 What think ye of Christ?
Lu. 2:1-20 Mary pondered these things in her heart
Ph. 4:8-13 Think on these things
1 Ti. 4 Meditate upon these things
Meekness, *See* Humility
Meeting, *See* Assembly
Melody, *See* Music
Member
Jn. 15:1-15 I am the vine, ye are the branches
1 Co. 6 Your bodies are the members of Christ
1 Co. 12 All the members suffer with one member
Ep. 4 We are members one of another
Col. 3 Mortify your members which are upon the earth
Memorial Day
Ex. 13 Remember this day
De. 8:11-20 Forget not the Lord thy God
De. 34:5-12 No prophet like unto Moses
Es. 9:17-32 Founding of the Jewish National Memorial Day
Ps. 72 His name shall endure for ever
Ps. 116 Precious is the death of his saints
Is. 2:1-5 He shall judge among the nations
Mat. 5:1-12 Blessed are they that mourn
Mat. 16:24-28 Whosoever will lose his life for my sake
Lu. 22:7-20 This do in remembrance of me
Ac. 5:17-42 Worthy to suffer shame for his name

2 Ti. 2:3-14 Put them in remembrance
He. 11 They obtained a good report through faith
Re. 14 Write, Blessed are the dead
Memory
Ex. 20:1-17 Remember the sabbath day, to keep it holy
De. 8 Thou shalt remember the way God led thee
De. 32:7-14 Remember the days of old
Ac. 20:28-38 Remember the words of the Lord Jesus
1 Co. 11:23-34 This do in remembrance of me
He. 11:1-16 He being dead yet speaketh
2 Pe. 3:1-9 I stir up your pure minds by way of remembrance
Mercy
Ge. 18:20-33 I will not destroy it for ten's sake
Ps. 23 Surely goodness and mercy shall follow me
Ps. 103 He crowneth thee with tender mercies
Pr. 3:1-12 Let not mercy and truth forsake thee
Is. 42:1-12 A bruised reed shall he not break
Ho. 6 I desired mercy, and not sacrifice
Mat. 5:1-12 Blessed are the merciful
Col. 3:1-17 Put on bowels of mercies
Merriment, *See* Gayety
Messenger, *See* Ambassador
Messiah, *See* Christ, the Messiah
Middle, *See* Center
Midnight, *See* Darkness
Might
Ps. 84 Blessed is the man whose strength is in thee
Je. 9:17-24 Let not the mighty man glory in his might
1 Co. 1:18-31 The weak things confound the mighty
2 Co. 5 The love of Christ constraineth us
Ep. 3 Strengthened with might by his Spirit
Ep. 6 Be strong in the power of his might
Millennium, *See* Kingdom, the Coming
Mind
Is. 26:1-11 He whose mind is stayed on thee
Mk. 12:28-34 Thou shalt love the Lord with all thy mind

Mind (*cont.*)

Ro. 8:1-28 He knoweth what is the mind of the Spirit

Ro. 12 Transformed by the renewing of your mind

1 Co. 14:1-16 I will pray with the understanding

2 Co. 3 Their minds were blinded

Ep. 1 The eyes of your understanding were enlightened

Ph. 4:1-9 The peace of God keep your hearts and minds

2 Ti. 1 God hath given us the spirit of a sound mind

He. 8 I will put my laws into their minds

1 Pe. 1 Gird up the loins of your mind

Ministry

Mat. 20:20-29 The Son of man came to minister

Jn. 10:1-18 I am the good shepherd

1 Co. 9:1-19 Woe is unto me, if I preach not the gospel!

2 Co. 3:1-6 Ministers of the new testament

2 Co. 4 We look not at the things which are seen

2 Co. 6 Approving ourselves as the ministers of God

Ep. 4 I, the prisoner of the Lord, beseech you

1 Ti. 1 The glorious gospel of the blessed God

1 Ti. 4:6-16 Thou shalt be a good minister of Jesus

2 Ti. 2:1-4 Endure hardness as a good soldier

2 Ti. 4:1-8 Make full proof of thy ministry

1 Pe. 2:1-10 Ye are a royal priesthood

Miracle

Lu. 11:29-36 An evil generation seeks a sign

Jn. 2:1-11 The first miracle in Cana of Galilee

Jn. 3:1-13 To do these miracles God must be with him

Jn. 6:1-14 A multitude followed because of the miracles

Jn. 10:22-42 John did no miracle

Ac. 15:1-12 God wrought miracles by them

1 Co. 12 To another the working of miracles

Mirth, *See* Gayety

Misery, *See* Adversity

Misfortune, *See* Adversity

Mission, *See* Ambassador

Missions, Foreign

Ps. 72 Let the whole earth be filled with his glory

Is. 55:1-7 Come ye, buy, and eat

Is. 56:3-8 Yet will I gather others

Eze. 33:1-9 I have set thee a watchman

Mat. 10:5-10 These twelve Jesus sent forth

Mat. 18:11-14 The one sheep gone astray

Mat. 25:34-40 I was in prison, and ye came unto me

Mat. 28:18-20 Go ye therefore, and teach all nations

Lu. 4:16-31 Anointed to preach the gospel

Ac. 1:1-8 Unto the uttermost part of the earth

Ac. 8:26-39 Philip preached unto him Jesus

Ac. 10:1-33 Peter preaches to the Gentiles

Ac. 11:5-18 God gave them the like gift as to us

Ac. 16:6-15 Come over into Macedonia, and help us

Ac. 19:8-20 So mightily grew the word of God

Ro. 8:19-22 The whole creation groaneth and travaileth

Ro. 15:8-21 They that have not heard shall understand

2 Co. 5:14-21 We are ambassadors for Christ

Money, *See* Mammon

Monotheism, *See* God, Unity of

Morality, *See* Character

Morning

Ex. 16:1-10 In the morning ye shall see the Lord's glory

Ps. 30 Joy cometh in the morning

Ps. 139 If I take the wings of the morning

Ec. 11 In the morning sow thy seed

S. of S. 2 Until the day break, and the shadows flee

Is. 21:1-12 The watchman said, The morning cometh

Is. 60:1-13 Arise, shine; for thy light is come

La. 3:22-26 The Lord's mercies are new every morning

Ho. 13:1-14 They shall be as the morning cloud

Am. 5:4-15 Seek him that turneth death into morning

Ro. 13 The night is spent, the day
is at hand
1 Th. 5 Ye are children of light
2 Pe. 1 Until the day dawn
Mortality, *See* Death
Mother's Day
Ge. 2:18-25 It is not good that man
should be alone
1 S. 1 Hannah presents Samuel to
the Lord
Pr. 23:22-26 Thy father and thy
mother shall be glad
Pr. 31:10-31 Her children call her
blessed
Mat. 15:21-28 My daughter is griev-
ously vexed
Mat. 27:54-66 Many women were
there
Jn. 2:1-11 The mother of Jesus was
there
Jn. 19:23-27 His mother stood by
the cross
1 Co. 13 Charity suffereth long and
is kind
Ep. 6:1-9 Children, parents, serv-
ants, masters
Mountain
Ex. 24:12-18 Moses went up into
the mount of God
Ps. 24 Who shall ascend into the
hill of the Lord?
Ps. 36 Thy righteousness is like
the mountains
Ps. 95 The strength of the hills is
his also
Ps. 121 I will lift up mine eyes unto
the hills
Is. 27 They shall worship the Lord
in the holy mount
Is. 40:1-11 Every mountain shall
be made low
Is. 55 The mountains shall break
forth into singing
Lu. 6:12-19 He went out into a
mountain to pray
Mourning, *See* Death
Multitude, *See* Crowd
Music
Ge. 4:16-26 Jubal was the father of
the harp and organ

Ps. 100 Come before his presence
with singing
Ps. 149 Sing unto the Lord a new
song
Ps. 150 Praise him with stringed
instruments
Ec. 12 The daughters of music
shall be brought low
S. of S. 1 The song of songs, which
is Solomon's
Is. 35 The ransomed shall come to
Zion with songs
Is. 65:11-16 My servants shall
sing for joy of heart
Am. 5:21-27 Take away from me
the noise of thy songs
Mystery
Ex. 33:12-23 No man shall see me,
and live
Jb. 11 Canst thou by searching
find out God?
Pr. 25:1-7 It is the glory of God to
conceal a thing
Mk. 4:1-13 To know the mystery
of the kingdom of God
Ro. 11:16-36 How unsearchable are
his judgments
1 Co. 15:47-58 Behold, I show you
a mystery
Ep. 3 By revelation he made known
the mystery
Ep. 6 Make known the mystery of
the gospel
1 Ti. 3 Great is the mystery of
godliness
Mysticism
De. 29:10-29 The secret things
belong unto the Lord
Ps. 18:1-19 He made darkness his
secret place
Ps. 25 The Lord's secret is with
them that fear him
Ps. 44 God knoweth the secrets of
the heart
Is. 45:1-13 I will give thee the
treasures of darkness
Mat. 13:33-43 I will utter things
which have been secret
1 Co. 2 The Spirit searcheth the
deep things of God

[N]

Name
Pr. 18 The name of the Lord is
a strong tower
Ec. 7:1-22 A good name is better
than precious ointment

Lu. 10:1-20 Your names are written
in heaven
Ac. 3:12-26 Faith in his name hath
made this man strong
Ph. 4 Their names are in the book

Name (cont.)

Re. 19 A name written, KING OF KINGS

Nation
Ge. 12:1-5 I will make of thee a great nation
Ex. 29:43-46 I will meet with the children of Israel
Ex. 40:34-38 The children of Israel went onward
Le. 20:22-26 I have severed you from other people
De. 7:1-11 Thou art an holy people unto the Lord
Ps. 122 Pray for the peace of Jerusalem
Ps. 144 Happy is that people, whose God is the Lord
Pr. 14 Righteousness exalteth a nation
Is. 1:1-9 My people doth not consider
Is. 30:1-17 This is a rebellious people
Is. 60 A small one shall become a strong nation
Eze. 37:21-28 I will make them one nation
Ro. 13:1-8 Tribute to whom tribute is due

Nations, League of, See Nations, United
Nations, United, See United Nations
Nativity, See Christmas
Nature
Ex. 3:1-6 The place is holy ground
De. 33:13-17 Blessed of the Lord be his land
1 K. 19:4-13 He sat down under a juniper tree
Jb. 12 Speak to the earth, and it shall teach thee
Ps. 19 The heavens declare the glory of God
Ps. 104:1-24 The earth is full of thy riches
Ec. 3:1-15 He hath made everything beautiful in his time
Is. 44:21-28 Break forth into singing, mountains and forests
Mat. 6:26-34 Consider the lilies of the field
Mk. 1:1-11 By the river Jordan
Lu. 3:3-6 A voice in the wilderness
1 Co. 11:1-15 Doth not even nature teach you

Nature, Human, See Man
Need
Ps. 40 I am poor and needy
Mat. 6:1-8 Your Father knoweth what things ye need

Mat. 9:10-13 They that be whole need not a physician
Mat. 21:1-11 The Lord hath need of them
Mk. 12:41-44 She of her want cast in all that she had
Lu. 10:38-42 One thing is needful
Ro. 12 Distributing to the necessity of saints
1 Co. 9:1-16 Necessity is laid upon me
Ph. 4 My God shall supply all your need
He. 11:17-40 Destitute, afflicted, tormented
Re. 22 They need no candle, nor light of the sun

Neglect, See Indifference
Neighbor
Ge. 13:1-12 Let there be no strife, for we are brethren
Is. 41:1-9 They helped every one his neighbour
Mk. 12:28-34 Thou shalt love thy neighbour as thyself
Lu. 10:25-37 Which now of these three was neighbour?
Ro. 13 Love worketh no ill to his neighbour
Ep. 4:17-32 We are members one of another

Newness
Ec. 1 There is no new thing under the sun
La. 3:1-26 The Lord's mercies are new every morning
Eze. 11:14-20 I will put a new spirit within you
Eze. 18:25-32 Make you a new heart and a new spirit
Mk. 16:14-20 They shall speak with new tongues
Ep. 4:17-32 Put on the new man
Re. 21:1-10 Behold, I make all things new

Night, See Darkness
Nobility, See Character
Nourishment
Ex. 16:4-15 I will rain bread
Jb. 8:11-17 Can the flag grow without water?
Is. 1:1-20 I have nourished children and they have rebelled
Mat. 10:1-15 The workman is worthy of his meat
Jn. 6:47-65 I am the living bread
1 Ti. 6:1-8 Having food and raiment let us be content
He. 5 Ye have need of milk, not of strong meat

[O]

Oath
Ex. 20:1-17 Take not the name of the Lord thy God in vain
Ps. 24 He who hath not sworn deceitfully shall stand
Zch. 8:1-17 Love no false oath
Mat. 5:33-37 Swear not at all
Mat. 23:16-22 Whosoever shall swear
Ja. 5 Let your yea be yea; and your nay, nay

Obedience
1 S. 15:10-23 To obey is better than sacrifice
Es. 1 Queen Vashti refused to come
Mat. 7:21-27 He that doeth the will of my Father
Ac. 26:1-19 I was not disobedient unto the vision
Ro. 13:1-7 The powers that be are ordained of God
Ep. 6:1-16 Be obedient to them that are your masters
He. 2:1-10 If we neglect so great salvation
He. 5 Though a Son he learned obedience
He. 10:1-10 Lo, I come to do thy will, O God
1 Pe. 1:13-25 As obedient children
Re. 22 Blessed are they that do his commandments

Obligation, *See* Duty
Oblivion, *See* Forgetfulness
Obscurity, *See* Darkness
Observance, *See* Ceremony

Obstacle
Je. 6:18-25 I will lay stumbling-blocks before them
Mk. 10:17-27 The rich man and the kingdom of God
Ro. 5 We glory in tribulations
Ro. 8:24-39 Who shall separate us from the love of Christ?
1 Jn. 2:7-11 There is none occasion of stumbling in him

Occupation, *See* Business

Ocean
Ge. 1:1-13 The gathering of the waters called he Seas
Ps. 29 The voice of the Lord is upon the waters
Ps. 42 All thy waves are gone over me
Ps. 93 The floods lift up their waves
Ps. 95 The sea is his, and he made it
Ps. 107 These see his wonders in the deep

Ec. 1 All the rivers run into the sea
Lu. 5:1-11 Launch out into the deep
2 Co. 11:22-33 In perils of waters
Re. 21:1-7 There was no more sea

Offence
Mat. 11:1-6 Blessed is he who shall not be offended in me
Mat. 18:7-20 Woe unto the world because of offences!
Ac. 24:10-21 A conscience void of offence toward God
Ro. 4 Jesus was delivered for our offences
1 Co. 8 I will not make my brother to offend
1 Co. 10 Give none offence

Offering
Le. 22:19-25 Offerings must be without blemish
Ps. 4 Offer the sacrifices of righteousness
Ps. 51 The sacrifices of God are a broken spirit
Mi. 6:1-9 Shall I come before him with burnt offerings?
Mat. 9:1-13 I will have mercy, and not sacrifice
Mk. 12:28-34 To love him is more than burnt offerings
Ep. 5:1-14 Christ hath given himself for us an offering
2 Ti. 4 I am now ready to be offered, my departure is at hand
1 Pe. 2:1-10 Offer up spiritual sacrifices

Old People's Sunday
Ge. 47:8-10, 27-31 How old art thou?
Le. 19:23-37 Thou shalt honour the face of the old man
1 S. 12:1-5 I am old and gray-headed
Ps. 71 Now when I am old and greyheaded
Ps. 91 With long life will I satisfy him
Ps. 92 They shall bring forth fruit in old age
Pr. 16:16-33 The hoary head is a crown of glory
Ec. 12 Remember now thy Creator in the days of thy youth
Is. 65:17-25 The child shall die an hundred years old
Ep. 6:1-4 Obey your parents in the Lord
2 Ti. 4:6-8 I have finished my course

Old People's Sunday (*cont.*)

Tit. 2 That aged men be sober, grave, sound in faith
1 Jn. 2:15-17 The world passeth away

Omission

Ps. 36 He hath left off to be wise
Mat. 23:13-33 Ye omit the weightier matters of the law
Mat. 25:31-46 I was hungry, and ye gave me no meat
Ro. 7 The good that I would I do not
1 Co. 13 If I have not charity I am nothing
Ja. 2:14-26 Can faith without works save him?

Omnipotence, *See* God, Omnipotence of
Omnipresence, *See* God, Omnipresence of
Omniscience, *See* God, Omniscience of
Oneness, *See* Unity
Opportunity

Mat. 24:42-51 Watch therefore, for ye know not the hour
Jn. 4 The fields are white already to harvest
Jn. 9:1-38 I must work while it is day
Ac. 26 Almost thou persuadest me
2 Co. 6 Now is the accepted time
Ph. 4 Ye lacked opportunity
He. 3 The Holy Ghost saith, To day
Re. 3:18-22 Behold, I stand at the door, and knock
Re. 22 Let him that is athirst come

Opposition, *See* Enemy
Oppression, *See* Persecution
Optimism

Jn. 20:24-31 They have not seen, yet have they believed
Ro. 8:16-28 All things work together for good
1 Co. 13 Charity believeth all things
Ep. 5:1-16 Walk as children of light

Col. 1 Christ in you, the hope of glory
He. 11:1-16 Faith is the substance of things hoped for

Ordinance, *See* Ceremony
Ordination

Je. 1:1-16 I ordained thee a prophet
Mat. 10:16-42 As sheep in the midst of wolves
Ac. 6 We will give ourselves to the ministry
Ro. 13 The powers that be are ordained of God
Ep. 3 Preaching the unsearchable riches of Christ
Ep. 4 He gave some, apostles; and some, pastors
1 Ti. 2 I am ordained a preacher, and an apostle
Tit. 1 Ordain elders in every city
1 Pe. 5 Feed the flock of God which is among you

Origin, *See* Beginning
Ornament, *See* Beauty
Orphan

Ex. 22:21-24 Ye shall not afflict any fatherless child
Ps. 10 Thou art the helper of the fatherless
Ho. 14 In thee the fatherless findeth mercy
Ja. 1 Pure religion is to visit the fatherless

Orthodoxy, *See* Doctrine
Otherworldliness, *See* Holiness
Overthrow, *See* Defeat
Ownership

1 Ch. 29:10-19 All things come of thee
Lu. 12:13-34 Soul, thou hast much goods laid up
1 Co. 3 All things are yours
2 Co. 6 As having nothing, and yet possessing all things
He. 10:23-39 Ye have in heaven a better substance

[P]

Pacifist, *See* Peace
Pagan, *See* Heathen
Pain

Jb. 15 The wicked man travaileth with pain
Ho. 6 He hath torn, and he will heal us
Mat. 4:17-25 They brought unto him people with torments

Ro. 8:18-39 The whole creation groaneth in pain
2 Co. 11:22-33 In weariness and painfulness
Ph. 1:12-26 To die is gain
He. 5 He learned obedience by the things which he suffered
Re. 21:1-7 Neither shall there be any more pain

Palm Sunday

Hag. 2:1-9 The desire of all nations shall come

Zch. 9:9-17 Behold, thy King cometh unto thee

Mat. 21:12-17 Hosanna to the Son of David

Mk. 11:1-11 They brought the colt to Jesus

Mk. 11:15-19 Jesus went into the temple

Lu. 19:28-48 When he was come near, he wept over the city

Jn. 12:12-19 The people took branches of palm trees

Ro. 8:18-39 More than conquerors

1 Jn. 5:1-5 The victory that overcometh

Re. 19:11-16 King of Kings, and Lord of Lords

Parable

Ps. 49 I will incline mine ear to a parable

Ps. 78:1-35 I will open my mouth in a parable

Mk. 4:1-13 All these things are done in parables

Lu. 8:4-15 He spake by a parable

Paradise, *See* Heaven

Pardon, *See* Forgiveness

Parenthood

Ge. 18:17-19 He will command his children

Ex. 20:1-17 Honour thy father and thy mother

De. 6:1-13 Thou shalt teach them to thy children

1 S. 1:9-28 I have lent him to the Lord

Pr. 22 Train up a child in the way he should go

Mk. 10:13-16 Suffer the little children to come

Lu. 2:39-52 They found him in the temple

Jn. 9:1-11 Who did sin, this man, or his parents?

Ep. 6:1-4 In the nurture and admonition of the Lord

2 Jn. 1-6 I found of thy children walking in truth

Partaker, *See* Communion

Parting, *See* Departure

Partnership, *See* Communion

Passion

Ge. 44 Let not thine anger burn

Pr. 16:16-33 The slow to anger are better than the mighty

Mk. 15:15-38 They crucified him

Ac. 14:1-18 We are men of like passions with you

2 Co. 12 I will gladly spend and be spent for you

Passover

Ex. 12:21-28 It is the sacrifice of the Lord's passover

Mat. 26:17-35 I will keep the passover at thy house

Lu. 22:1-20 The feast of unleavened bread drew nigh

1 Co. 5 Christ our passover is sacrificed for us

He. 11:17-40 Through faith he kept the passover

Past

Ge. 6:1-8 There were giants in the earth in those days

De. 8 Thou shalt remember the way the Lord led thee

1 S. 3:1-14 The word of the Lord was precious in those days

Ps. 90 A thousand years are as yesterday to thee

Ec. 3:1-15 That which hath been is now

Is. 46 Remember the former things of old

2 Co. 5 Old things are passed away

Ep. 2 In time past ye walked according to the world

Tit. 3 Avoid genealogies

He. 1 God spake in times past unto the fathers

Pastor, *See* Ministry

Path

Ps. 16 Thou wilt show me the path of life

Ps. 77 Thy path is in the great waters

Ps. 139:1-12 Thou compassest my path and my lying down

Pr. 3:1-20 He shall direct thy paths

Pr. 4:14-19 The path of the just is as the shining light

Mat. 7:1-14 Narrow is the way, which leadeth unto life

1 Co. 12 I show unto you a more excellent way

Patience

Ps. 130 My soul waiteth for the Lord

Mk. 14:26-42 Couldest not thou watch one hour?

He. 10:30-39 Ye have need of patience

He. 12:1-14 Let us run the race with patience

Patience *(cont.)*

Ja. 1 The trying of your faith worketh patience

Ja. 5 Ye have heard of the patience of Job

2 Pe. 1 Add to temperance patience

Re. 1 In the kingdom and patience of Jesus

Re. 2:1-7 I know thy labour and thy patience

Patriotic Holidays

De. 4:1-10 What nation is there so great?

De. 6 The Lord shall give thee goodly cities

De. 12:1-16 Dwell in the land which God giveth you

De. 26:1-11 The Lord hath given us this land

Ps. 33 Blessed the nation whose God is the Lord

Ps. 85 That glory may dwell in our land

Ps. 122 Pray for the peace of Jerusalem

Pr. 14:28-35 Righteousness exalteth a nation

He. 11:1-16 They desire a better country

Pattern, *See* Perfection

Payment, *See* Reward

Peace

Ge. 26:12-25 Isaac and his wells

Ps. 46 Be still, and know that I am God

Is. 2:1-5 Neither shall they learn war any more

Is. 9:5-7 The Prince of Peace

Is. 11:1-10 A little child shall lead them

Is. 32 The work of righteousness shall be peace

Is. 66:5-18 I will extend peace to her like a river

Mi. 4:1-7 They shall sit every man under his vine

Zch. 2:1-5 The Lord will be unto her a wall of fire

Mat. 5:1-12 Blessed are the peacemakers

Mat. 5:9, 38-48 Resist not evil

Lu. 2:1-14 On earth peace, good will toward men

Jn. 14:1-14 Let not your heart be troubled

1 Th. 5 Be at peace among yourselves

Penance, *See* Repentance

Penitence, *See* Repentance

Pentecost, *See* Whitsunday

People

De. 7:1-11 The Lord hath chosen thee as a special people

De. 33:1-3 He loved the people

Ru. 1:6-18 Thy people shall be my people

1 S. 8:1-9 Hearken unto the voice of the people

1 S. 12:20-25 The Lord will not forsake his people.

Ps. 3 I will not be afraid of ten thousands

Is. 62 Prepare ye the way of the people

He. 8 They shall be to me a people

Perfection

Le. 22:19-25 Ye shall offer a male without blemish

Ps. 37:27-40 Mark the perfect man

Mat. 5:43-48 Be ye therefore perfect

Mat. 19:16-26 If thou wilt be perfect, go and sell

Ph. 4:4-13 Whatsoever things are true

2 Ti. 3:14-17 That the man of God may be perfect

Ja. 1:17-27 The perfect law of liberty

Ja. 2:12-26 By works was faith made perfect

Ja. 3 If he offend not in word, he is a perfect man

1 Jn. 4 Perfect love casteth out fear

Peril, *See* Danger

Perplexity, *See* Doubt

Persecution

Ex. 1:8-14 Lives bitter with hard bondage

Ps. 44:13-26 For thy sake we are killed

Mat. 5:1-12 Blessed are ye, when men shall persecute you

Lu. 21:5-19 They shall persecute you

Jn. 16:1-7 Jesus foretells the disciples' persecution

Ac. 7:51-60 Your fathers persecuted the prophets

Ac. 9:1-9 I am Jesus whom thou persecutest

Ro. 8:31-39 Shall persecution separate us from Christ?

Ro. 12 Bless them which persecute you

2 Co. 4 Persecuted, but not forsaken

2 Co. 12:1-10 I take pleasure in persecutions

1 Pe. 4:12-19 The fiery trial which is to try you

Re. 17:1-6 The blood of the martyrs of Jesus

Perseverance, *See* Persistence

Persistence

Ps. 55:16-23 Evening, morning, and noon will I pray

Mat. 18:15-22 Until seventy times seven

Mk. 13:1-13 He that shall endure shall be saved

Lu. 9:57-62 Having put his hand to the plough

Lu. 11:1-13 Because of his importunity he will rise

Ac. 2:37-47 They continued stedfastly

Ac. 12:1-19 Peter continued knocking

2 Co. 4 Seeing we have this ministry, we faint not

Ga. 6 Let us not be weary in well doing

1 Th. 5 Hold fast that which is good

He. 6:1-11 Let us go on unto perfection

Persons, Respect of

De. 1:13-18 Ye shall hear the small as well as the great

Pr. 28 To have respect of persons is not good

Mat. 5:43-48 He sendeth rain on the just and the unjust

Mk. 12:13-17 Thou regardest not the person of men

Ac. 10:34-48 God is no respecter of persons

Ro. 10 No difference between the Jew and the Greek

Ep. 6 There is no respect of persons with him

Col. 3:1-15 There is neither bond nor free

Ja. 2 If ye have respect of persons ye commit sin

Persuasion

Ac. 26 Almost thou persuadest me to be a Christian

Ro. 8:31-39 I am persuaded that death shall not separate

Ro. 14:1-9 Let every man be fully persuaded in his mind

2 Co. 5 We persuade men

2 Ti. 1 I am persuaded that he is able to keep

He. 11:1-16 They were persuaded of the promises

Pessimism

Jb. 10 Where the light is as darkness

Ps. 97 Clouds and darkness are round about him

Ec. 1:12-18 All is vanity and vexation

Ec. 2:18-23 All his days are sorrows, and his travail grief

Ec. 5:9-17 Of what profit is labour for the wind?

Ec. 6 All the labour of man is for his mouth

Eze. 9 The Lord hath forsaken the earth

Petition, *See* Entreaty

Pettiness, *See* Smallness

Pharisee, *See* Bigotry

Philanthropy, *See* Charity

Philosophy

Jb. 12 With the ancient is wisdom

Pr. 9 Wisdom hath builded her house

Jn. 1:1-5 In the beginning was the Word

Ac. 17:16-31 Certain philosophers encountered him

1 Co. 2 We speak the wisdom of God in a mystery

1 Co. 3 The wisdom of this world is foolishness

Col. 2 Let no man spoil you through philosophy

Physician, *See* Healing

Piety, *See* Holiness

Pilgrim

Ge. 28:1-15 I will keep thee whereever thou goest

Ex. 6:1-8 The land of their pilgrimage

Nu. 10:29-36 We are journeying

Ps. 119:49-64 In the house of my pilgrimage

He. 11:1-13 Strangers and pilgrims on the earth

1 Pe. 2:11-25 As strangers and pilgrims

Pioneer

Ex. 14:1-15 Go forward

Jos. 1 Go in and possess the land

Jos. 7:1-9 Go up and view the country

Lu. 10:1-12 I send you forth as lambs among wolves

Ph. 3:13-16 Reaching forth

He. 11:1-16 He went out, not knowing whither

Pity, *See* Solicitude

Plea, *See* Entreaty

Pleasure, *See* Joy

Pledge, *See* Promise
Plenty, *See* Abundance
Poise, *See* Peace
Possession, *See* Ownership
Poverty
　1 S. 2:1-11　The Lord maketh poor and maketh rich
　Is. 14:24-32　The needy shall lie down in safety
　Lu. 4:14-21　He hath sent me to preach to the poor
　Lu. 6:20-38　Blessed be ye poor
　2 Co. 6　As poor, yet making many rich
　2 Co. 8　Though rich, for your sakes he became poor
　Ja. 2　Hath not God chosen the poor of this world
　Re. 2:1-11　I know thy poverty (but thou art rich)
Power, *See* Might
Praise
　Ps. 33　Praise is comely for the upright
　Ps. 34　O taste and see that the Lord is good
　Ps. 147　It is good to sing praises unto God
　Ps. 150　Praise ye the Lord
　Pr. 27:1-11　Let another praise thee
　Is. 60　Thou shalt call thy gates Praise
　Lu. 2:1-18　A multitude of the heavenly host praising God
　Jn. 12:37-50　They loved the praise of men
　He. 13　The sacrifice of praise
Prayer
　Ge. 18:17-33　Abraham stood before the Lord
　1 S. 7:5-17　I will pray for you unto the Lord
　2 Ch. 7:14-16　Pray and seek my face
　Pr. 15:25-33　The Lord heareth the prayer of the righteous
　Mat. 6:5-15　The Lord's prayer
　Mat. 7:1-12　Ask, and it shall be given you
　Mat. 18:19,20　If two of you shall agree
　Lu. 11:5-13　Because of his importunity
　Lu. 18:1-14　Men ought always to pray, and not to faint
　Jn. 17　Jesus prays for the disciples
　Ro. 10:1-13　The Lord is rich unto all that call upon him
　Ep. 3:14-21　I bow my knees unto the Father
　1 Th. 5　Pray without ceasing

　Ja. 5　The prayer of a righteous man availeth much
　1 Pe. 3:1-12　His ears are open unto their prayers
　Re. 5　The prayers of saints are golden vials
Preaching
　Is. 61　The Lord hath anointed me to preach
　Da. 12　They that turn many to righteousness
　Mk. 4:14-20　The sower soweth the word
　Ac. 4:1-14　Peter, filled with the Holy Ghost, spoke
　Ro. 10:8-15　How shall they hear without a preacher?
　1 Co. 2:1-5　I came not with excellency of speech
　Ph. 1:3-21　Every way Christ is preached
　2 Ti. 4:1-8　Preach the word
Predestination
　Mat. 25:31-46　Inherit the kingdom prepared for you
　Jn. 17　Thou lovedst me before the foundation
　Ro. 8:28-39　Whom he did predestinate he called
　Ro. 11:1-21　God foreknew his people
　Ep. 1　Predestinated according to his purpose
　1 Pe. 1　Elect according to the foreknowledge of God
Preëminence, *See* Best
Prejudice
　De. 1:16,17　Ye shall hear the small as well as the great
　2 K. 5:1-14　Are not the rivers of Damascus better?
　Mat. 9:1-13　Why eateth your Master with publicans?
　Lu. 4:16-32　No prophet is accepted in his own country
　Jn. 7:40-53　Out of Galilee ariseth no prophet
　Jn. 8:14-17　Ye judge after the flesh
　Ac. 23:1-11　I am a Pharisee, the son of a Pharisee
Preparation
　Ps. 23　Thou preparest a table before me
　Is. 40:1-8　Prepare ye the way of the Lord
　Ho. 6　His going forth is prepared as the morning
　Lu. 1:5-25　To make ready a people prepared for the Lord

Lu. 12:22-40 Let your loins be girded about

1 Co. 2 Things that God hath prepared

Tit. 3 Be ready to every good work

Presence

Ge. 3:1-21 Adam and Eve hid themselves from his presence

Ex. 33:12-23 My presence shall go with thee

1 Ch. 16:23-36 Glory and honour are in his presence

Ps. 100 Come before his presence with singing

Ps. 114 Tremble, thou earth, at the presence of the Lord

Zph. 1 Hold thy peace at the presence of the Lord God

Present, *See* Gift

Preservation

Ps. 5 Thou defendest them

Ps. 25 Let integrity and uprightness preserve me

Ps. 31 The Lord preserveth the faithful

Ps. 36 O Lord, thou preservest man and beast

Ps. 91 He shall give his angels charge over thee

Ps. 97 He preserveth the souls of his saints

Ps. 116 The Lord preserveth the simple

Lu. 17:20-37 Whosoever shall lose his life shall preserve it

Presumption

Pr. 27:1-11 Boast not thyself of to morrow

Pr. 30:1-14 O how lofty are their eyes!

Ob. 1-9 I will bring thee down from among the stars

2 Pe. 2:1-12 Presumptuous are they, self-willed

Price, *See* Cost

Pride

Jos. 6:12-20 The walls of Jericho fall

Pr. 13 By pride cometh contention

Is. 14:4-23 Thy pomp is brought down to the grave

Is. 28:1-6 Woe to the crown of pride

Da. 4:28-37 Is not this great Babylon?

Ob. :3-9 The pride of thine heart hath deceived thee

Mk. 7:14-23 Out of the heart of men proceeds pride

Lu. 18:1-14 I thank thee, that I am not as other men

Jn. 8:33-47 We be Abraham's seed

2 Co. 10 He that glorieth, let him glory in the Lord

2 Ti. 1:1-14 I am not ashamed

1 Jn. 5:1-15 Who is he that overcometh the world?

Priesthood, *See* Ministry

Principle

Ps. 119:17-32 Make me to understand the way of thy precepts

Da. 9:1-16 We have sinned by departing from thy precepts

2 Ti. 2:22-26 Follow righteousness, faith, charity, peace

He. 5 The first principles of the oracles of God

He. 6 The principles of the doctrine of Christ

Prison, *See* Captivity

Prize, *See* Reward

Proclamation

Ex. 33:12-23 I will proclaim the name of the Lord

Is. 61 Anointed to proclaim liberty to the captives

Je. 31:1-9 Publish ye, and say, O Lord, save thy people

Lu. 12:1-12 It shall be proclaimed upon the housetops

Prodigal

Pr. 18 The slothful is brother to the waster

Is. 55 Why spend money for that which is not bread?

Mat. 7:1-12 Cast not your pearls before swine

Mk. 14:3-9 Why was this waste of ointment made?

Lu. 15:11-32 The parable of the prodigal son

Profanity, *See* Curse

Profession

Is. 61 Men shall call you Ministers of our God

Ro. 1:1-12 Called to be saints

Ro. 1:16-25 Professing themselves wise, they became fools

1 Co. 7:17-24 As God hath called every one, so let him walk

1 Ti. 6 Thou hast professed a good profession

Tit. 1 They profess that they know God

He. 3 Apostle and High Priest of our profession

He. 4 Let us hold fast our profession

Profit

De. 4:25-40 Keep his commandments that it may go well

Pr. 10:1-16 Treasures of wickedness profit nothing

Pr. 14:23-35 In all labour there is profit

Ec. 5:8-17 The profit of the earth is for all

Is. 3:1-11 They shall eat the fruit of their doings

Mk. 8:34-38 What shall it profit a man?

Jn. 6:47-65 The flesh profiteth nothing

1 Ti. 6:1-16 Godliness with contentment is great gain

Tit. 3 Good works are profitable unto men

He. 12:1-11 He chastened us for our profit

Progress, *See* Advance

Prohibition

Ex. 20:1-17 The ten commandments

Le. 19:11-18 Thou shalt not lie one to another

Pr. 23:1-21 Be not among winebibbers

Ep. 5:6-21 Be not drunk with wine, wherein is excess

Promise

Ge. 9:8-17 I do set my bow in the cloud

Ge. 12:1-9 I will make thy name great

Ju. 2:1-10 I will never break my covenant with you

1 S. 1:9-11, 20-28 He shall be lent to the Lord

1 Ch. 17:1-15 I took thee from the sheepcote

Ec. 5:1-8 When thou vowest a vow unto God, pay it

Proof, *See* Evidence

Prophet

Nu. 11:24-30 Would that all the Lord's people were prophets

1 S. 3:1-18 Speak, Lord, for thy servant heareth

Mat. 11:1-15 A prophet, and more than a prophet

Lu. 1:57-80 Thou shalt be called the prophet of the Highest

Ac. 3:12-26 Ye are the children of the prophets

1 Co. 13 We know in part, and we prophesy in part

1 Th. 5 Despise not prophesyings

2 Pe. 1 Holy men of God spake as they were moved

Re. 19:1-10 His testimony is the spirit of prophecy

Propitiation, *See* Reconciliation

Prosperity

1 S. 2:1-11 The Lord maketh poor, and maketh rich

Ps. 1 Whatsoever he doeth shall prosper

Ps. 37:1-11 Fret not because of him who prospereth

Ps. 52 He trusted in the abundance of his riches

Ps. 62 If riches increase, set not your heart upon them

Ps. 73 The ungodly prosper in the world

Ps. 118 O Lord, I beeseech thee, send now prosperity

Ps. 122 They shall prosper that love thee

Ec. 7:11-22 In the day of prosperity be joyful

Mat. 6:19-34 Lay not up treasures upon earth

Lu. 1:46-55 The rich he hath sent empty away

Protection, *See* Security

Providence

Ge. 22:1-14 God will provide

Ex. 16:1-18 I will rain bread from heaven for you

Ps. 55 Cast thy burden upon the Lord, he shall sustain

Ps. 90:1-12 Our dwelling place in all generations

Mat. 6:5-15 Your father knoweth what things ye have need of

Mat. 6:24-34 Take no thought for your life

Lu. 12:13-21 Soul, thou hast much goods laid up

Ro. 8:1-28 All things work together for good

Prudence

Pr. 8 I wisdom dwell with prudence

Pr. 15 He that regardeth reproof is prudent

Pr. 18 The heart of the prudent getteth knowledge

Pr. 22 A prudent man foreseeth the evil, and hideth

Ho. 14 Who is prudent, and he shall know these things?

Lu. 10:17-24 Thou hast hid these things from the prudent

Ep. 1 He hath abounded in all wisdom and prudence

Psalm, *See* Hymn
Punishment
  1 K. 12:6-11 I will chastise you with scorpions
  Pr. 13:14-25 He that spareth his rod hateth his son
  Pr. 19 Chasten thy son while there is hope
  Pr. 26:1-10 A rod for the fool's back
  Je. 11:11-17 Behold, I will bring evil upon them
  Lu. 12:41-48 He shall be beaten with many stripes
  He. 12:1-14 No chastening seemeth to be joyous
Purification, *See* Purity
Purity
  Ps. 51 Wash me, and I shall be whiter than snow
  Is. 1:10-20 Wash you, make you clean
  Mat. 5:1-16 Blessed are the pure in heart
  Mat. 5:27-32 If thine eye offend thee, pluck it out
  Mat. 23:23-33 Cleanse first that which is within the cup

  1 Co. 5 Purge out the old leaven
  Ph. 4 Whatsoever things are pure, think on these things
  Tit. 1 Unto the pure all things are pure
  Ja. 1:19-27 To keep himself unspotted from the world
  1 Pe. 1:13-25 Love one another with a pure heart
  1 Jn. 3 Even as he is pure
  Re. 22 A pure river of water of life, clear as crystal
Purpose
  Ps. 17 I am purposed
  Lu. 4:16-21 He hath anointed me to preach the gospel
  Jn. 10:1-18 I am come that they might have life
  Ac. 26:1-19 I have appeared unto thee for this purpose
  2 Co. 9 According as he purposeth in his heart
  Ep. 3:1-12 According to the eternal purpose
  Ph. 3:13-16 I press toward the mark
  2 Ti. 1:1-9 According to his own purpose and grace

[Q]

Quality, *See* Character
Quarrel, *See* Strife
Quest
  Ge. 28:10-22 Surely the Lord is in this place
  Nu. 13:1-2, 17-27 Send thou men to search the land
  Ps. 34 Seek peace, and pursue it
  Am. 5:4-20 Seek the Lord, and ye shall live

  Mat. 2:1-12 There came wise men from the east
  Mat. 7:1-12 Seek, and ye shall find
  Mat. 13:44-52 Like unto a merchant man, seeking goodly pearls
  Mat. 18:1-14 The Son of man is come to save
  Jn. 12:20-36 We would see Jesus
Quickening, *See* Revival
Quiet, *See* Peace

[R]

Rabbi, *See* Master
Race Relations Sunday
  Jn. 15:8-17 Love one another
  Ac. 10:19-28 I should not call any man common
  Ac. 17:22-28 He hath made of one blood all nations
  Ro. 15:1-7 The strong must aid the weak
  Ga. 3:26-29 If ye be Christ's, then are ye Abraham's seed
  Col. 3:9-17 Where there is neither Greek nor Jew

Radiance, *See* Glory
Rage, *See* Anger
Raiment, *See* Clothes
Rain
  Ge. 7 The rain was upon the earth forty days
  Ps. 72 He shall come down like rain
  Eze. 34:20-31 There shall be showers of blessing
  Ho. 6 He shall come unto us as the rain
  Mat. 5:43-48 He sendeth rain on just and on the unjust

Rain *(cont.)*

Mat. 7:24-29 The rain descended, and beat upon that house

Rainbow, *See* Covenant

Rally Day

Ge. 35:1-14 I will make there an altar unto God

Ne. 4 The people had a mind to work

Ps. 111 Praise the Lord in the assembly

Is. 6 Here am I; send me

Eze. 43:18-27 They shall consecrate themselves

Jo. 2:15-32 Gather the people, sanctify the congregation

Mat. 18:15-20 Where two or three are gathered

Ac. 12:1-19 Many were gathered together praying

Ro. 12 Present your bodies a living sacrifice

He. 10:23-39 Not forsaking the assembling of ourselves

Ransom, *See* Christ, the Saviour

Readiness

Mat. 25:1-13 They that were ready went in

Mk. 14:26-42 The spirit truly is ready, but the flesh is weak

Lu. 1:5-23 A people prepared for the Lord

Lu. 12:31-40 Let your loins be girded about

Lu. 22:31-46 Lord, I am ready to go with thee

Jn. 7:1-9 Your time is always ready

Ac. 17:10-15 They received the word with all readiness

Ep. 6:10-17 The preparation of the gospel of peace

2 Ti. 4:1-8 I am now ready to be offered

1 Pe. 3:8-22 Ready always to give an answer

Re. 19:1-9 Ready for the marriage of the Lamb

Realization, *See* Completion

Reaping, *See* Harvest

Reason

Jb. 13 Hear now my reasoning

Is. 1:16-27 Come now, and let us reason together

Mk. 12:28-34 Love the Lord with with all thy mind

Ro. 7 Another law, warring against the law of my mind

1 Co. 14:1-15 I will pray with the understanding also

He. 8 I will put my laws into their mind

1 Pe. 3:8-22 The reason of the hope that is in you

Rebirth, *See* Birth, New

Rebuke, *See* Condemnation

Receptivity

Mat. 13:1-17 Blessed are your ears, for they hear

Lu. 8:4-15 Some seed fell on good ground

Lu. 8:37-40 They were all waiting for him

Ac. 17:10-15 They received the word with all readiness

1 Th. 2 Ye received it as the word of God

Recognition

Mat. 11:1-15 Art thou he that should come?

Mk. 5:1-15 They come to Jesus

Jn. 1:19-27 One whom ye know not

Jn. 17 Life eternal is to know thee

Ac. 9:1-9 Who art thou, Lord?

1 Co. 13 Then shall I know even as also I am known

Recollection, *See* Memory

Recompense, *See* Reward

Reconciliation

Ge. 33:1-15 Let me find grace in thy sight

2 Ch. 30:1, 6-13 The Lord your God is gracious and merciful

Mal. 4 He shall turn the heart of fathers to the children

Mat. 5:21-26 First be reconciled to thy brother

2 Co. 5 Be ye reconciled to God

Col. 1:1-21 Now hath he reconciled you

He. 2 To make reconciliation for the sins of the people

Reconstruction, *See* Restoration

Rectitude, *See* Character

Redemption, *See* Salvation

Reformation Sunday

Jn. 1:1-28 Grace for grace

Ro. 1:1-17 The just shall live by faith

1 Co. 2 Jesus Christ, and him crucified

Ep. 2:1-10 By grace are ye saved through faith

Ep. 6:10-18 Stand against the wiles of the devil

1 Th. 2 In trust with the gospel

2 Ti. 1:1-14 I know whom I have believed

He. 1 God hath spoken to us by his Son

He. 11:1-16 These all died in faith

Refuge

Nu. 35:9-15 Ye shall appoint you cities of refuge

2 S. 22:1-20 The Lord is my refuge, my saviour

Ps. 46 God is our refuge and strength

Ps. 62:1-8 God is a refuge for us

Is. 32:1-8 A man shall be as a hiding place

Regeneration, *See* Revival

Regret

Ps. 51 Against thee, thee only, have I sinned

Ps. 77 I remembered God, and was troubled

Da. 9:3-19 We have sinned, and have committed iniquity

Mat. 27:1-8 I have betrayed the innocent blood

Lu. 9:57-62 No man, looking back, is fit for the kingdom

Lu. 15:11-32 I have sinned against heaven, and before thee

Reign, *See* Dominion

Rejection

1 S. 8:1-9 They have not rejected thee, but me

Is. 53:1-9 He is despised and rejected of men

Mk. 7:1-13 Ye reject the commandment of God

Jn. 6:53-69 Many of the disciples went back

Jn. 12:37-50 He that rejecteth me hath one that judgeth him

Ro. 8:1-17 If he have not the Spirit of Christ, he is none of his

Rejoicing, *See* Joy

Reliance

Ps. 118 It is better to trust in the Lord

Na. 1 The Lord knoweth them that trust in him

Mat. 17:14-21 If ye have faith as a grain of mustard seed

Mk. 4:30-41 How is it that ye have no faith?

Mk. 9:14-29 All things are possible to him that believeth

Jn. 14:1-14 Ye believe in God, believe also in me

2 Co. 8 The great confidence which I have in you

Col. 2:1-9 Established in the faith

Relief, *See* Charity

Religion

Ro. 12:9-21 Overcome evil with good

2 Co. 13 Examine yourselves, whether ye be in the faith

Ga. 1 I profited in the Jews' religion

Ja. 1:19-27 Pure religion and undefiled

Jude 1-17 The faith once delivered unto the saints

Religious Education Week

De. 6:3-15 Teach them diligently unto thy children

Pr. 22:1-19 Train up a child in the way he should go

Is. 28:5-13 Precept upon precept

Mat. 28 Go ye therefore, and teach all nations

Lu. 2:39-52 The child grew, filled with wisdom

Jn. 3:1-17 We know that thou art a teacher

Ep. 6 Bring up your children in the nurture of God

1 Ti. 4 These things command and teach

Remembrance, *See* Memory

Remission, *See* Forgiveness

Remorse, *See* Repentance

Renewal, *See* Revival

Renunciation, *See* Sacrifice

Repentance

2 Ch. 33:9-19 He humbled himself greatly before God

Ps. 34 The Lord saveth such as be of a contrite spirit

Is. 55 Let the wicked forsake his way

Mat. 3 Repent ye: for the kingdom of heaven is at hand

Mat. 4:12-17 Jesus began to preach, and to say, Repent

Mat. 11:20-27 They repented not

Lu. 3:7-17 Bring forth therefore fruits worthy of repentance

Lu. 15:1-10 Joy in heaven over one sinner that repenteth

Lu. 15:11-32 Father, I have sinned against heaven

Lu. 18:9-14 God be merciful to me a sinner

Re. 2:1-7 Repent, and do the first works

Repose, *See* Rest

Reproach, *See* Condemnation

Reproof, *See* Condemnation

Reputation, *See* Best

Request, *See* Entreaty
Rescue, *See* Salvation
Resignation, *See* Contentment
Resolution, *See* Steadfastness
Responsibility, *See* Duty
Rest
  Ex. 23:1-12 On the seventh day thou shalt rest
  Ps. 23 He maketh me to lie down in green pastures
  Ps. 37:1-18 Rest in the Lord, and wait patiently for him
  Ps. 116 Return unto thy rest, O my soul
  Am. 6:1-6 Woe to them that are at ease in Zion
  Mat. 11:28-30 My yoke is easy
  He. 4 There remaineth a rest to the people of God
  Re. 14 That they may rest from their labours
Restoration
  Ps. 23 He restoreth my soul
  Ps. 51 Restore unto me the joy of thy salvation
  Is. 40:18-31 They shall renew their strength
  Is. 58:1-12 The restorer of paths to dwell in
  Je. 30:10-17 I will restore health unto thee
  Jo. 2:21-32 I will restore to you the years the locust hath eaten
  Hab. 3 Revive thy work in the midst of the years
  Ep. 4 Be renewed in the spirit of your mind
Restraint, *See* Compulsion
Result
  Ec. 11:1-4,6 Cast thy bread upon the waters
  Is. 5:1-6 My vineyard brought forth wild grapes
  Is. 32 The effect of righteousness shall be quietness
  Mat. 7:15-29 Ye shall know them by their fruits
  Mk. 4:26-29 As if a man should cast seed into the ground
  1 Co. 1:17-31 Lest the cross of Christ be made of none effect
  Ga. 5 The fruit of the Spirit is love, joy, peace
Resurrection
  Eze. 37:1-10 Can these bones live?
  Lu. 20:27-38 They are the children of the resurrection
  Jn. 5:17-31 All in the graves shall come forth

  Jn. 11:1-44 The raising of Lazarus
  Ac. 26:1-19 Why incredible that God should raise the dead?
  2 Co. 1 We should trust in God which raiseth the dead
  2 Co. 4 He shall raise up us also by Jesus
  Ep. 2 God hath raised us up together
  Col. 3:1-15 If ye then be risen with Christ
  He. 11:17-40 That they might obtain a better resurrection
  Re. 20 I saw the dead stand before God
Retribution, *See* Punishment
Return, *See* Restoration
Reunion, *See* Assembly
Revelation
  Is. 45:19-25 I have not spoken in secret
  Mk. 4:21-29 Nothing hid, which shall not be manifested
  Jn. 1:14-18 The only begotten Son hath declared him
  Jn. 16:1-20 The Spirit will guide you into all truth
  1 Co. 2 God hath revealed them unto us by his Spirit
  1 Co. 12:1-11 The manifestation of the Spirit
  2 Co. 3 With open face beholding the glory of God
  Ep. 1 He made known unto us the mystery of his will
Revenge
  Is. 35 Your God will come with vengeance
  Na. 1 The Lord revengeth, and is furious
  Mat. 5:38-48 Turn the other cheek
  Ro. 12 Vengeance is mine; I will repay
  Ro. 13 A revenger to execute wrath
  2 Th. 1 Taking vengeance on them that know not God
  Jude 1-12 Sodom suffered the vengeance of eternal fire
Reverence, *See* Worship
Revival
  2 Ch. 7:1-3,11-16 I will forgive their sin
  Ps. 51 Restore unto me the joy of thy salvation
  Ps. 85 Revive us again
  La. 5 Renew our days as of old
  Jo. 2:21-29 I will pour out my spirit
  Mi. 4:1-7 I will gather her that is driven out

Lu. 15:1-10 The lost sheep and the lost coin

Lu. 15:11-32 This thy brother was dead, and is alive

Jn. 3:1-17 Except a man be born again

Jn. 4:1-29 Jesus and the Samaritan woman

Ac. 2:1-13 They were all filled with the Holy Ghost

2 Co. 5:1-17 We must all appear before the judgment seat

1 Pe. 1:1-21 An inheritance reserved in heaven for you

Revolution

Ps. 2 The kings set themselves against the Lord

Is. 30:1-21 Woe to the rebellious children

Je. 5:19-24 This people hath a revolting heart

Eze. 20:33-49 I will purge out from among you the rebels

Mk. 13:1-8 There shall not be left one stone upon another

Reward

2 Ch. 25:5-9 The Lord is able to give thee much more

Ps. 19 In keeping of them there is great reward

Ps. 58 Verily there is a reward for the righteous

Is. 1:16-27 Every one followeth after rewards

Is. 62 Behold, his reward is with him

Mat. 10:16-42 He shall in no wise lose his reward

Mat. 25:14-23 I will make thee ruler over many things

Lu. 23:39-49 Remember me when thou comest into thy kingdom

Ga. 6 Whatsoever a man soweth he shall reap

Ph. 3 The prize of the high calling of God

2 Ti. 4:1-8 There is laid up for me a crown

Ja. 1 He shall receive the crown of life

Re. 14:1-13 Their works do follow them

Riches

De. 8:11-18 He giveth thee power to get wealth

Pr. 13:1-11 Wealth gotten by vanity

Mat. 6:19-34 Lay up treasures in heaven

Mat. 13:44-48 A treasure hid in a field

Mk. 10:17-27 Go thy way, sell whatsoever thou hast

Lu. 11:1-11 Seek, and ye shall find

Lu. 12:16-34 A treasure in the heavens that faileth not

Lu. 16:19-31 Dives and Lazarus

Lu. 19:1-10 The half of my goods I give to the poor

Ac. 2:41-47 They sold their possessions and goods

Ac. 3:1-10 Silver and gold have I none

1 Co. 3:10-23 All things are yours

1 Ti. 6:17-19 Trust not in uncertain riches, but in God

Re. 2:8-11 I know thy poverty (but thou art rich)

Right

Ju. 17 Every man did that which he thought right

Ps. 19 The statutes of the Lord are right

Ps. 51 Renew a right spirit within me

Lu. 12:49-59 Why of yourselves judge ye not what is right?

Re. 22 That they may have right to the tree of life

Righteousness, *See* Character

Ritual, *See* Ceremony

Rivalry

Ge. 25:20-34 Esau despised his birthright

Pr. 6 Jealousy is the rage of a man

Is. 19:1-4 They shall fight every one against his brother

Lu. 22:24-30 Which should be accounted the greatest

2 Co. 12 Lest there be envyings

Ph. 2:1-18 Let nothing be done through vainglory

2 Ti. 2:1-5 To be crowned he must strive lawfully

Ja. 5 Grudge not one against another

Robe, *See* Clothes

Rock

Ge. 28:10-22 He took the stones for his pillows

De. 32:1-14,30,31 He is the Rock

Ps. 27 He shall set me up upon a rock

Ps. 71 Thou art my rock

Is. 32 As the shadow of a great rock in a weary land

Is. 51:1-6 Look unto the rock whence ye are hewn

Mat. 7:21-29 The wise man built his house upon a rock

Rock *(cont.)*
Mat. 16:13-23 Thou art Peter and upon this rock will I build
Lu. 8:4-15 Some fell upon a rock
1 Co. 10 They drank of that spiritual Rock
1 Pe. 2:1-9 As lively stones, built up in a spiritual house
Rod, *See* Punishment
Room
Ps. 118 The Lord set me in a large place
Is. 49:18-23 The place is too strait for me
Is. 54 Enlarge the place of thy tent
Lu. 2:1-16 There was no room for them in the inn
Lu. 14:15-24 Yet there is room
Root
Pr. 12 The root of the righteous yieldeth fruit

Is. 11:1-9 A Branch shall grow out of his roots
Mat. 13:1-13 Because they had no root, they withered away
Ro. 11:16-36 If the root be holy, so are the branches
Ep. 3 Rooted and grounded in love
Col. 2 Rooted and built up in him
1 Ti. 6 The love of money is the root of all evil
Jude 1-13 Trees plucked up by the roots
Ruin, *See* Destruction
Rule, *See* Dominion
Rule, Golden
Le. 19:1-18 Thou shalt love thy neighbour as thyself
Mat. 7:1-12 Whatsoever ye would that men should do to you
Lu. 6:27-38 Do ye also to them likewise

[S]

Sabbath
Ex. 20:1-17 Remember the sabbath
Ps. 118 This is the day the Lord hath made
Mat. 12:1-13 Plucking corn on the sabbath
Mk. 2:23-28 The sabbath was made for man
Mk. 3:1-6 It is lawful to do good on the sabbath
Lu. 13:10-17 Because Jesus healed on the sabbath
Lu. 14:1-6 Is it lawful to heal on the sabbath?
Sacrament
Ec. 12:1-7 Remember thy Creator in the days of thy youth
Je. 1:1-10 I ordained thee a prophet unto the nations
Mat. 13:1-13 It is given unto you to know the mysteries
Mat. 19:1-9 What therefore God hath joined together
Mk. 14:13-16 Suffer the little children to come unto me
Ac. 2:38-41 Repent and be baptized
1 Co. 11:23-29 This cup is the new testament in my blood
Re. 14:1-13 Blessed are the dead which die in the Lord
Sacrifice
Mat. 10:16-39 He that loseth his life shall find it
Mk. 8:34-38 Whosoever shall lose his life shall save it

Lu. 9:51-62 Let the dead bury their dead
Lu. 14:25-33 Cost of discipleship
Jn. 10:10-15 I lay down my life for the sheep
Jn. 15:12-17 Greater love hath no man than this
Ac. 20:13-38 I count not life dear
Ro. 12 Present your bodies a living sacrifice
2 Co. 11:23-28 Paul's sufferings
Ph. 2:1-18 He became obedient unto death
2 Ti. 4 I am now ready to be offered
Sadness, *See* Sorrow
Safety, *See* Security
Saint
Jos. 3 Sanctify yourselves
1 S. 2:1-10 He will keep the feet of his saints
Ps. 37:1-29 The Lord forsaketh not his saints
Mk. 6:14-29 He was a holy man
Ro. 1:1-12 Called to be saints
Ep. 2 Ye are fellowcitizens with the saints
Ph. 4 All the saints salute you
Salvation
Ps. 31:1-5 Pull me out of the net
Ps. 34 This poor man cried
Ps. 103:1-5 He redeemeth thy life
Is. 35:1-10 The ransomed of the Lord shall return
Lu. 2:25-40 Mine eyes have seen thy salvation

Lu. 19:1-10 This day is salvation come to this house

Ac. 16:25-34 What must I do to be saved?

2 Co. 6:1-10 Now is the day of salvation

Ph. 2:1-13 Work out your salvation with fear and trembling

He. 2:1-9 If we neglect so great salvation

He. 7 He is able to save to the uttermost

Sanctification, *See* **Holiness**

Sanctuary

Ge. 28:10-22 Ascending and descending angels

Ge. 35:1-15 Make there an altar unto God

Ps. 11 The Lord is in his holy temple

Ps. 26 Lord, I have loved the habitation of thy house

Ps. 96 Strength and beauty are in his sanctuary

Is. 56 A house of prayer for all people

Lu. 2:41-52 They found him in the temple

Ac. 17:16-31 God dwelleth not in temples made with hands

1 Co. 3 The temple of God is holy, which temple ye are

1 Co. 6 Your body is the temple of the Holy Ghost

Ep. 2 The building groweth into a holy temple

Re. 7:9-17 They serve him day and night in his temple

Re. 21:10-27 I saw no temple therein

Satan

Jb. 1:1-12 Satan went forth from the presence of the Lord

Is. 14:4-23 How art thou fallen from heaven, O Lucifer!

Mat. 4:1-11 Get thee hence, Satan

Mk. 1:1-13 He was in the wilderness, tempted of Satan

Lu. 10:1-20 Even the devils are subject unto us

Jn. 8:33-59 Ye are of your father the devil

Ac. 26:1-19 To turn them from Satan unto God

1 Co. 10 The cup of the Lord, and the cup of devils

2 Co. 11:1-15 Satan is transformed into an angel of light

He. 2 That through death he might destroy the devil

Ja. 4 Resist the devil, and he will flee from you

1 Pe. 5 Your adversary the devil walketh about

1 Jn. 3:1-11 He that committeth sin is of the devil

Satisfaction, *See* **Contentment**

Saviour, *See* **Salvation**

Schism, *See* **Heresy**

Science

Pr. 8 Knowledge of witty inventions

Ec. 7 I applied mine heart to seek out wisdom

Is. 47 Wisdom and knowledge have perverted thee

Da. 1:3-7 Skilful in wisdom and understanding science

Ro. 15:1-14 Filled with all knowledge

1 Co. 2 The natural man receiveth not things of Spirit

1 Ti. 6 Avoiding oppositions of science

Scorn

Ps. 1 The seat of the scornful

Is. 53 He is despised and rejected of men

Mat. 18:1-10 Despise not one of these little ones

Mk. 10:32-34 They shall mock him and scourge him

Lu. 8:49-56 They laughed him to scorn

1 Th. 4 He despiseth not man, but God

He. 11:17-40 Cruel mockings and scourgings

Scourge, *See* **Punishment**

Scout

Nu. 13:17-33 They went up, and searched the land

Is. 40:1-8 Make straight in the desert a highway

Is. 40:28-31 They shall mount up with wings like eagles

Lu. 1:67-80 He was in the deserts

Lu. 12:31-40 Be ye therefore ready also

Jn. 1:19-28 The voice of one crying in the wilderness

Tit. 3 To be ready to every good work

He. 11:1-16 He went out, not knowing whither he went

Scribe

Mat. 5:1-20 Your righteousness must exceed that of scribes

Mat. 7:24-29 As one having authority, and not as the scribes

Scribe *(cont.)*

Mat. 13:47-58 A scribe instructed unto the kingdom of heaven
Mk. 11:15-19 The scribes sought to destroy him
Mk. 12:38-44 Beware of the scribes
1 Co. 1:19-31 Where is the wise? Where is the scribe?

Scripture, *See* Bible
Sea, *See* Ocean
Search, *See* Quest
Secrecy

Ps. 44 He knoweth the secrets of the heart
Ps. 90 Our secret sins are in the light
Ps. 91 He that dwelleth in the secret place
Ec. 12 God shall bring every secret thing to judgment
Mat. 26:17-30 One of you shall betray me
Lu. 8:16-18 The secret shall be made manifest
Lu. 12:1-12 Nothing covered that shall not be revealed
Jn. 3:14-36 Every one that doeth evil hateth the light
Ac. 26:19-32 This thing was not done in a corner
Ro. 2:11-23 God shall judge the secrets of men
Ro. 13 Let us put off the works of darkness

Sect, *See* Division
Security

De. 33:26-29 Underneath are the everlasting arms
Ps. 4 Thou, Lord, makest me dwell in safety
Ps. 91 He shall give his angels charge over thee
Is. 11:1-9 The wolf shall dwell with the lamb
Is. 26:1-13 Thou wilt keep him in perfect peace
Is. 32 My people shall dwell in sure dwellings
Mi. 4:1-8 None shall make them afraid
He. 13 I will not fear what man shall do
1 Pe 3:8-22 Who will harm you, if you follow the good?

Seed

Ge. 8 Seedtime and harvest shall not cease
Ge. 22:1-18 In thy seed shall all nations be blessed

Is. 32 Blessed are ye that sow beside all waters
Lu. 8:4-15 The seed is the word of God
1 Co. 3 I planted, Apollos watered, God gave increase
1 Co. 15:35-50 Sown in weakness, raised in power
Ga. 6 He that soweth to the Spirit shall reap

Segregation

Ge. 9:18-27 A servant of servants shall he be
Ge. 11:1-9 The tower of Babel
Le. 20:22-26 I have severed you from other people
Ac. 2:1-12 The day of Pentecost
Ac. 10:9-28 No man is common or unclean
Ac. 11:1-18 What God hath cleansed is not common
1 Co. 12:14-27 Many members, yet one body
Ga. 4:22-31 Cast out the bond-woman and her son
Ep. 2:11-22 The middle wall of partition
Col. 3:1-11 There is neither bond nor free

Selection, *See* Choice
Self-Confidence, *See* Reliance
Self-Control

Ps. 141 Set a watch, O Lord, before my lips
Pr. 13 He that keepeth his mouth keepeth his life
Pr. 16 The slow to anger is better than the mighty
Pr. 25 He that hath no rule over his own spirit
Ro. 6 Let not sin reign in your mortal body
1 Co. 9 The man that striveth for mastery is temperate
Ga. 5 The fruit of the Spirit is temperance
Ja. 3 Able to bridle the whole body
Re. 21:1-7 He that overcometh shall inherit all things

Self-Denial, *See* Sacrifice
Selfishness

Jb. 1:1-12 Doth Job fear God for nought?
Pr. 11 The people shall curse him that withholdeth
Ho. 10 Israel bringeth forth fruit unto himself
Mat. 25:31-46 I was a stranger, and ye took me not in

Lu. 12:13-21 Beware of covetousness

1 Co. 13 Charity seeketh not her own

Ph. 2:1-18 Look not every man on his own things

Ph. 2:19-24 All seek their own

Self-Realization, *See* Life, the Full

Self-Sacrifice, *See* Sacrifice

Self-Satisfaction, *See* Pride

Sensuality, *See* Lust

Sentiment, *See* Emotion

Separation, *See* Division

Serenity, *See* Peace

Servant, *See* Service

Servant, Suffering

Is. 42:1-12 He shall not fail nor be discouraged

Is. 53:1-12 Despised and rejected

Service

Mat. 24:45-51 Who then is a faithful and wise servant?

Mat. 25:14-30 Well done, good and faithful servant

Mat. 25:34-46 Inasmuch as ye have done it

Mk. 9:33-37 He who would be first must be servant of all

Jn. 13:1-17 He began to wash the disciples' feet

Jn. 21:15-17 Feed my sheep

Ro. 12 Your reasonable service

Ro. 15:1-13 We ought to bear the infirmities of the weak

1 Co. 9:19-27 I made myself servant unto all

Ep. 6:1-13 With good will doing service

He. 12:1-14 Lift up the hands which hang down

Service, Social

Le. 19:32-37 Just balances, just weights

Ps. 144 That there be no complaining in our streets

Ec. 5:8-20 The profit of the earth is for all

Is. 41:6-7 They helped every one his neighbour

Am. 5:14-24 Establish judgment in the gate

Ac. 4:31-37 Unto every man according as he had need

Ac. 6:1-4 Their widows were neglected

2 Co. 9:1-7 As touching the ministering to the saints

Col. 4 Give unto your servants that which is just

Severity, *See* Cruelty

Sex

Ge. 1:26-28 Male and female created he them

Ge. 2:15-25 A man shall cleave unto his wife

Jn. 6:44-65 The spirit quickeneth; the flesh profiteth nothing

1 Co. 6:15-20 Glorify God in your body

Ga. 3:21-29 There is neither male nor female

Ga. 5 The flesh lusteth against the Spirit

2 Ti. 2 Flee youthful lusts

Shadow

Ps. 17 Hide me under the shadow of thy wings

Ps. 57 In the shadow of thy wings will I make my refuge

Ps. 91 Under the shadow of the Almighty

Ps. 102:1-12 My days are like a shadow that declineth

Ps. 121 The Lord is thy shade upon thy right hand

Is. 32 As the shadow of a great rock in a weary land

Ac. 5:12-16 The shadow of Peter

He. 10:1-9 The law having a shadow of good things to come

Shame

Ge. 3:1-13 I was naked and I hid myself

Ps. 44:8-26 Thou makest us a byword

Ps. 69:1-20 I was the song of the drunkards

Je. 23:33-40 I will bring an everlasting reproach upon you

Ho. 4:1-11 I will change their glory into shame

Lu. 9:23-27 Of him shall the Son of man be ashamed

Ro. 1:1-17 I am not ashamed of the gospel

Sheep, *See* Shepherd

Shepherd

Ge. 4:1-8 Abel was a keeper of sheep

Ps. 23 The Lord is my shepherd

Ps. 95 We are the people of his pasture

Je. 23:1-8 Pastors that scatter the sheep

Eze. 34 David shall be their shepherd

Mat. 9:27-38 Scattered abroad as sheep having no shepherd

Mat. 12:10-21 How much better is a man than a sheep?

Shepherd *(cont.)*

Lu. 2:1-20 The shepherds returned, glorifying and praising God

Jn. 10:1-18 I know my sheep

Shield, *See* Security

Shortness, *See* Brevity

Sickness

Ps. 103 He healeth all thy diseases

Je. 8:18-22 Is there no balm in Gilead?

Mat. 4:23-25 He healed them

Mk. 2:1-17 They that are sick need the physician

Lu. 18:35-43 Thy faith hath saved thee

Ja. 5:1-16 The prayer of faith shall save the sick

Sight

2 K. 6:1-17 Open his eyes, that he may see

Jb. 29 I was eyes to the blind

Ps. 115 Eyes have they, but they see not

Ps. 146 The Lord openeth the eyes of the blind

Is. 11:1-9 He shall not judge after the sight of his eyes

Mat. 5:1-12 The pure in heart shall see God

Mat. 18:7-14 If thine eye offend thee, pluck it out

Lu. 11:29-36 The light of the body is the eye

Lu. 18:31-43 Jesus said unto him, Receive thy sight

Jn. 9:1-25 Whereas I was blind, now I see

2 Co. 5 We walk by faith, not by sight

Re. 1 Every eye shall see him

Sign, *See* Marvel

Silence

Ne. 8:9-12 Hold your peace, for the day is holy

Jb. 4 There was silence, and I heard a voice

Ps. 39 I will keep my mouth with a bridle

Ps. 46 Be still, and know that I am God

Pr. 17:17-28 He that hath knowledge spareth his words

Ec. 3:1-8 A time to keep silence

Is. 42:1-12 He shall not cry

Zph. 1 Hold thy peace at the presence of the Lord God

Mat. 27:11-14 He answered him to never a word

1 Th. 4:1-12 Study to be quiet

Re. 8 There was silence in heaven

Simplicity

Ps. 19 Making wise the simple

Ps. 116 The Lord preserveth the simple

Pr. 1:20-33 How long will ye love simplicity?

Ro. 12:6-21 He that giveth, let him do it with simplicity

2 Co. 1:1-12 In simplicity and godly sincerity

2 Co. 11:1-6 The simplicity that is in Christ

Sin

Ge. 3 The serpent beguiled me and I did eat

Ge. 6:1-8 The wickedness of man was great

Ps. 19 Presumptuous sins

Ps. 32 His transgression is forgiven

Ps. 103:8-18 He will not always chide

Is. 1:16-20 Your sins shall be white as snow

Is. 13:19-22 Babylon shall be as Sodom and Gomorrah

Is. 59:1-19 Their feet run to evil

Mal. 2:11-17 Ye have wearied the Lord

Mat. 6:5-15 Forgive us our debts

Mat. 12:43-45 The last state is worse than the first

Mk. 3:22-30 He that blasphemes against the Holy Ghost

Lu. 7:36-50 Her sins are forgiven, for she loved much

Lu. 15:1-10 The lost sheep and the lost coin

Lu. 15:11-32 He wasted his substance with riotous living

Lu. 18:9-14 God be merciful to me a sinner

Jn. 8:1-11 Go, and sin no more

Ro. 6 The wages of sin is death

Ro. 12 Overcome evil with good

1 Jn. 1 The blood of Jesus cleanseth us from all sin

Re. 17:1-5 Babylon, the great, the mother of harlots

Sin, Original

Ro. 5 By one man's offence death reigned

Ro. 7 Who shall deliver me from this death?

1 Co. 15:1-22 In Adam all die

Ja. 1 Sin, when it is finished, bringeth death

Sincerity
Jos. 24:14-25 Serve the Lord in sincerity
Mat. 6:1-8 Thou shalt not be as the hypocrites are
Mat. 7:15-28 Ye shall know them by their fruits
Ro. 12 Let love be without dissimulation
1 Co. 5 The unleavened bread of sincerity and truth
2 Co. 8:1-9 To prove the sincerity of your love
Ep. 6:1-17 Doing the will of God from the heart
Ph. 1:1-11 That ye may be sincere
Tit. 2 Showing uncorruptness, gravity, sincerity
1 Pe. 2:19-25 No guile was found in his mouth

Sinlessness, *See* Holiness
Skepticism, *See* Doubt
Skill, *See* Ability
Sky, *See* Heaven
Slander
Pr. 11 He destroyeth his neighbour with his mouth
Pr. 12 The tongue of the wise is health
Pr. 17 He that repeateth a matter separateth friends
Pr. 26 Where there is no talebearer, strife ceaseth
1 Ti. 4 Refuse profane and old wives' fables
2 Pe. 2:1-15 Not afraid to speak evil of dignities

Slavery, *See* Captivity
Sleep, *See* Rest
Sloth, *See* Idleness
Smallness
Pr. 6:6-11 Yet a little sleep, a little slumber
Pr. 16:1-9 Better a little with righteousness
Pr. 30:24-28 There be four things which are little
Is. 28:9-17 Here a little, and there a little
Is. 60 A little one shall become a thousand
Mi. 5 Though thou be little
Lu. 19:12-26 Thou hast been faithful in a very little
1 Co. 5 A little leaven leaveneth the whole lump
Ja. 3 The tongue is little, and boasteth

Snow, *See* Winter

Society, *See* Communion; Community, Christian
Solace, *See* Comfort
Soldier
Ex. 15:1-13 The Lord is a man of war
2 Ch. 20:14-19 The battle is not yours, but God's
Is. 2:1-5 Neither shall they learn war any more
Is. 31 Woe to them that trust in chariots
Mat. 8:5-13 I have soldiers under me
Ep. 6:10-17 Put on the whole armor of God
2 Ti. 2:3-7 Endure hardness as a good soldier

Solicitude
Ps. 55 He shall sustain thee
Ps. 119:129-144 Rivers of water run down mine eyes
Mat. 14:14-21 Jesus was moved with compassion
Mat. 23:34-39 As a hen gathereth her chickens
Mk. 4:35-41 Master, carest thou not that we perish?
Ac. 20:28-38 I warned you every day with tears
Ro. 9:1-18 I have great heaviness and sorrow
Ro. 15:1-7 Bear the infirmities of the weak
Ga. 6 Bear ye one another's burdens
He. 4 Touched with the feeling of our infirmities
He. 5 Compassion on the ignorant
1 Pe. 5 He careth for you
Jude 17-25 Of some have compassion

Solitude
Ge. 2:18-25 It is not good that man should be alone
1 K. 19:1-18 Now, O Lord, take away my life
Ps. 68:1-8 God setteth the solitary in families
Ps. 102 As a sparrow alone upon the house top
Ec. 4 How can one be warm alone?
Is. 35 The solitary place shall be glad for them
Is. 63:1-6 I have trodden the winepress alone
La. 1:1-12 How doth the city sit solitary!

Solitude (cont.)

Mat. 4:1-11 Jesus was led up into the wilderness
Mat. 26:36-46 Jesus in Gethsemane
Mk. 1:35-45 He departed into a solitary place
Mk. 6:30-46 Come ye into a desert place
Jn. 16:1-7, 16-20, 32, 33 Ye shall leave me alone

Son

Is. 9:1-7 Unto us a son is given
Am. 2:6-16 I raised up of your sons for prophets
Mat. 21:28-41 Last of all he sent unto them his son
Lu. 11:1-13 Will a father give his son a stone for bread?
Lu. 12:49-57 The father shall be divided against the son
Lu. 15:11-32 My son was dead, and is alive again
Jn. 19:25-27 Woman, behold thy son!

Song, See Hymn

Sorrow

Ps. 130 Out of the depths have I cried unto thee
Ec. 7:1-10 Sorrow is better than laughter
Is. 61 The oil of joy for mourning
Mat. 26:36-46 My soul is exceeding sorrowful
Lu. 6:20-26 Blessed are ye that weep now
Jn. 16:1-20 Your sorrow shall be turned to joy
2 Co. 6 As sorrowful, yet always rejoicing
2 Co. 7 The sorrow of the world worketh death
Ja. 4 Let your laughter be turned to mourning
Re. 7:9-17 God shall wipe away all tears from their eyes

Soul

Ge. 2:1-7 Man became a living soul
De. 6:1-15 Thou shalt love the Lord with all thy soul
Ps. 23 He restoreth my soul
Ps. 42 Why art thou cast down, O my soul?
Ps. 107:1-9 He satisfieth the longing soul
Ps. 121 The Lord shall preserve thy soul
Pr. 11 He that winneth souls is wise

Eze. 18:1-9 Behold, all souls are mine
Lu. 1:46-55 My soul doth magnify the Lord
Lu. 9:23-27 What is a man advantaged?
Lu. 12:13-31 This night thy soul shall be required of thee
1 Co. 15:39-50 The last Adam was made a quickening spirit
2 Co. 4 The inward man is renewed day by day
1 Pe. 2:19-25 The Shepherd and Bishop of your souls

Sovereignty, See Dominion
Speech, See Conversation
Speed, See Haste

Spirit

Pr. 20 The spirit of man is the candle of the Lord
Mat. 5:1-12 Blessed are the poor in spirit
Jn. 6:53-65 The words that I speak unto thee are spirit
1 Co. 2 The Spirit searcheth all things
1 Co. 15:39-55 The natural body and the spiritual body
Ga. 5 Let us also walk in the Spirit
Ep. 4:1-16 There is one body and one Spirit
1 Th. 5 Quench not the Spirit
He. 1 He maketh his angels spirits
1 Jn. 4 Try the spirits whether they are of God

Spirit, Fruit of

Mat. 7:7-20 Ye shall know them by their fruits
Ro. 8:1-14 To be spiritually minded is life and peace
Ga. 5 The fruit of the Spirit is love, joy, peace
Ga. 6 He that soweth to the Spirit shall reap
Ep. 5:1-14 The fruit of the Spirit is in all goodness

Spirit, Holy

Is. 61:1-3 The Spirit of the Lord God is upon me
Lu. 4:16-24 The Spirit of the Lord is upon me
Jn. 3:1-13 That which is born of the Spirit is spirit
Jn. 14:15-31 The Comforter will teach you all things
Jn. 16 The Spirit will guide you into all truth
Ac. 2:1-13 They were all filled with the Holy Ghost

Ac. 4:8-12 Peter was filled with the Holy Ghost

Ac. 19:1-12 Have ye received the Holy Ghost?

Ro. 15:13-25 Sanctified by the Holy Ghost

1 Co. 12:1-13 By one Spirit we are all baptized into one body

Ga. 5 Walk in the Spirit

1 Jn. 5 It is the Spirit that beareth witness

Jude 20-25 Praying in the Holy Ghost

Splendor, *See* Glory

Spring

Ps. 1 He shall be like a tree

Ps. 65 Thou visitest the earth and waterest it

Ps. 104 Thou renewest the face of the earth

Ec. 3 There is a time to plant

S. of S. 2 Lo, the winter is past

Is. 41:10-20 I will make the dry land springs of water

Is. 49:1-12 He shall lead them by the springs of water

Is. 61 The earth bringeth forth her bud

Is. 65:17-25 I create new heavens and a new earth

Lu. 8:4-15 The parable of the sower

Ro. 12 Be ye transformed by the renewing of your mind

Ga. 6:1-9 What a man soweth, that shall he also reap

Star, *See* Heaven

Starvation, *See* Famine

State, *See* Nation

Statute, *See* Commandment

Steadfastness

Ps. 78:1-39 They were not steadfast in his covenant

Ps. 90 Our dwelling place in all generations

Mat. 10:16-42 He that endureth to the end shall be saved

Lu. 9:51-62 He steadfastly set his face

Jn. 15:1-15 Continue ye in my love

Ac. 2:37-47 They continued steadfastly

1 Co. 16:1-13 Stand fast in the faith

Ga. 6 Let us not be weary in well doing

He. 10:1-25 Hold fast without wavering

He. 12:22-29 A kingdom which cannot be moved

Ja. 1:1-8 A double minded man is unstable

Re. 3:1-13 Hold that fast which thou hast

Steward, *See* Service

Stillness, *See* Peace

Stomach, *See* Bread

Stone, *See* Rock

Stranger

De. 10:12-22 Love ye therefore the stranger

Ru. 2:4-13 Go not to glean in another field

Ps. 146 The Lord preserveth the strangers

Ep. 2 Now therefore ye are no more strangers

He. 11:1-16 They confessed that they were strangers

He. 13 Be not forgetful to entertain strangers

1 Pe. 2 I beseech you as strangers

Strength, *See* Health

Strictness, *See* Bigotry

Strife

Le. 26:21-39 I will bring a sword upon you

Ps. 144 The Lord teacheth my hands to war

Pr. 20 It is an honour to cease from strife

Pr. 25:8-28 A soft tongue breaketh the bone

Pr. 28:17-28 A proud heart stirreth up strife

Is. 40:1-11 Her warfare is accomplished

Jo. 1 Alas for the day!

Jo. 3:9-18 Beat your plowshares into swords

Mat. 5:43-48 Love your enemies

Mat. 10:34-42 I came not to send peace, but a sword

Lu. 21:5-24 Nation shall rise against nation

1 Co. 16:1-14 Quit you like men, be strong

2 Co. 10 The weapons of our warfare are not carnal

Ep. 6:10-17 The whole armour of God

1 Ti. 6:11-21 Fight the good fight of faith

2 Ti. 2:14-21 Strive not about words to no profit

2 Ti. 2:22-26 The servant of the Lord must not strive

2 Ti. 4:1-8 I have fought a good fight

Strife *(Cont.)*

Tit. 3:1-11 Avoid foolish questions
Re. 9 He opened the bottomless pit
Re. 12:7-17 There was war in heaven
Struggle, *See* Strife
Study, *See* Instruction
Stumbling-Block, *See* Obstacle
Subjection, *See* Captivity
Submission, *See* Obedience
Suffering, *See* Pain
Suffering, Vicarious

Is. 53:1-9 The Lord hath laid on him the iniquity of us all
Ep. 1:1-14 We have redemption through his blood
He. 9 Christ was offered to bear the sins of many
1 Pe. 2:11-25 Christ also suffered for us
1 Pe. 3:8-22 The just for the unjust
1 Jn. 1 The blood of Jesus cleanseth us from all sin
1 Jn. 2:1-17 He is the propitiation for our sins
Summer

Ge. 8:15-22 Summer and winter shall not cease
Ps. 74 Thou hast made summer and winter
Pr. 6:6-11 The ant provideth her meat in the summer
Pr. 10:1-14 He that gathereth in summer is a wise son
Ec. 11 A pleasant thing it is to behold the sun
Je. 8:18-22 The harvest is past, the summer is ended
Lu. 21:29-38 Ye know that summer is now nigh at hand
Summit, *See* Mountain
Summons, *See* Call
Sun

Ge. 1:14-19 God made the greater light to rule the day
Ps. 19 He hath set a tabernacle for the sun
Ps. 84 The Lord God is a sun and shield
Ps. 121 The sun shall not smite thee by day

Ps. 136:1-9 He made the sun to rule by day
Ps. 139:1-12 The night shineth as the day
Ec. 11 It is a pleasant thing to behold the sun
Mat. 13:1-9; 36-43 Then shall the righteous shine as the sun
1 Co. 15:39-58 There is one glory of the sun
Re. 21:9-27 The city had no need of the sun
Sunday

Ex. 20:1-17 Six days shalt thou labour
Ps. 73:12-28 It is good to draw near to God
Ps. 118:14-29 This is the day which the Lord hath made
Mk. 16:1-11 Jesus is risen on the first day of the week
Ro. 14:1-13 One man esteemeth one day above another
Sunday, Palm, *See* Palm Sunday
Sunrise, *See* Morning
Sunset, *See* Evening
Superiority, *See* Chief
Superstition, *See* Gods
Supper, the Last, *See* Communion, Service of
Supper, the Lord's, *See* Communion, Service of
Supplication, *See* Entreaty
Supremacy, *See* Chief
Surprise, *See* Astonishment
Sweetness

Ju. 14:12-18 Out of the strong came forth sweetness
Ps. 19 His judgments are sweeter than the honeycomb
Ps. 104:24-35 My meditation of him shall be sweet
Ps. 119:97-112 How sweet are thy words to my taste!
Pr. 13:12-25 Desire accomplished is sweet to the soul
Ec. 5:9-20 The sleep of a labouring man is sweet
Is. 5:20-30 Woe unto them that put bitter for sweet
Swiftness, *See* Haste
Sympathy, *See* Solicitude
Synagogue, *See* Church

[T]

Tabernacle, *See* Sanctuary
Talent, *See* Ability
Talk, *See* Conversation
Tardiness
　Pr. 6:6-11 Go to the ant, thou sluggard
　Je. 8:13-22 The summer is ended, and we are not saved
　Mat. 25:1-13 The parable of the ten virgins
　Mat. 25:31-46 Lord, when saw we thee athirst?
　Ac. 24:22-27 When I have a convenient season
Task, *See* Labor Day
Taste
　Ps. 34 O taste and see that the Lord is good
　Ps. 119:97-112 How sweet are thy words to my taste!
　Mat. 16:24-28 Some here shall not taste of death
　Lu. 14:25-35 If the salt has lost its savor
　Col. 2 Touch not; taste not; handle not
　He. 2 Jesus tasted death for every man
Teaching, *See* Education
Tear, *See* Sorrow
Temperance Sunday
　1 K. 20:13-21 A battle lost by drunkenness
　Pr. 23:15-25 Be not among winebibbers
　Pr. 23:29-35 Who hath woe? who hath contentions?
　Is. 5:8-24 Mighty to drink wine
　Is. 28:1-8 They have erred through wine
　Ro. 13:12-14 Not in rioting and drunkenness
　Ro. 14 None of us liveth to himself
　1 Co. 6:9-20 Drunkards shall not inherit the kingdom
　Ga. 5:16-26 The fruit of the Spirit is temperance
　2 Pe. 1:1-11 Add to knowledge temperance
Temple, *See* Sanctuary
Temptation
　Ge. 3:1-6 The serpent deceives Eve
　Mat. 4:1-11 The temptation of Jesus
　Mat. 6:5-15 Lead us not into temptation

Mat. 26:36-58 Watch that ye enter not into temptation
Lu. 4:1-13 He was forty days tempted of the devil
Lu. 22:39-46 Pray, lest ye enter into temptation
1 Co. 10:1-13 With the temptation a way to escape
Ep. 6:10-17 That ye may be able to withstand
Ja. 1:1-15 Count it all joy when ye fall into temptation
2 Pe. 3:9-18 Beware lest ye fall from your own steadfastness
Re. 3:7-13 I will keep thee from the hour of temptation
Test
　Ge. 32:24-32 There wrestled a man with him
　Ju. 7:1-8 Gideon's three hundred men
　Pr. 16 The Lord weigheth the spirits
　Am. 7 I will set a plumbline in the midst of my people
　Mal. 3:1-18 Prove me now herewith
　Mat. 16:21-28 To every man according to his works
　Ro. 12 Prove what is the perfect will of God
　1 Th. 5 Prove all things; hold fast that which is good
　1 Jn. 4 Try the spirits whether they are of God
Testament, New
　Je. 31:31-34 I will make a new covenant
　Lu. 22:7-23 This cup is the new testament in my blood
　2 Co. 3 We are ministers of the new testament
　Ep. 2 Ye were strangers from the covenants of promise
　He. 7 Jesus became the surety of a better testament
　He. 8 He hath made the first covenant old
　He. 12:18-29 Jesus the mediator of the new covenant
Testament, Old
　Ge. 6:13-22 With thee will I establish my covenant
　Ge. 9:1-17 My bow shall be for a token of a covenant
　Ge. 17:1-14 My covenant shall be in your flesh
　Je. 50:1-5 A perpetual covenant with the Lord

Testimony, *See* Witness
Text, *See* Bible
Thanklessness, *See* Ingratitude
Thanksgiving
Ex. 16:3-15 I will rain bread from heaven for you
De. 8 When thou hast eaten, thou shalt bless God
1 S. 2:1-11 My heart rejoiceth in the Lord
1 Ch. 29:10-14 All things come of thee
Ps. 22:4, 5, 22-31 Our fathers trusted in thee
Ps. 23 My cup runneth over
Ps. 33 Blessed the nation whose God is the Lord
Ps. 34:1-10 I will bless the Lord at all times
Ps. 67 Let all the people praise thee
Ps. 77 God gave ear unto me
Ps. 100 Enter into his gates with thanksgiving
Ps. 103 Forget not all his benefits
Ps. 107:1-22 O give thanks unto the Lord
Ps. 111 The Lord is full of compassion
Ps. 116 I will offer the sacrifice of thanksgiving
Ps. 117 Praise him, all ye people
Ps. 136 His mercy endureth forever
Ps. 139 They are more in number than the sand
Ps. 147:5-20 Sing unto the Lord with thanksgiving
Ps. 150 Praise God in his sanctuary
Is. 5:1-12 My well-beloved hath a vineyard
Is. 9:2-7 The joy in harvest
Mat. 11:25-30 I thank thee, Lord of heaven and earth
Mat. 26:26-28 He took the cup, and gave thanks
Lu. 8:26-39 The great things Jesus had done
Lu. 17:11-19 Where are the nine?
2 Co. 9 His unspeakable gift
Ep. 5 Giving thanks always for all things
Ph. 4:1-13 By prayer and supplication with thanksgiving
1 Th. 5:6-18 In every thing give thanks
1 Ti. 6:17-19 Be not highminded
Re. 5:8-14 Worthy is the Lamb that was slain
Thirst, *See* Desire

Thorn
Is. 55 Instead of the thorn the fir tree
Je. 12:1-13 They have sown wheat, but shall reap thorns
Mat. 7:15-20 Do men gather grapes of thorns
Mat. 27:29-37 They put a crown of thorns on his head
Lu. 8:4-15 Some fell among thorns
2 Co. 12:1-10 A thorn in the flesh
Thought, *See* Meditation
Tidings, *See* Gospel
Time
Ps. 34 I will bless the Lord at all times
Ps. 90 Our dwelling place in all generations
Ec. 3 He made everything beautiful in his time
Ec. 9:11-18 Time and chance happeneth to them all
Mat. 16:1-4 Can ye not discern the signs of the times?
1 Co. 7:29-40 The fashion of this world passeth away
Ga. 4 Ye observe days, and months, and times
2 Pe. 3 One day with the Lord is as a thousand years
Timidity, *See* Fear
Tithe
Ge. 28:10-22 I will surely give the tenth unto thee
Le. 27:30-34 The tenth shall be holy unto the Lord
Mal. 3:8-10 Will a man rob God?
Mat. 23:23-33 Ye pay tithes, but have omitted other things
Lu. 18:9-14 I give tithes of all that I possess
Today
Ex. 32:15-35 Consecrate yourselves today unto the Lord
Ps. 118 This is the day which the Lord hath made
Mat. 6:5-18 Give us this day our daily bread
Lu. 23:39-49 Today shalt thou be with me in paradise
2 Co. 6 Now is the day of salvation
He. 3:1-15 While it is called today
Toil, *See* Labor Sunday
Tolerance, *See* Charity
Tomb, *See* Death
Tomorrow
Pr. 27 Boast not thyself of tomorrow
Is. 22:1-14 Let us eat and drink; for tomorrow we die

Mat. 6:24-34 Take therefore no
thought for the morrow
Ja. 4 Ye know not what shall be
on the morrow
Tongue, *See* Conversation
Torment, *See* Pain
Tower, *See* Security
Trade, *See* Business
Tradition
Pr. 23:1-11 Remove not the old
landmark
Mat. 5:21-48 But I say unto you
Mat. 15:1-20 Why do they trans-
gress the tradition?
Jn. 4:1-26 Our fathers worshipped
in this mountain
Ac. 16:16-24 They teach customs
which are not lawful for us
Ga. 1 I was zealous of the tradi-
tions of my fathers
Tragedy, *See* Adversity
Training, *See* Education
Tranquillity, *See* Peace
Transfiguration
Mat. 17:1-8 He was transfigured
before them
Mk. 9:2-10 This is my beloved Son:
hear him
Transformation, *See* Change
Transgression, *See* Sin
Travail, *See* Trouble
Travel, *See* Journey
Treachery, *See* Betrayal
Treason, *See* Betrayal
Treasure, *See* Riches
Tree
Ps. 1 Like a tree planted by the
rivers of water
Mat. 7:15-29 Every good tree bring-
eth forth good fruit
Ga. 3:1-13 Cursed is every one
that hangeth on a tree
1 Pe. 2:11-25 He bare our sins in
his own body on the tree
Re. 2:1-7 I will give him to eat of
the tree of life
Re. 22 The leaves of the tree were
for healing
Trial, *See* Trouble
Tribulation, *See* Trouble
Trinity
Jn. 16:7-15 The Father, the Spirit
of truth, and I
2 Co. 13 Jesus Christ, God, the
Holy Ghost
Ep. 2 Through him we come by
one Spirit to the Father
1 Jn. 5:1-13 The Father, the Word,
and the Holy Ghost

Triumph, *See* Victory
Trouble
Ge. 42:29-38 All these things are
against me
Ps. 3 I will not be afraid of ten
thousands
Ps. 18:1-19 He drew me out of
many waters
Ps. 46 God is a very present help
in trouble
Ps. 137 By the rivers of Babylon
we wept
Is. 54:1-10 With great mercies
will I gather thee
Mat. 5:1-12 Blessed are ye, when
men shall persecute you
Jn. 14:1-14 Let not your heart be
troubled
Ac. 14:19-28 Through much trib-
ulation we enter the kingdom
2 Co. 4 Our light affliction worketh
glory for us
2 Ti. 1 Partaker of the afflictions
of the gospel
2 Ti. 2:1-9 I suffer trouble
1 Pe. 5 Casting all your care upon
him
Trust
Jb. 13 Though he slay me, yet will
I trust in him
Ps. 42 Why art thou cast down,
O my soul?
Ps. 62 Trust in him at all times
Ps. 112 His heart is fixed, trusting
in the Lord
Ps. 121 The Lord shall preserve
thee from all evil
Is. 12 I will trust, and not be afraid
Is. 26:1-9 Thou wilt keep him in
perfect peace
Jn. 20:24-31 Be not faithless, but
believing
2 Co. 7 I have confidence in you
in all things
1 Ti. 6 Keep that which is com-
mitted to thy trust
Truth
Ps. 15 He that speaketh the truth
in his heart
Ps. 43 Let thy light and thy truth
lead me
Mat. 5:33-37 Let your communica-
tion be Yea, Nay
Jn. 8:25-32 Ye shall know the truth
Jn. 18:15-27 Peter's denial
Jn. 18:28-40 What is truth?
Ac. 5:1-11 Thou hast lied unto God
2 Co. 13 We can do nothing against
the truth

Truth *(cont.)*

Ep. 4 Speaking the truth in love
Ep. 6 Having your loins girt about with truth
3 Jn. Thou walkest in the truth

Tumult, *See* Confusion

Tyranny

Ex. 1:7-14 All their service was with rigour
Ps. 62 Trust not in oppression
Is. 3:12-26 Ye beat my people
Mi. 2 They take by violence
Am. 8:1-6 Ye swallow up the needy

[U]

Unbelief, *See* Denial

Uncertainty, *See* Doubt

Understanding

1 K. 3:4-15 Give thy servant an understanding heart
Pr. 4:1-13 Wisdom is the principal thing
Pr. 8 Wisdom was set up from everlasting
Mk. 12:28-34 Thou shalt love God with all thy mind
1 Co. 14:10-20 In understanding be men
He. 11:1-16 Through faith we understand
Ja. 3 The wisdom from above is first pure

Unfaithfulness, *See* Betrayal

Ungodliness, *See* Sin

United Nations

2 Ch. 34:29-33 The king made a covenant before the Lord
Ps. 72 All nations shall serve him
Is. 2:2-4 Nation shall not lift up sword against nation
Is. 66:5-24 I will gather all nations and tongues
Mat. 25:31-46 Before him shall be gathered all nations
Mat. 28:16-20 Teach all nations
Lu. 13:18-30 They shall come from east, west, north, and south
Ac. 10:34-43 God is no respecter of persons
Ac. 17:22-31 God hath made of one blood all nations
Ro. 10:11-21 Unto the ends of the world
Re. 22 The leaves were for the healing of nations

Unity

Ge. 2:18-25 They shall be one flesh
De. 6:1-15 The Lord our God is one Lord
Mat. 18:19, 20 If two of you shall agree

Ac. 2:38-47 They had all things common
Ac. 17:22-33 God hath made of one blood all nations
1 Co. 12:12-27 Ye are the body of Christ
Ep. 4:1-16 One Lord, one faith, one baptism
Col. 1:1-17 By him all things consist

Universality

Ge. 18:16-33 All nations shall be blessed in him
Jo. 2:21-32 I will pour out my spirit upon all flesh
Mk. 16:14-20 Go ye into all the world
Lu. 2:8-16 Good tidings to all people
Jn. 10:1-18 Other sheep I have, which are not of this fold
Ac. 1:1-11 Witnesses unto the uttermost part of the earth
Re. 14:1-7 The everlasting gospel for every nation

Universe

Ge. 1:1-5 God created the heaven and the earth
1 K. 8:22-30 The heaven of heavens cannot contain thee
Ps. 33 The earth is full of the goodness of the Lord
Ps. 68:26-35 Sing unto God, ye kingdoms of the earth
Is. 48:12-22 My right hand hath spanned the heavens
Is. 54:1-10 The God of the whole earth shall he be called

Unrest, *See* Confusion

Unrighteousness, *See* Sin

Unselfishness

Mk. 12:28-34 Thou shalt love thy neighbour as thyself
Jn. 21:15-17 Feed my lambs
Ac. 20:28-35 It is more blessed to give than to receive

Ro. 14:1-9 None of us liveth to himself

Ro. 15:1-7 Even Christ pleased not himself

1 Co. 10:24-33 Not seeking mine own profit

1 Co. 13 Charity seeketh not her own

2 Co. 8:9-15 For your sakes he became poor

Ph. 2:1-16 Look on the things of others

He. 13:1-3 Let brotherly love continue

Unworldliness, *See* Holiness
Unworthiness

Mat. 3:1-12 The tree which bringeth not forth good fruit

Mat. 5:1-16 If the salt hath lost his savour

Mat. 13:18-23 He becometh unfruitful

Lu. 9:51-62 No man, looking back, is fit for the kingdom

1 Co. 11:18-34 Whosoever shall drink this cup unworthily

Re. 5 No man was found worthy

Uprightness, *See* Purity

[V]

Vacation

Ge. 2:1-3 God rested on the seventh day

Ju. 9:8-15 The trees went forth to anoint a king

1 K. 19:1-18 A day's journey into the wilderness

Ps. 8 When I consider thy heavens

Ps. 23 He maketh me to lie down in green pastures

Ps. 55:1-8 I would fly away, and be at rest

Is. 40:18-31 The Creator of the earth fainteth not

Mk. 6:7-32 Come ye apart and rest a while

Valor, *See* Courage
Value, *See* Worth
Vanity, *See* Pride
Variety, *See* Diversity
Vengeance, *See* Revenge
Vice, *See* Sin
Vicissitude, *See* Trouble
Victory

Is. 25 He will swallow up death in victory

Mat. 12:10-20 Till he send forth judgment unto victory

Ro. 8:24-39 We are more than conquerors

1 Co. 15:47-58 O grave, where is thy victory?

2 Co. 2 God causeth us to triumph in Christ

1 Jn. 5 This is the victory that overcometh the world

Re. 2:1-11 I will give thee a crown

Re. 6 He went forth conquering, and to conquer

Re. 17 The Lamb shall overcome them

Virgin, *See* Chastity
Virtue, *See* Character
Vision

Ge. 21:14-19 God opened her eyes

Ex. 3:1-12 The bush burned with fire

Is. 6:1-8 Whom shall I send?

Da. 6 Windows open toward Jerusalem

Jo. 2:21-32 Your young men shall see visions

Hab. 2:1-3 Though the vision tarry, wait for it

Mat. 13:1-17 Blessed are your eyes, for they see

Mk. 9:1-10 He was transfigured before them

Jn. 1:35-51 Behold the Lamb of God!

Ac. 9:1-22 There shined about him a light from heaven

Ac. 11:5-18 Peter's vision

Ac. 16:6-10 A vision appeared to Paul in the night

1 Co. 9:1-16 Have I not seen Christ our Lord?

2 Co. 12:1-5 Caught up to the third heaven

Re. 1:4-18 I was in the Spirit and heard a great voice

Re. 22 They shall see his face

Vocation, *See* Calling
Vow, *See* Promise

[W]

Wage, *See* Reward
Wait
 Ps. 37:1-11 They that wait upon the Lord shall inherit
 Ps. 145 The eyes of all wait upon thee
 Is. 40:28-31 They that wait upon the Lord shall renew
 La. 3:22-36 Quietly wait for the salvation of the Lord
 Hab. 2:1-4 Though the vision tarry, wait for it
 Ac. 1:1-14 Wait for the promise of the Father
 Ro. 8:16-28 Waiting for the adoption
 Ga. 5 We wait for the hope of righteousness
Wall, *See* Security
Wandering, *See* Journey
Want, *See* Need
War, *See* Strife
Washington's Birthday
 Ex. 18:13-27 Thou shalt provide able men
 De. 26:1-11 The Lord brought us into this place
 Ps. 85 Thou hast been favourable unto thy land
 Ps. 90 Establish thou the work of our hands
 Is. 11:1-9 The spirit of the Lord shall rest upon him
 He. 12:1-15 Follow peace with all men
Waste, *See* Prodigal
Watch
 Ge. 31:43-55 The Lord watch between thee and me
 Ps. 63 I meditate on thee in the night watches
 Ps. 127 The watchman waketh but in vain
 Ps. 130 More than they that watch for the morning
 Is. 21:11-12 The watchman said, The morning cometh
 Eze. 33:1-9 I have set thee a watchman
 Hab. 2:1-4 I will stand upon my watch
 Mat. 26:36-46 Could ye not watch with me one hour?
 Lu. 2:8-16 Shepherds keeping watch over their flock
 Lu. 12:35-40 Blessed those whom the Lord finds watching

 1 Co. 16:1-14 Watch ye, stand fast in the faith
 1 Pe. 4 Be sober, and watch unto prayer
 Re. 16:15-21 Blessed is he that watcheth
Water
 Ps. 23 He leadeth me beside the still waters
 Ec. 11 Cast thy bread upon the waters
 S. of S. 8 Many waters cannot quench love
 Is. 32 Blessed are ye that sow beside all waters
 Is. 55 Ho, every one that thirsteth, come ye
 Is. 58:8-14 Thou shalt be like a watered garden
 Am. 5:21-27 Let judgment run down as waters
 Mat. 10:37-42 Whosoever shall give a cup of cold water
 Jn. 3:1-13 Except a man be born of water and Spirit
 Jn. 4:7-26 Water springing up to everlasting life
 Jude 1-13 Clouds are they without water
 Re. 7:9-17 To living fountains of waters
Way, *See* Highway
Weakness
 Jb. 4 Thou hast strengthened the weak hands
 Jn. 5:2-9 I have no man to help me
 1 Co. 1:20-31 God hath chosen the weak things of the world
 1 Co. 15:39-58 It is sown in weakness, it is raised in power
 2 Co. 11 Who is weak, and I am not weak?
 2 Co. 12 My strength is made perfect in weakness
 He. 11:17-40 Out of weakness were made strong
Wealth, *See* Riches
Weapon, *See* Strife
Weariness
 Ge. 3:13-24 In the sweat of thy face shalt thou eat bread
 Jb. 3 There the weary be at rest
 Ps. 55 Cast thy burden upon the Lord
 Pr. 24:1-10 If thou faint in the day of adversity

Ec. 5:8-17 The sleep of a labouring man is sweet

Is. 32 The shadow of a great rock in a weary land

Is. 40:28-31 They shall run, and not be weary

2 Co. 11:22-30 In weariness and painfulness

Ga. 6 Let us not be weary in well doing

Wedding, *See* Marriage

Weeping, *See* Sorrow

Weight, *See* Burden; Measure

Welcome, *See* Hospitality

Well-Doing, *See* Benevolence

Whitsunday

Jo. 2:28-32 I will pour out my spirit upon all flesh

Jn. 16:1-14 I will send the Comforter unto you

Ac. 2:1-18 When the day of Pentecost was come

Ac. 2:37-47 There were added about three thousand souls

Re. 3:1-13 I will write upon him my new name

Whole

Ps. 72 Let the whole earth be filled with his glory

Ec. 12 This is the whole duty of man

Ac. 9:32-42 Jesus Christ maketh thee whole

Ep. 4 Till ye come unto a perfect man

Col. 2 Ye are complete in him

Ja. 1 That ye may be perfect and entire

Wickedness, *See* Sin

Wife, *See* Marriage

Wilderness, *See* Solitude

Will, *See* Purpose

Will, Free

Is. 55 Buy wine and milk without money or price

Mat. 11:25-30 Come unto me, all ye that labour

Jn. 6:22-40 Him that cometh to me I will not cast out

Ac. 2:14-21 Whosoever calls on the Lord shall be saved

Ro. 8 He will give us all things freely

Re. 22:12-21 Let him take the water of life freely

Will, Good, *See* Benevolence

Winter

Ge. 8:15-22 Summer and winter shall not cease

Jb. 37 He saith to the snow, Be thou on the earth

Jb. 38:1-30 Out of whose womb came the ice?

Ps. 74 Thou hast made summer and winter

Ps. 147 He giveth snow like wool

Wisdom, *See* Knowledge

Withering

Ps. 1 His leaf also shall not wither

Ps. 102 I am withered like grass

Is. 40:1-11 The grass withereth, the flower fadeth

Is. 64:1-8 We all do fade as a leaf

Jo. 1 All the trees of the field are withered

Mat. 12:10-13 The man with the withered hand

Lu. 8:4-15 When it sprang up it withered away

Witness

Ex. 20:1-17 Thou shalt not bear false witness

Jb. 16 My witness is in heaven

Jb. 42:1-6 Now mine eye seeth thee

Is. 55 I have given him for a witness

Mk. 5:1-19 Go home and tell thy friends

Jn. 8:12-32 My record is true

Jn. 20:24-29 Unless I see I will not believe

Ac. 1:1-11 Ye shall be witnesses unto me

Ac. 14:8-18 He left not himself without witnesses

Tit. 1 This witness is true

He. 11:32-40; 12:1,2 The cloud of witnesses

2 Pe. 1:16-21 We were eyewitnesses of his majesty

1 Jn. 5 There are three that bear record in heaven

Woe, *See* Sorrow

Woman

Ge. 2:18-25 She shall be called Woman

Ge. 3:1-21 Eve was the mother of all living

Jb. 14 Man born of woman is of few days

Pr. 6:20-35 Keep thee from the evil woman

Pr. 31 A woman that feareth God shall be praised

1 Co. 11:1-15 The woman is of the man, the man not of the woman

1 Co. 14:23-40 Let the women keep silence in the churches

Woman, the Virtuous
Pr. 11:16-22 A gracious woman retaineth honor
Pr. 12:1-12 A virtuous woman is a crown to her husband
Pr. 14:1-11 Every wise woman buildeth her house
Pr. 31:10-31 Who can find a virtuous woman
Lu. 1:26-38 Blessed art thou among women
Ac. 9:36-43 This woman was full of good works

Wonder, *See* Awe

Word
Pr. 15:23-33 The words of the pure are pleasant words
Mat. 12:31-37 By thy words thou shalt be justified
Lu. 1:1-4 Ministers of the word
Lu. 11:14-28 Blessed are they that hear the word of God
Ac. 20:28-38 Remember the words of the Lord Jesus
1 Co. 4 The kingdom of God is not in word
Ep. 5:1-16 Let no man deceive you with vain words
2 Ti. 4:1-8 Preach the word
Ja. 1:16-27 Be ye doers of the word, not hearers only

Work, *See* Labor Day

World, *See* Universe

Worldliness, *See* Mammon

Worry
Ps. 37:1-11 Fret not thyself because of evildoers
Mat. 6:19-34 Take therefore no thought for the morrow
Mk. 4:14-20 The cares of this world choke the word
Lu. 10:38-42 Martha, thou art troubled about many things
2 Co. 4 We are troubled on every side
2 Co. 11:24-33 The care of the churches cometh upon me daily
1 Pe. 5 Casting all your care upon him

Worship
Ex. 3:1-6 The place where thou standest is holy ground
Ps. 34:1-11 O magnify the Lord with me
Ps. 55 We walked into the house of God in company
Ps. 95 O come, let us worship and bow down
Ps. 99 Worship at his holy hill
Ps. 100 Enter his courts with praise
Ps. 122 Let us go into the house of the Lord
Is. 1:1-20 Bring no more vain oblations
Mat. 6:5-18 When thou prayest, enter into thy closet
Jn. 4:20-24 The true worshippers shall worship the Father
1 Ti. 2 I will therefore that men pray everywhere
Re. 4 Holy, holy, holy, Lord God almighty
Re. 15 The temple was filled with smoke from the glory of God

Worth
Pr. 31 The price of a virtuous woman
Mat. 10:1-15 The workman is worthy of his meat
Mat. 10:16-39 Ye are of more value than many sparrows
Mat. 13:45-46 The pearl of great price
Mk. 8:34-38 What shall a man give for his soul?
Jn. 12:20-36 He that loveth his life shall lose it
Col. 1:1-19 Walk worthy of the Lord unto all pleasing
2 Th. 1 That God count you worthy of this calling
Re. 5 Thou art worthy to take the book

Wound, *See* Injury

Wrath, *See* Anger

Wretchedness, *See* Adversity

Writing, *See* Book

Wrong, *See* Sin

[Y]

Year, End of
De. 8 The Lord bringeth thee into a good land
Ps. 90:1-17 Our dwelling place in all generations

Ec. 3:1-15 God requireth that which is past
Ec. 7:7-19 Better the end than the beginning
Mat. 25:1-10 The door was shut

Mk. 13:33-37 Take ye heed, watch and pray
Jn. 14:1-6 Let not your heart be troubled
Ro. 12:1-8 Transformed by the renewing of your mind
Ph. 1:12-26 I shall abide and continue with you
Ph. 3:12-21 Our conversation is in heaven
He. 11:32-40 God hath provided some better thing for us
He. 13:1-8 Jesus Christ the same for ever
1 Pe. 1:1-17 Hope to the end for grace
Re. 20:11-15 Another book was opened
Re. 22 I am Alpha and Omega

Year, New
Ge. 12:1-5 Get thee out of thy country
Ex. 14:5-15 Speak unto them that they may go forward
Ex. 33:7-14 My presence shall go with thee
De. 1:21-46 God hath set the land before thee
De. 2:1-3 Ye have compassed this mountain long enough
De. 30:11-19 I have set before thee life and death
Jos. 1:1-5 Moses is dead; now therefore arise
Jos. 3:5-9, 11, 13-17 Tomorrow the Lord will do wonders
1 K. 19:1-8 The journey is too great for thee
Ps. 9:1-11 The Lord shall endure for ever
Ps. 23 The Lord is my shepherd
Ps. 27 All the days of my life
Ps. 31:15-24 My times are in thy hand
Ps. 34 What man is he that desireth life?
Ps. 37:1-27 Do good; and dwell for evermore
Ps. 43 Let thy light and thy truth lead me
Ps. 46 The Lord of hosts is with us
Ps. 90 Teach us to number our days
Ps. 96 Sing unto the Lord a new song
Ps. 97 The Lord reigneth
Ps. 102:1-12, 24-28 Thy years shall have no end

Ps. 107:1-8 He led them forth by the right way
Ps. 107:23-31 He bringeth them unto their desired haven
Pr. 3:1-13 Long life shall they add to thee
Ec. 8:1-12 Man knoweth not that which shall be
Is. 6:1-8 Whom shall I send?
Is. 40:1-11, 28-31 Prepare ye the way of the Lord
Is. 45:1-8 The gates shall not be shut
Lu. 13:6-10 Let it alone this year also
Jn. 3:1-13 Ye must be born again
Jn. 9:1-11 I must work while it is day
Ro. 12 Fervent in spirit; serving the Lord
1 Co. 15:50-58 Always abounding in the work of the Lord
Ga. 6:2-10 Let us not be weary in well doing
Ep. 4:1-16 Walk worthy of your vocation
Ep. 5:6-16 Redeeming the time
Ph. 1:12-27 To me to live is Chirst
Ph. 3:7-14 I press toward the mark
Col. 3 Set your affection on things above
2 Ti. 2:1-15 Show thyself approved unto God
He. 3:7-14 Today if ye will hear his voice
He. 6:1-12 Let us go on unto perfection
Ja. 4:8-15 Your life is a vapour
1 Pe. 1:3-19 Pass the time of your sojourning in fear
Re. 21:1-7 Behold I make all things new

Yearning, *See* Desire
Yesterday
1 S. 7 Hitherto hath the Lord helped us
Jb. 8 We are but of yesterday
Ps. 77 I have considered the days of old
Ps. 90 A thousand years are as yesterday
He. 1 God spake in times past unto the fathers
He. 13 The same yesterday, today, and for ever
Yield, *See* Harvest
Yoke, *See* Bond

Young People's Sunday
1 S. 16:1-13 Samuel anoints David
1 S. 17:31-51 David and Goliath
2 Ch. 34:1-7 While he was yet young
Ps. 119:9-16 Wherewithal shall a young man cleanse his way?
Pr. 8:32-36 Hearken unto me, O ye children
Pr. 20:11-30 The glory of young men is their strength

Ec. 11:6-10 In the morning sow thy seed
Ec. 12:1-7 Remember now thy Creator
Mat. 19:16-22 All these things have I kept from my youth
Ac. 2:1-18 Your young men shall see visions
1 Ti. 4:12-16 Let no man despise thy youth

Youth, *See* Young People's Sunday

[Z]

Zeal, *See* Ardor

Zion, *See* Jerusalem